SLAVERY AND THE
POST-BLACK IMAGINATION

SLAVERY AND THE POST-BLACK IMAGINATION

Edited by
Bertram D. Ashe and Ilka Saal

UNIVERSITY OF WASHINGTON PRESS

Seattle

Slavery and the Post-Black Imagination was made possible in part by a grant from the V Ethel Willis White Endowment, which supports the publication of books on African American history and culture.

Printed and bound in the United States of America
Composed in Warnock Pro, typeface designed by Robert Slimbach

24   23   22   21   20   5   4   3   2   1

UNIVERSITY OF WASHINGTON PRESS
uwapress.uw.edu

LIBRARY OF CONGRESS CATALOGING-IN-PUBLICATION DATA
Names: Saal, Ilka, editor. | Ashe, Bertram D., 1959- editor.
Title: Slavery and the post-black imagination / edited by Bertram D. Ashe and Ilka Saal.
Description: 1st. | Seattle : University of Washington Press, 2020. | Includes bibliographical references and index.
Identifiers: LCCN 2019018122 (print) | LCCN 2019981446 (ebook) |
ISBN 9780295746647 (hardcover) | ISBN 9780295746630 (paperback) |
ISBN 9780295746654 (ebook)
Subjects: LCSH: American literature—African American authors—History and criticism. | American literature—21st century—History and criticism. | Slavery in literature. | Slavery in mass media.
Classification: LCC PS153.N5 S223 2020 (print) | LCC PS153.N5 (ebook) |
DDC 810.9/896073—dc23
LC record available at https://lccn.loc.gov/2019018122
LC ebook record available at https://lccn.loc.gov/2019981446

CONTENTS

ACKNOWLEDGMENTS

The project was "born" during a prolonged telephone conversation between Toronto and Richmond in the spring of 2016. It's been a fun and exciting and sometimes quite tumultuous ride ever since. We would like to thank everyone who kept us going, in one way or another, at some point or another. Sincere thanks to our contributors for their fabulous work and to our editors, Larin McLaughlin and Caitlin Tyler-Richards, for their unwavering and generous support of the project from start to finish. We are grateful to Branden Jacobs-Jenkins for sharing an afternoon with us and indulging our myriad questions as well as to Chenjerai Kumanyika, Jack Hitt, and Chris Neary of the *Uncivil* podcast team at Gimlet Media for allowing us to publish the transcript of "The Song." Furthermore, we appreciate the astute and helpful comments sent to us by the external reviewers as well as the financial and logistic support from the universities of Richmond and Erfurt. Bert would also like to thank Valerie—I can't imagine life without you. And Ilka would like to thank Tristan and Anselm for giggles and cuddles and, above all, Jan for having her back, for his incredible love and patience, and for putting the commas in the right places.

SLAVERY AND THE
POST-BLACK IMAGINATION

INTRODUCTION

ILKA SAAL AND BERTRAM D. ASHE

"EACH GENERATION OF BLACKS DEMANDS MORE OF THE PAST," WRITES British-Guyanese poet and novelist Fred D'Aguiar. "Not because they are suffering short-term memory loss or some such syndrome (after all, didn't the generation before have lots to say about slavery) but because they need their own version of the past, to see the past in their own images, words. To have slavery nuanced their way."[1] Taking our cue from D'Aguiar's observation, the question we pose in this essay collection is how artists growing up in the post–civil rights era—which critics have variously dubbed the post-soul or post-black era—attempt to nuance slavery their way. How do their attempts differ from those of their predecessors, particularly from the authors of literary and visual neo-slave narratives of the 1970s and 80s, and where do they affirm significant continuities? What are the images, rhythms, and narratives that matter to today's artists? What politics of remembrance and what visions of the future do they articulate?

Inviting our contributors to reflect on these and similar questions, the collection of essays assembled here seeks to trace major ways in which artists have addressed the issue of transatlantic slavery and its legacies over the past thirty years—that is, ever since the publication of Toni Morrison's *Beloved* (1987). Morrison's landmark novel represents in many regards the culmination of the neo-slave narrative tradition, which has emerged steadily from the late 1960s onward. At the same time, *Beloved* also marks, as scholars such as Judith Misrahi-Barak, Stephen Best, and Margot Natalie Crawford have pointed out, a watershed moment with regard to the cultural and poetic scope of neo-slave narratives as well as with regard to the kind of relationship to the past they articulate. Misrahi-Barak, for instance, observes that in the wake of *Beloved*, neo-slave narratives have significantly expanded their geographic scope and poetological range. "African American neo-slave narratives stopped being only African American: they became Caribbean, Black British, African and African-Caribbean-Canadian etc. . . . They became transnational and global."[2] In terms of their poetics, they have also moved beyond Ashraf Rushdy's initial definition of the genre as first-person prose narratives that adopt the conventions of the antebellum slave narrative: "They became plays and poems as well as third-person novels, pseudo-autobiographies and pseudo-testimonials."[3] In this opened-up geographic and poetic space of the black Atlantic, important processes of "cross-pollination" have taken place. What Misrahi-Barak calls "post-*Beloved*" writing therefore tends to be highly aware of its inter- and transtextual influences, articulating this awareness of the polyphony of past and present voices engaged in the construction of contemporary narratives of slavery in a much more "forceful, deliberate, and obvious way" than its predecessor, the classic neo-slave narrative, pre-*Beloved*. "A dialogic consciousness now exists that probably did not exist on such a scale thirty years ago," Misrahi-Barak notes.[4]

Similarly, there are indications that the more recent body of writing on slavery has begun to articulate a very different relationship to the past than the one exemplarily expressed by Morrison's *Beloved*, which Stephen Best describes as an essentially melancholic one. As Best considers the implications of such a melancholic attachment to the past for contemporary scholarship, he also points to a prominent change in Morrison's writing, the 2008 novel *A Mercy*. Here, he writes, the slave past is no longer depicted as a compulsory haunting, as an obsessive return similar to *Beloved*, but "as that which falls away—a separateness resistant to being either held or read in melancholic terms."[5] In contrast to *Beloved*, *A Mercy* does not hail its readers as witnesses to the losses sustained during slavery, but "abandons us to a more baffled, cut-off, foreclosed position with regard to the slave past."[6] The programmatic title of the essay, "On Failing to Make the Past Present" and the author's pronounced intention to "write the epitaph to the *Beloved* moment" clearly bespeak Best's hope that contemporary scholarship and art might continue to build on *A Mercy*'s fresh relationship to the past.[7] In this regard, it might also bring about a decisive shift from a politics of melancholia to a politics of mourning, from sustaining an affective bond with the past to the "undoing of the affective history project" that has undergirded not only *Beloved* but, we might add, the majority of the neo-slave narratives of the 1970s and 80s.[8] Margo Natalie Crawford responds to Best's thesis by pointing out that while she sees "black mo'nin'" as necessarily and productively entangled with melancholia, she, too, notices in a number of contemporary texts a pronounced "*space-clearing* and *opening up* to such an extent that they [these texts] could be called post-neo-slave narratives."[9] While these narratives continue to point up continuities between the antiblack racism of the past and the antiblack racism of the present, they also "hail a future that does not have to be the past."[10] To Crawford this pronounced space-clearing gesture presents a crucial *conceptual* difference from the neo-slave narratives, though it does not present a chronological one for her. Yet her examples— Morrison's *A Mercy* (2008), E. P. Jones's *The Known World* (2003), and Monifa Love's *Freedom in the Dismal* (1998)—demonstrate that, such early examples as Amiri Baraka's play *The Slave* (1964) notwithstanding, the tendency to push away from an aesthetics of haunting, made programmatic with Morrison's *Beloved*, to an aesthetics "of the not yet formulated possibilities of the future" appears to be more prominent in the recent literature on slavery.[11]

Our collection seeks to build on this groundbreaking work by Misrahi-Barak, Best, and Crawford by identifying important shifts in recent artistic engagements with the past with regard to changing poetics as well as politics. How have narratives of slavery evolved poetologically over the past thirty years? What does post-*Beloved* writing reveal about changing attitudes toward the past? In this collection we decided to focus exclusively on recent African American cultural productions, even as we are keenly aware that many of these texts partake in a larger poetics of literary and visual narratives of slavery marking the circum-Atlantic world.[12] By limiting our inquiry to the United States of America, we want to underscore the question of to what extent changing conceptions of freedom and identity that have emerged in the wake of the civil rights and Black Power movements are impacting contemporary attitudes toward the past. For this reason, our collection intentionally limits itself to works by artists who were born or came of age *after* the end of the civil rights movement, so that we can gauge the particularities of this generation's "structure of feeling," to evoke Raymond Williams's influential concept. Williams here refers to "a particular quality of social experience and relationship, historically distinct from other particular qualities, which gives the sense of a generation or a period."[13] Not yet a worldview or ideology, a "structure of feeling" indicates "meanings and values as they are actively lived and felt"; it bespeaks experience "still in process."[14] It is often in literature and art that we find semantic and formal expressions of the structure of feeling generated by the shared space of sociopolitical and cultural experience of an age cohort.[15]

Several scholars have theorized the generational feeling of the post–civil rights era as post-soul or post-black. We here understand post-blackness very much in the sense of Thelma Golden and Glenn Ligon's 2001 original coinage of the term as shorthand for resisting narrow definitions of African American identity and for expressing a profound interest in "redefining complex notions of blackness."[16] Golden insists that *post-black* decidedly does not signify the abandonment of or moving past blackness but rather the articulation of "ideological and chronological dimensions and repercussions."[17] It warrants stressing that the Golden-Ligon definition does not understand *post-black* as postracial, and neither does this collection of essays. Post-blackness seeks to emphasize an evolving understanding of meanings of blackness. Much like Golden and Ligon, Nelson George, Trey Ellis, Mark Anthony Neal, Ytasha L. Womack, Touré, and Bertram D. Ashe have pointed to a decisive artistic and ideological break in the works of artists who were either born or came of age after the civil rights movement.[18]

This break displays three distinctive characteristics: (a) "a hybrid, fluid, elastic, cultural mulattoesque sense of blackness,"[19] which works alongside (b) the playful, often humorous, and frequently iconoclastic Signifyin(g) on established narratives, tropes, images of blackness in order to (c) trouble habitual notions of blackness, or, as Ashe suggests, to execute a sense of "blaxploration." These millennial black cultural productions "worry blackness; they stir it up, touch it, feel it out, and hold it up for examination in ways that depart significantly from previous—and necessary—preoccupations with struggling for political freedom, or with an attempt to establish and sustain a coherent black identity."[20] Derek Conrad Murray importantly adds that *post-black* signifies the resistance to and departure from normative understandings of blackness, especially those that "negate forms of difference, particularly the subjectivities of women and those that are queerly identified. For many in the African American community the visual and ideological emblems of normative blackness have not spoken to the complexities of their experience."[21] Murray therefore understands post-blackness as a "generationally-specific ethos,"[22] or consciousness, that challenges "the hegemony of hetero-patriarchal expressions of blackness that, in their essentialist logics and racial nostalgia, relegate African-American identity to a series of limiting scripts."[23] As an aesthetic, post-blackness troubles especially those scripts that narrowly prescribe the boundaries of an "authentic" blackness and endorse a politics of respectability. As a theory of representation, it furthermore becomes a means for artists and critics to unpack the complexities and shifting modalities of representing blackness: "It is a means to both understand and characterize a set of aesthetic, conceptual, political, and artistic tendencies that are present in the creative practices of post–civil rights generation artists," Murray writes here in this volume.

Satire and humor play an important role in post-blackness's assault on normative scripts and its playful unpacking of discursive constructions of blackness. Not surprisingly, contemporary artistic explorations of American slavery often, but not always, use satire or humor to explore slavery. They do so not to demean those who were actually enslaved or to underestimate the seriousness of slavery, but to approach slavery in much the way Ralph Ellison suggested blues singers sang the blues: "By singing of pain and simultaneously laughing at it one faces the pain in such a way that it is transcended. It is not overcome or defeated in an unrealistic or romantic sense; it is simply brought under control and deprived of its demoralizing power over the individual."[24] Thus, the searing satire of Paul Beatty's *The Sellout*, Kara Walker's layered, absurdist silhouettes, Jordan Peele's hilarious and disturbing *Get Out*, as well as Branden Jacobs-Jenkins's poignant, outrageous *Neighbors*, to name just a few, attempt each in its own way to bring slavery "under control," insisting on depriving it of its "demoralizing power."

These artists also make, as a collective, a bold declaration of artistic agency, pushing back against both respectability and a portentous solemnity all too common when discussing American slavery. Derek Conrad Murray, in his essay on Kara Walker collected here, speaks directly to the idea of satire as intellectual practice:

> Walker's incendiary formalism makes explicit reference to the violence inflicted upon black bodies—as well as to the relation among "vision, visualizing and visibility," identifications that are deeply entangled in the logics of power and social authority. Given the representational entanglements between images of antiblack violence in American visual culture and an increased consumer demand for black bodies in contemporary art, it is necessary to consider how satire upends a compulsory politics of racial fidelity—and begins to embark upon a contentious intracultural debate about the social function of blackness (as culture) in the twenty-first century.

Such is the vital cultural work of these artists, who were originally theorized under the rubric of the "post-soul" and have lately increasingly been described as "post-black."[25]

While we consider the terms *post-soul* and *post-black* as largely synonymous with regard to their poetics and politics, we here choose to refer to the imaginative engagement with the various legacies of slavery at the turn of the millennium as post-black. In doing so, we aim to intervene in recent debates concerning the validity, usefulness, and meanings of the term by removing it from the semantic field of *postrace* or *color blindness*, with which it has frequently and incorrectly been associated in the mass media, particularly during Barack Obama's presidency, as well as more recently in scholarship, such as in the 2015 collection *The Trouble with Post-Blackness*.[26] Margo Natalie Crawford usefully introduces the term *black post-blackness* to clarify that the aesthetics and politics of the late twentieth and early twenty-first centuries continue to be indebted to older articulations of blackness even as they attempt to break the boundaries of those previous definitions.[27] Moreover, as Crawford puts it, "Black post-blackness is the circular inseparability of the lived experience of blackness and the translation of that lived experience into the world-opening possibilities of art."[28] It is precisely with regard to the world-opening possibilities of art that *Slavery and the Post-Black Imagination* aims to bring the category of the post-black to bear on contemporary discussions on the afterlife of slavery as it continues to manifest itself in the material, institutional, psychological, affective, and discursive structures of everyday life in the United States.[29]

As the essays in this collection demonstrate, artists born after the civil rights era remain intensely cognizant of the legacies of racial slavery and the systemic patterns of antiblack racism that have grown out of it. But as also becomes apparent, many do not subscribe to what Best describes as the "melancholic historicism" of a Morrisonian poetics that demands our persistent affective identification with the past and welds the present inextricably to the collective trauma of slavery.[30] Rather, the artists discussed in this collection—all of whom came of artistic age in the late 1980s and early 1990s or even later—tend to use their artwork to push both against the oppressive constraints imposed by the psychic and representational legacies of slavery that continue to affect their everyday lives and against the injunction to "remain 'faithful to the lost object.'"[31] Kara Walker, Thylias Moss, Cheryl Dunye, Branden Jacobs-Jenkins, Paul Beatty, Colson Whitehead, Natashia Déon, Yaa Gyasi, Jordan Peele, the Carolina Chocolate Drops, Damian Duffy and John Jennings—as the assembled readings and interviews demonstrate, these artists negotiate the legacies of history as well as the burden of representations placed on them in order to articulate "the past in their own images, words"[32] and to imagine possibilities and change even within persisting systemic constraints. Importantly, they do so in both content *and* form, seeking to intervene politically and poetically in established discourses of slavery and black identity. To be sure, these two lines of inquiry are often, though not always, tightly interwoven. Most essays in this collection demonstrate how the exploration of black identities frequently goes hand in hand with formal playfulness, with the purposeful refiguration of prevailing tropes, narratives, and images in the discursive and representational legacies of slavery. Drawing on the definitions of *post-soul* and *post-black* delineated above, which encompass both aesthetic and sociocultural criteria, our collection, then, seeks to position post-blackness as a valid and productive category of analysis with regard to the poetics and politics of contemporary engagements with slavery in African American culture.

In this context, *Slavery and the Post-Black Imagination* also aims to enter into a fruitful conversation with the recently published essay collection *The Psychic Hold of Slavery: Legacies in American Expressive Culture* (2016), edited by Soyica Diggs Colbert, Robert J. Patterson, and Aida Levy-Hussen, which similarly looks at late twentieth- and early twenty-first-century cultural productions on slavery but starts from a very different premise: "our inability—or unwillingness—to 'get over' slavery."[33] Accordingly, the book sets out to investigate the "desires, investments, or identitarian logics [that] account for our inability—or unwillingness—to get over slavery."[34] While *Slavery and the Post-Black Imagination* also acknowledges the persisting relevance of the afterlife of transatlantic slavery for contemporary social, political, and cultural life in the United States, the majority of the essays in our collection do not consider slavery as "the metonym for understanding blackness and inequality in the contemporary moment."[35] While contemporary artists clearly continue to engage the legacies of slavery and attempt to give them a place in contemporary understandings of black identities and race relations, few continue to place it front and center. The essays by Derek Conrad Murray, Cameron Leader-Picone, Ilka Saal, Malin Pereira, and Bertram D. Ashe highlight the multifarious attempts in contemporary black cultural productions to decenter slavery from its privileged position in African American thought.[36]

On a related note, several scholars and artists in *Slavery and the Post-Black Imagination* shift the debate from a focus on the history and/or temporality of slavery to questions of historiography and representation.[37] "I'm just going to say this right now so we can get it over with," Branden Jacobs-Jenkins provocatively remarks in his play *An Octoroon* (2015). "I don't know what a real slave sounds like. And neither do you."[38] With this he posits an apt contemporary rejoinder to an observation the fugitive slave William Wells Brown articulated already in 1847 to readers and audiences on the abolitionist circuit: "I may try to represent to you Slavery as it is; another may follow me and represent the condition of the Slave; we may all represent it as we think it is; and yet we shall all fail to represent the real condition of the Slave. . . . Slavery has never been represented; Slavery can never be represented."[39] The artists discussed in this volume would agree on this score: with their artworks they do not attempt to know or own the past, to make it "yield up a kind of a truth," as Toni Morrison famously writes in her programmatic essay "The Site of Memory."[40] Rather, starting from the poststructuralist premise that the past can be known only "through its textual traces,"[41] they are invested in excavating, interrogating, and playfully engaging precisely these discourses of the past: the various narratives; verbal, visual, and sonic tropes; as well as *lieux de mémoire* that have been used by white and black Americans alike to render the facts of slavery. These discourses have shaped not only our ways of knowing the past but also our ways of acting in the present, and in this sense they have become part of history itself. Several of the artworks discussed here therefore interrogate the stakes of writing, troping, visualizing, sounding, and performing history. Rather than positing the continuing structures of antiblack domination in Western societies as the fundamental conditions that delimit contemporary engagements with slavery, *Slavery and the Post-Black Imagination* starts with the moments of possibility inherent in the ludic engagement with canonical, counter-mnemonic, and popular tropes, narratives, and iconographies of American history and memory. The essays in this collection are interested in examining the various ways in which the literary, visual, and performing arts not only take stock of contemporary conditions of freedom and unfreedom but, through their artistic work, attempt to upset and, in Soyica Diggs Colbert's words, "flip" dominant "epistemological scripts," to open up possibilities for knowing the past differently and for creating new representations of blackness.[42]

Slavery and the Post-Black Imagination takes a vital and critical interest in questions of periodization. As the chapters in this volume demonstrate, this does not mean that our book endorses conventional methods of historiography, nor that it subscribes to what Aida Levy-Hussen calls an "historical altericism," which she defines as "a discrete and declarative style of historical narration, and the inflexible priority of fact over fiction."[43] Like Levy-Hussen, we believe that trauma is passed on trans- and intergenerationally well beyond any living recollection of the original experience. But as Marianne Hirsch also reminds us, these forms of postmemory are "mediated not by recall but by *imaginative* investment, projection, and creation."[44] This certainly applies to cultural productions on slavery, where the imagination— or, in Toni Morrison's words, "a little bit of guess work"[45]—has long played a major role. Yet, within the steady stream of imaginative investment in slavery that has emerged from the late 1960s onward, we can discern important differences in kind and degree, reflective of how attitudes to the traumatic past evolve due to the changing cultural and sociopolitical contingencies of those who do the imagining. We therefore think it valid and useful to parse out more finely how African American culture's engagement with slavery has evolved, to stake out relevant continuities as well as shifts in emphasis—both of a political and poetological kind. While post-blackness might not be the only structure of feeling that manifests itself in the contemporary moment, we believe that it holds considerable viability and traction in late twentieth- and early twenty-first-century culture and therefore warrants closer critical reflection. As a generational ethos, an aesthetic praxis, and a theory of representation, it can productively contribute to current discussions regarding the place of slavery in the contemporary cultural imagination.

Finally, as our choice of title indicates, we have conceived of this book as an homage to Deborah E. McDowell's and Arnold Rampersad's pioneering work *Slavery and the Literary Imagination* (1989). This slim but important volume, which in August 2019 turned thirty years old, proved groundbreaking in opening up the field of study and discussion on "the interplay between slavery and the American literary imagination."[46] It was the first essay collection to trace the evolution of this interplay from Frederick Douglass to Sherley Anne Williams. McDowell and Rampersad's "hope that ideas and approaches generated in these essays will be applied to other texts, so that a more accurate and comprehensive sense of the subject will emerge" came true.[47] Numerous studies on African American cultural productions of slavery followed, bringing a new genre, the neo-slave narrative, to critical attention. Yet, while the by now classic canon of literary neo-slave narratives—including novels by Sherley Anne Williams, Toni Morrison, Octavia Butler, Ishmael Reed, David Bradley, and Charles Johnson—has received broad coverage, few scholarly works have kept up with more recent cultural productions: the literary neo-slave narratives of the 1990s and 2000s as well as the emergence of such narratives in nonprose fiction, such as poetry and drama, as well as in different media, such as in the visual arts, music, and the performing arts.[48] This is where our study sets in: taking inspiration from McDowell and Rampersad's book as well as D'Aguiar's assertion that each generation needs its own version of slavery, we here begin to map these more recent developments in African American culture from the 1990s to the 2010s.

Our volume, furthermore, seeks to highlight how the subject of slavery has branched out in the black cultural imagination to encompass a great variety of artistic media and genres: from the pages of the novel to the screens of TV and movie productions, the canvases of the visual arts, the sonic texture of popular music, and bodily performances on stage. Discussing recent works of prose fiction, verse, drama, the graphic novel, film, music, and the performing and visual arts—many of which have so far received little scholarly attention—the essays in *Slavery and the Post-Black Imagination* demonstrate the ubiquity and vibrancy of the post-black imagination in contemporary African American culture. To emphasize not only the enormous scope but also the vitality of the contemporary artistic imagination, we have, moreover, sought to combine the voices of critics with the voices of actual practitioners. For this reason, the collection includes alongside scholarly essays two interviews with artists. While our volume thus attempts to sketch out a varied yet broad-stroked picture of how a generation of artists who were born or came of age after the civil rights movement have engaged the various material, affective, and representational legacies of transatlantic slavery, we are also aware that this attempt remains incomplete and at best provisional. Like McDowell and Rampersad, we hope that other scholars will sketch in the blanks and nuance the shades.

We start off this book with two critical reflections on the aesthetic capacity, political utility, and theoretical value of post-blackness at the start of the twenty-first century, in a climate marked, somewhat paradoxically, by rampant antiblack racism, on the one hand, and neoliberal discourses of tolerance and diversity, on the other. Derek Conrad Murray's essay, "The Blackest Blackness," sets the stage for our collection with a provocative discussion of the meanings of representing blackness in African American art as well as African American scholarship. In his discussion of Kara Walker's carnivalesque silhouettes of antebellum plantation slavery, he identifies biting satire as the central operative form of self-criticality in post-black representational practice. Murray essentially reads Walker's cutouts in the spirit of a Žižekian "dirty joke" about slavery that not only completely ignores and undermines established protocols of propriety but also satirizes the relationship "between the social victim and those who are intent on (at least symbolically) healing the wounds of historical equality." He sees Walker's satirical engagement with canonical and popular representations of slavery articulating and modeling an intellectual practice that makes fun of "racial appropriates and the dogmas of historical memory" and embarks "upon a contentious intracultural debate about the social function of blackness (as culture) in the twenty-first century." This debate, Murray contends, is long overdue not only in the arts but also in institutionalized scholarship, where "blackness (as *the* subject of representation) has emerged as a kind of liberal cliché that allows for the performance of politically correct liberal sentiment." The satirical bite, aesthetic opacity, and ethical messiness of Walker's slavery silhouettes upend any attempt to fix and police the meanings of blackness—those anchored in the long history of antiblack racism, those sanctioned by institutional ideologies of liberal tolerance, or those endorsed by intracultural respectability politics. For Murray, then, in the spirit of Walker's artwork, post-blackness demarks "cultural positions that are beyond belongingness and, in many respects, embrace a condition of illegibility."

Derek C. Maus follows by recuperating a slightly older articulation of post-blackness, the post-soul, as a viable practice of representation, which he, like Murray, understands as functioning as "a liberating ethos" in times emboldened by white supremacy and its various blunt and subtle assertions of antiblack racism. In his reading of four recent novels on slavery—Colson Whitehead's *Underground Railroad*, Natashia Déon's *Glory*, Yaa Gyasi's *Homegoing*, and Ben Winters's *Underground Airlines*, all published in 2016, the year that saw the election of a president whose populist campaign hinged on the power of whiteness—Maus demonstrates how these various fictionalizations of slavery effectively tackle both the limits and the possibilities of our present moment. He sees the post-soul aesthetic functioning as an "intensely self-aware" historiographic metanarrative that not only "challenges Americans' ignorance . . . regarding slavery and its relationship to black identity in the twenty-first century" but also "repurposes," "blaxplores," and "bastardizes" established historiographical accounts to "contest and to complicate semantically impoverished cultural narratives . . . related to blackness." With his study Maus returns us to a more precise definition of post-black (compared to the one espoused by both advocates and critics of the postracial) in order to underscore how post-soul's original impetus for troubling established categories of blackness and devising new black historiographies counteracts both the resurgent "white supremacist ideology of recent years and the overly sunny assertions of racism's demise in the wake of Obama's election."

The subsequent essays examine the dynamics sketched out by Maus and Murray with close readings of individual works of art. In their readings of novels, films, and graphic novels, Cameron Leader-Picone, Mollie Godfrey, and Kimberly Nichele Brown show how contemporary artists engage modes of satire, intertextuality, and visuality by way of challenging the neoliberal rhetoric of color blindness and postracialism and revealing the continuing operations of systemic racism in contemporary society. They underline how post-black interrogations of the afterlife of slavery attempt to intervene formally and politically in established discourses of blackness. Cameron Leader-Picone discusses the role of satire in Paul Beatty's Booker Prize–winning 2015 novel *The Sellout*, where an autodiegetic narrator, "BonBon" Me, revives slavery and segregation in the fictional South Central Los Angeles town of Dickens. The novel, Leader-Picone argues, critiques American progress narratives rooted in the slow granting of citizenship and rights to black people. While it ostensibly sets up the illusory revival of slavery and segregation as the narrator's great offense against society, its ultimate satirical targets are "the market forces, state actors, legal structures, and intracommunity claims" that continue to restrict the freedom of black people. Deploying satire as its main mode of aesthetic inquiry and, similar to what Murray recognizes in Kara Walker's work, as a form of intellectual practice, Beatty unmasks narratives of racial progress and post–civil rights race neutrality as superficial and illusory. But he also challenges expectations of what African American literature should look like and how black characters should behave, particularly in relation to a genealogy of collective struggles for emancipation and equal rights. The ultimate targets of Beatty's satire are "discourses of authenticity"—confining discourses of identity imposed from both without and within the culture. It is in this sense that Leader-Picone sees post-blackness at work in Beatty's satire as favoring an "unmitigated blackness" that doesn't "giv[e] a fuck" and "doesn't sell." This post-blackness locates freedom not in claims to progressive collective change, past and future, but in individual liberation that defies essentializing categories.

Mollie Godfrey's discussion of Damian Duffy and John Jennings's 2017 graphic novel *Kindred*, an adaptation of Octavia Butler's 1976 novel of the same name, provides an interesting counterargument to Beatty's insistence on "unmitigated blackness." She explores how both the original and its adaptation use popular modes of presentation—science fiction and the graphic novel—to speak to the political needs of their respective moments. Where Butler's novel uses the device of time travel to pose complex questions about the intersectionality of race and gender in the struggle against racism in the context of black nationalist and second-wave feminist discourses of the 1970s, Duffy and Jennings's contemporary visual adaptation attempts to reimagine black activism for a young generation "coming of age surrounded by images of violence and brutality against black people." Where the original *Kindred* interrogates the value and limits of endurance and resistance as viable modes of survival and opposition, its younger cousin probes the value and limits of visual evidence and witnessing in that continuing struggle. Godfrey positions both works as "transitional moments in the rise and subsequent transformation" of the post-black aesthetic. Where Butler's novel, similar to Beatty's later work, complicates unified and exclusive visions of black collectivity under Black Power to foreground an intersectional feminism, Duffy and Jenning's graphic adaptation insists on the need to forge a new sense of "black collectivity without sacrificing the commitment to plurality, intersectionality, and inclusion upon which black feminists, black queer folk, and others insist." When read alongside each other, Beatty's 2015 novel and Duffy and Jenning's 2017 graphic novel thus point to a provocative convergence within the spectrum of post-black engagements with the past: assertions of a radical individualism, on the one hand, and insistence on the need for new forms of collectivity, albeit differential ones, on the other. We see this as a vital sign that post-blackness enables a variety of non-essentializing positionalities.

Kimberly Nichele Brown's essay sounds this conjunction further. In her analysis of Jordan Peele's 2017 horror film *Get Out*, she discusses how Peele effectively critiques the alleged advent of a postracial and color-blind society by bringing the film's implicit and symbolic commentary on American slavery to the surface. The Coagula Order, a sect composed of whites who transfer white psyches into the bodies of talented blacks, is Peele's way of signifying on both cultural appropriation and what Brown calls a "new millennial reframing of slavery in the United States." Further, Brown connects the Middle Passage reality of the Sunken Place to Peele's appeal to blacks that they "stay woke"—to "remain cognizant of slavery's afterlife."

The next group of contributions—by Chenjerai Kumanyika, Jack Hitt, and Chris Neary; Bertram D. Ashe; Ilka Saal; Malin Pereira; and Branden Jacobs-Jenkins—focuses on the performative dimensions of blackness, on the ways that contemporary artists playfully appropriate and refigure tropes, images, sounds, and narratives of slavery. We here publish the transcript of the *Uncivil* podcast episode "The Song," released by Gimlet Media in November 2017, which powerfully bespeaks the complex and often fraught histories of performative appropriation and reappropriation. In "The Song," podcast authors Chenjerai Kumanyika, Jack Hitt, and Chris Neary dig into the various layers of the history of "I Wish I Was in Dixie's Land"—a song that for many people has come to signify a sonic *lieu de mémoire* of slavery and white supremacy, having served during the Civil War as the unofficial anthem of the Confederacy. The podcast reveals the origins of "Dixie" in a free black family of musicians in Ohio and traces its laden history of appropriation by white minstrelsy musicians. It also highlights post-black attempts at reappropriation by the African American string band the Carolina Chocolate Drops. That the post-black refiguration of troubled representational legacies does not always work out is illustrated by the story of Drop member Justin Robinson, who eventually left the band when he felt that his performance of "Dixie" could no longer expose and trouble audience expectations.

In a similar vein, Ilka Saal's essay examines contemporary theater's penchant for rehearsing racializing stereotypes that have emerged in the context of slavery, including minstrelsy performances. Drawing on Branden Jacobs-Jenkins's play *Neighbors* (2010) and Young Jean Lee's *The Shipment* (2009) for case studies, Saal reads the use of stereotypes as partaking in complex layers of theatricality that seek to implicate audiences in the performance of race. Tapping into the affective and epistemological hold of the racist stereotype, these performances not only seek to shock and provoke; they aim to bring into focus the stereotype's inherent intersubjective dimension: the various scopic, psychic, and epistemic processes through which the audience is made complicit in the construction and performance of the racial object. At the same time, the self-aware and stylized performance of stereotypes can also allow performers to articulate resistance to the objectification inherent in the stereotype. Theatricalized performances of racist stereotypes, at their best, thus partake in the post-black assault on reified notions of blackness and reaffirm the fluidity of concepts of identity. However, Saal argues, as with all performances of affect, there is a risk that these performances might backfire—a risk the post-black artist is willing to take.

The force of the performative also plays an important role in Malin Pereira's reading of Thylias Moss's 2004 verse novel *Slave Moth*. Pereira examines how Moss revisits the familiar motifs of freedom, literacy, and identity in the traditional slave narrative in order to formulate a liberatory narrative of female agency. The lyrical subject, fourteen-year-old Varl, ultimately "wills herself to freedom" through various acts of critical and imaginative writing, despite external constraints resulting from her physical enslavement on a Tennessee plantation. In addition, Pereira zooms in on the various performances with which the poet-performer Moss accompanies the written text, such as staged dissent, oral performance, and the repurposing of a collectible object through sewing and photography. The extended artwork helps us identify embodied and disembodied "avatars of black female subjectivity" that challenge foundational and fetishized notions of truth about slavery, disrupt presumptive knowledge of black subjectivity, and reimagine black female objecthood as a strategy toward agency.

Bertram D. Ashe's discussion of Cheryl Dunye's mockumentary *The Watermelon Woman* (1996) focuses on the filmmaker's deployment of several frames of narrative and visual mediation. This technique, Ashe argues, enables Dunye not only to highlight the extent to which in the contemporary imagination slavery is always already mediated, always already a representation, but also to position her interrogations of these representational legacies in relation to contemporary black lesbian subjecthood. Blurring the boundaries between her own life and the life of her research subject, between mimesis and diegesis, as well as purposefully intermingling fact and fiction and interspersing a series of self-reflective commentaries, Dunye foregrounds the very contemporary meaning-making processes and politics at work in the performative archival reconstruction and artistic reproduction of slavery's subjects.

We round off this discussion with a brand-new interview with Obie Award–winning playwright Branden Jacobs-Jenkins, who has garnered nationwide and international acclaim with three plays addressing the legacies of American slavery: *Neighbors* (2010), *An Octoroon* (2014), and *Appropriate* (2014). Among other things, Jacobs-Jenkins here explains the profound role that audiences play in his theater productions and how he attempts to make audiences aware of their emotional reactions to racial representations, thus drawing them into a larger, communal conversation about contemporary meanings of blackness, its histories, and the spectator's own complicity in them. Humor plays an important role in his endeavor to induce spectators to leave the comfort zones of their habitual thinking about race—even as it sometimes walks a fine line between provocation and reification. Jacobs-Jenkins also mentions the formative influence that post-black visual artists, such as Kara Walker, Glenn Ligon, Lorna Simpson, and Kerry James Marshall, have had on his conception of theater as a visual event that thematizes and explores the scopic dynamics of constructing blackness.

In closing, then, the essays collated here powerfully demonstrate the complex ways a contemporary generation of artists is intensely aware of how the material, psychological, and representational afterlife of transatlantic slavery continues to affect present-day perceptions of blackness, whiteness, and race relations. And they engage these legacies head-on. They playfully, and often provocatively, refigure canonical, popular, and sacrosanct narratives, motifs, memes, and iconographies not only of dominant white historiographies but also of the counter-historiographies and counter-memories produced by previous generations of African American artists in order to give voice to what slavery means to them today in their own words and images.

NOTES

1 Fred D'Aguiar, "The Last Essay about Slavery," in *The Age of Anxiety*, ed. Sarah Dunant and Roy Porter (London: Virago Press, 1997), 126.

2 Judith Misrahi-Barak, "Post-*Beloved* Writing: Review, Revitalize, Recalculate," *Black Studies Papers* 1, no. 1 (2014): 39, http://elib.suub.uni-bremen.de/edocs /00103775-1.pdf.

3 Misrahi-Barak, "Post-*Beloved* Writing," 39. For Rushdy's definition, see Ashraf Rushdy, *Neo-Slave Narratives: Studies in the Social Logic of a Form* (New York: Oxford University Press, 1999).

4 Misrahi-Barak, "Post-*Beloved* Writing," 42.

5 Stephen Best, "On Failing to Make the Past Present," *Modern Language Quarterly* 73, no. 3 (September 2012): 466.

6 Best, "On Failing to Make the Past Present," 472.

7 Best, "On Failing to Make the Past Present," 465.

8 Best, "On Failing to Make the Past Present," 466.

9 Margo Natalie Crawford, "The Inside-Turned-Out Architecture of the Post-Neo Slave Narrative," in *The Psychic Hold of Slavery: Legacies in American Expressive Culture*, ed. Soyica Diggs-Colbert, Robert J. Patterson, and Aida Levy-Hussen (New Brunswick, NJ: Rutgers University Press, 2016), 70, italics in original.

10 Crawford, "The Inside-Turned-Out Architecture," 70.

11 Crawford here uses a phrase from Colin Davis's reading of Jacques Derrida's *Specters of Marx* in his article "Hauntology, Spectres, and Phantoms." Crawford, "The Inside-Turned-Out Architecture," 81.

12 Joseph Roach builds with the concept of the "circum-Atlantic" on Paul Gilroy's seminal study *The Black Atlantic* (1993) by way of foregrounding the co-creative, performative oceanic interculture that was created and deeply impacted by the diasporic and genocidal histories of the transatlantic slave trade. See Joseph Roach, *Cities of the Dead: Circum-Atlantic Performance* (New York: Columbia University Press, 1996).

13 Raymond Williams, *Marxism and Literature* (Oxford: Oxford University Press, 1971), 131.

14 Williams, *Marxism and Literature*, 132.

15 See Astrid Erll's notion of generationality in this regard. Astrid Erll, "Generation in Literary History: Three Constellations of Generationality, Genealogy, and Memory," *New Literary History* 45, no. 3 (Summer 2014): 385–409.

16 Thelma Golden, "Introduction," in *Freestyle* (New York: Studio Museum in Harlem, 2001), 14.

17 Golden, "Introduction," 14.

18 Bertram D. Ashe, "Theorizing the Post-Soul Aesthetic: An Introduction," *African American Review* 41, no. 4 (2007): 610. See also Mark Anthony Neal, *Soul Babies: Black Popular Culture and the Post-Soul Aesthetic* (New York: Routledge 2002); Nelson George, *Buppies, B-Boys, Baps & Bohos: Notes on Post-Soul Black Culture* (New York: Da Capo Press, 1992); Trey Ellis, "The New Black Aesthetic," *Callaloo* 12, no. 1 (Winter 1989): 233–43; Ytasha L. Womack, *Post Black: How a New Generation Is Redefining African American Identity* (Chicago: Chicago Review Press, 2010); and Touré. *Who's Afraid of Post-Blackness? What It Means to Be Black Now* (New York: Free Press, 2011).

19 Ashe, "Theorizing the Post-Soul Aesthetic," 614.

20 Ashe, "Theorizing the Post-Soul Aesthetic," 614.

21 Derek Conrad Murray, *Queering Post-Black Art: Artists Transforming African-American Identity after Civil Rights* (London: I. B. Taurus, 2016), 2.

22 Murray, *Queering Post-Black Art*, 25

23 Murray, *Queering Post-Black Art*, 3.

24 Shelby Steele, "Ralph Ellison's Blues," *Journal of Black Studies* 7, no. 4 (Dec 1976): 153.

25 For a discussion of nuances of difference, see Paul C. Taylor, "Post-Black, Old-Black," *African American Review* 41, no. 4 (Winter 2007): 625–40.

26 See Houston A. Baker Jr. and K. Merinda Simmons, eds., *The Trouble with Post-Black* (New York: Columbia University Press, 2015).

27 Margo Natalie Crawford, *Black Post-Blackness: The Black Arts Movement and Twenty-First-Century Aesthetics* (Urbana: University of Illinois Press, 2017).

28 Crawford, *Black Post-Blackness*, 2.

29 On this score, see for instance Michelle Alexander, *The New Jim Crow: Mass Incarceration in the Age of Colorblindness* (New York: New Press, 2010); Ta-Nehisi Coates, *We Were Eight Years in Power: An American Tragedy* (New York: One World, 2017).

30 Best, "On Failing to Make the Past Present," 460.

31 Best, "On Failing to Make the Past Present," 460. Best cites Slavoj Žižek here.

32 D'Aguiar, "The Last Essay about Slavery," 126.

33 Soyica Diggs Colbert, "Introduction: 'Do You Want to Get Well?,'" in Colbert, Patterson, and Levy-Hussen, *The Psychic Hold of Slavery*, 3.

34 Robert J. Patterson, "Conclusion: Black Lives Matter, Except When They Don't: Why Slavery's Psychic Hold Matters," in Colbert, Patterson, and Levy-Hussen, *The Psychic Hold of Slavery*, 213.

35 Patterson, "Conclusion," 215.

36 On this score, see also Douglas A. Jones Jr., "The Fruit of Abolition: Discontinuity and Difference in Terrance Hayes's 'The Avocado,'" in Colbert, Patterson, and Levy-Hussen, *The Psychic Hold of Slavery*, 39–54, as well as the above-mentioned essay by Margot Natalie Crawford, "The Inside-Turned-Out Architecture of the Post-Neo Slave Narrative," in the same volume.

37 See, for instance, the essays by Aida Levy-Hussen, "Trauma and the Historical Turn in Black Literary Discourse," and Calvin Warren, "Black Time: Slavery, Metaphysics, and the Logic of Wellness," both in Colbert, Patterson, and Levy-Hussen, *The Psychic Hold of Slavery*.

38 Branden Jacobs-Jenkins, *An Octoroon* (New York: Dramatists Play Service, 2015), 17.

39 William Wells Brown, "A Lecture Delivered before the Female Anti-Slavery Society of Salem," in *The Works of William Wells Brown: Using His 'Strong, Manly Voice,'* ed. Paula Garrett and Hollis Robbins (Oxford: University of Oxford Press, 2006), 4.

40 Toni Morrison, "The Site of Memory," in *Inventing the Truth: The Art and Craft of Memoir*, ed. William Zinsser (New York: Houghton Mifflin, 1998), 192. Consider similar statements by Margret Walker, who, with her 1966 novel *Jubilee*, aims "to set the record straight where Black people are concerned" or by Sherley Anne Williams, who, with her neo-slave narrative *Dessa Rose* (1986), wants "to own a summer in the 19th century." See Charles H. Rowell, "Poetry, History, and Humanism: An Interview with Margaret Walker," in *Conversations with Margaret Walker*, ed. Maryemma Graham (Jackson: University Press of Mississippi, 2002), 23; and Sherley Anne Williams, "Author's Note," in *Dessa Rose* (1986; repr., New York: Harper 1999), 6.

41 Linda Hutcheon, *Poetics of Postmodernism: History, Theory, Fiction* (New York: Routledge, 1988), 75.

42 Soyica Diggs Colbert, *The African American Theatrical Body* (Cambridge: Cambridge University Press, 2011), 8.

43 Levy-Hussen, "Trauma and the Historical Turn," 207.

44 Marianne Hirsch, *The Generation of Postmemory: Writing and Visual Culture after the Holocaust* (New York: Columbia University Press, 2012), 5, emphasis added.

45 Morrison, "The Site of Memory," 192.

46 Deborah E. McDowell and Arnold Rampersad, "Introduction," in *Slavery and the Literary Imagination*, ed. Deborah E. McDowell and Arnold Rampersad (Baltimore: Johns Hopkins University Press, 1989), x.

47 McDowell and Rampersad, "Introduction," x.

48 On recent developments in literature, see for instance Arlene R. Keizer, *Black Subjects: Identity Formation in the Contemporary Narrative of Slavery* (Ithaca, NY: Cornell University Press, 2004); Lars Eckstein, *Re-membering the Black Atlantic: On the Poetics and Politics of Literary* Memory (Amsterdam: Rodopi, 2006); Abigal Ward, *Caryl Phillips, David Dabydeen, and Fred D'Aguiar: Representations of Slavery* (Manchester: Manchester University Press, 2011). For recent developments in the visual arts, see, for instance, Gwendolyn Dubois Shaw, *Seeing the Unspeakable: The Art of Kara Walker* (Durham: Duke University Press, 2004); Celeste-Marie Bernier, *African American Visual Arts* (Edinburgh: Edinburgh University Press, 2008); and Huey Copeland, *Bound to Appear: Art, Slavery, and the Site of Blackness in Multicultural America* (Chicago: University of Chicago Press, 2013).

CHAPTER ONE

THE BLACKEST BLACKNESS

Slavery and the Satire of Kara Walker

DEREK CONRAD MURRAY

HAS BLACKNESS SIMPLY BECOME *CULTURE*—A MERE PAGEANT TO BE performed in the halls of the ivory tower? As African American art historians, with our impressive degrees, speaking with impassioned grace about the historical and present-day traumas of black life and its various relics and spectacles, do we merely polish what I've come to characterize as the *memorabilia of marginalia*? In the midst of an African American art history event at an institution that has been historically indifferent to that very field, I began to ponder these questions. The irony, of course, is that without that very institution's support, the event would likely not have occurred in the first place. Possibly for that reason, not one paper broached the topic of the discipline's long-standing erasure of African American art and culture: the theoretical dismissiveness, the paucity of black students in art history, and the appalling lack of African American art historians on the faculty of art history programs—including the one that was hosting the event. With each lecture, I became more agitated, as it grew clear I could no longer play the role of the ennobled suffering black academic: the one who poetically muses about the beauty and dignity of blackness in the face of benign neglect. Our job is to celebrate, to commemorate, to recover what has been lost and ignored: to perform a cultural appreciation of the margins.

These feelings were not new. In fact, they have bubbled to the surface in my writing for years, but this was different. It was a primal scene of sorts. I had hit the wall. I was less concerned about the scholarship itself. All of these emergent academics were bright, their papers interesting, and their subjects illuminating. My concern was the performance of proper blackness: a combination of posturing and racial sermonizing mixed with a politics of authenticity laced with the markers of art-historical appropriateness. Needless to say, I've become increasingly concerned that the African American art historian's role is to perform a pleasing yet nonthreatening display of blackness. But there is also a logic that subtends this performative positionality: a logic that suggests that our self-love is the greatest love of all. It is, in fact, a beacon of self-love, a guiding force for all those laboring on the periphery. It is the *blackest blackness*. Our very institutional presence hinges upon our performance of racial health and dignified suffering, our well-adjusted sense of ethnic pride—*and, perhaps most importantly*, our unwillingness to challenge institutional, disciplinary, and methodological exclusions.

When it was time for me to speak, rather than respond directly to the papers I had been asked to address, I read the following joke by Slovenian philosopher Slavoj Žižek:

> THERE IS A NICELY VULGAR JOKE about Christ: the night before he was arrested and crucified, his followers started to worry—Christ was still a virgin; wouldn't it be nice to have him experience a little bit of pleasure before he dies? So they asked Mary Magdalene to go to the tent where Christ was resting and seduce him; Mary said she would do it gladly and went in, but five minutes later, she ran out screaming, terrified and furious. The followers asked her what went wrong, and she explained: "I slowly undressed, spread my legs and showed Christ my pussy; he looked at it, said 'What a terrible wound! It should be healed!' and gently put his palm on it."
>
> So beware of people too intent on healing other people's wounds—what if one enjoys one's wound? In exactly the same way, directly healing the wound of colonialism (effectively returning to the pre-colonial reality) would have been a nightmare: if today's Indians were to find themselves in pre-colonial reality, they would have undoubtedly uttered the same terrified scream as Mary Magdalene.[1]

The reading of the joke was not premeditated. It was a spontaneous act and it was met with silence and shock, if not also revulsion. But I was liberated. In that instance, I had unwittingly stepped outside the borders of racial appropriateness and proper blackness. The act itself was satirical; it was meant to provoke *everyone* in the room, including myself—not simply to indict histories of white racism, but to also redirect the critique inward and

DEREK CONRAD MURRAY

back upon itself. I felt a need to turn away, albeit somewhat clumsily, from the institutional theatrics of black pride. It did not go over well.

The joke resonates with me because it utilizes biting satire to call into question the often-farcical relation between the social victim and those who are intent (at least symbolically) on healing the wounds of historical inequity. And in my closing comments, I left the audience with a question: "Is it our role as black art historians to merely (and performatively) *enjoy our wounds* as social spectacle?" In other words, is it our institutional position to find new entertaining and expressive means to perform blackness as intellectual entertainment? The public enactment of black rage, black sorrow, black pride, and black fear have become as routinized and predictable as the institutional exclusions and forms of discrimination that continue to marginalize people of African descent. These absurd pageants, which I tend to view as a form of ventriloquism, have not transformed academic and intellectual cultures into more equitable spaces. So what purpose do they serve?

I recount this narrative as a metaphor for the unique representational troubling of post-blackness envisioned in the artistic production of Kara Walker. The introduction of Walker's infamous narrative tableaux into the American art scene created a violent rupture in the genteel and self-consciously dignified space of African American art. Her images were not stifled by respectability politics, even while they were unflinching in their indictment of histories of antiblack racism. Walker's approach was more holistic, more Foucauldian in its discursive exploration of power and its abuses. In its engagement with black people, her work did not shy away from *the mess*, so to speak: the forms of self-abuse, the intracultural nihilism, and our complicity with antiblackness. Satire is her weapon of choice, and for that reason, her images were met with condemnation and calls for censorship from within the black community itself. Walker's work serves as an exemplar for the mobilization of satire as a form of self-criticality.

This type of work needs to be done in order for black artists and scholars alike to reject the stifling dictates of compulsory essentialism: a limitation that hinders progress and forbids self-criticality. However, this potentially breaches the sacrosanct intracultural demand for racial fidelity, one of the fundamental dimensions of African American community. The boundaries of black authenticity, which are most readily expressed in a set of visual and behavioral markers that define one's rootedness in blackness (black cultural distinctiveness), are rigidly policed—and ultimately define one's racial legitimacy.

Post-blackness, as a theory of representation, has enabled us to unpack these complexities as they manifest visually, yet as scholars and historians of color, there needs to be a post-black satire as intellectual praxis that transcends the mere performance of racial authenticity. Many in the African American artistic and intellectual communities have reacted to post-black with condemnation and hostility. These attitudes have largely been the result of two core misinterpretations. The first is its mischaracterization as a postracial stance (an antiblack blackness). The second is a failure to understand that post-black is a theory of representation: it is a means to both understand and characterize a set of aesthetic, conceptual, political, and artistic tendencies that are present in the creative practices of post–civil rights generation artists. It is not, in contrast to its rampant mischaracterization, a genre of art—nor should its critical engagement be regarded as a form of advocacy. The role of the critic (as a public witness) is to characterize cultural forms: to explicate them and to render judgment—but not to promote them. Post-black functions as a means to unpack a shifting set of attitudes and expressive modalities about blackness that are steeped in satire.

The aim of this analysis is to explore the intricacies of Walker's unique brand of satirical troubling, an approach that is intent on pushing through the boundaries of respectability politics and racial obligation that continue to inform (if not also limit) the genre of contemporary African American art, not to mention its interpretive possibilities and historiography. Post-black satire continues to be a fraught and largely misunderstood polemical tool, and Walker has utilized it to forge a representational path that has indelibly transformed how artists and intellectuals conceptualize the possibilities of black artistic production in the twenty-first century. This paper will unpack how Walker mobilizes a post-black sensibility to reimagine and reanimate cultural and representational engagements with the legacy of slavery.

A MESSY REFUSAL OF RESPECTABILITY POLITICS

African American artist Kara Walker has built a considerable body of work that tackles the most controversial and thorny issues in American history—specifically, the legacy of chattel slavery, its complex power relations, and attendant physical and psychic violence. As a post–civil rights artist, Walker's formal and critical approach has evolved alongside the rise of post-blackness, a divisive terminology that has most popularly been utilized to characterize the conceptual, aesthetic, and political particularities of African American contemporary art production in the post–civil rights era. Walker is a deft formalist whose work has pushed the boundaries and representational conventions of contemporary art; however, her oeuvre continues to confound audiences and cultural commentators alike—not least because she has managed to blend formal lyricism and material sophistication with post-blackness and its subversive and biting racial satire.

I embark on this writing with a healthy dose of cynicism because, since Walker's emergence in the art world in the '90s, there has been a regressive turn in the historiography of African American art toward a combination of respectability politics and racial sermonizing that has produced less of what could be characterized as a discourse and more a platform for recuperation and celebration. Blackness has become a type of fetish, a symbol of either social suffering or cultural spectacle—or perhaps a combination of both. And in our digitally inflected society, I increasingly view blackness as a type of playable and inhabitable media. It is, in many respects, the coolest suffering and the most resplendent of abjections. But along those lines, the apparent rise of, or at least increased visibility of, antiblack violence in American life and its visual culture (i.e., the current cultural fascination and moral outrage around the ubiquity of police shootings) has been responsible for several related phenomena, one of the most significant being a renewed interest in antiracist activism and the rise of the Black Lives Matter movement—which has greatly impacted cultural consciousness around the continued persistence of antiblackness in America's cities, not to mention corrupt and racially skewed systems of criminal justice and incarceration. These social ills are well known and often debated; yet on the level of representation, there is a greater need to interrogate what amounts to a pornographics of violence implicit within the visual spectacles of these media images.

Walker's incendiary formalism makes explicit reference to the violence inflicted upon black bodies—as well as to the relation among "vision, visualizing and visibility," identifications that are deeply entangled in the logics of power and social authority.[2] Given the representational entanglements between images of antiblack violence in American visual culture and an increased consumer demand for black bodies in contemporary art, it is necessary to consider how satire upends a compulsory politics of racial fidelity and begins to embark upon a contentious intracultural debate about the social function of blackness (as culture) in the twenty-first century.

The curation of blackness has always been a fault line and an enduring source of institutional consternation. Case in point: the melee over artist Dana Schutz's painting *Open Casket* (a recreation of the notorious photograph of the slain Emmett Till), which caused a stir when included in the 2017 Whitney Biennial in New York. Schutz, a white American artist, was attacked for laying claim to an image of antiblack violence: an iconic photograph that many in the black arts community felt was the domain of African American culture.

What ensued was a highly contentious and very public debate about the presence of such images in our media-saturated culture. While not taking a partisan position in this debate, I will say that I found it particularly generative that there was a public discussion about the proliferation of images of black suffering. What do these images mean? And what is their social function? In many respects, both the images and the very predictable response to their presence have become culture—and therefore, I am beginning to question the larger social role that blackness (as an imago and a positionality) plays in the cultural landscape. Nicole Fleetwood suggests that it is understood within visual culture scholarship that "optical technologies have been used to discipline racialized bodies," and as she reminds us, "vision and visual technologies, in this context, are seen as hostile and violent forces that render blackness as aberration."[3] Fleetwood effectively captures the inescapability of racial marking that is implicit to vision and visuality—and which functions as a powerful means to maintain power relations rooted in containment, repression, and social control. I'm also thinking here of Christian Metz's concept *scopic regime*, which has been instrumental in theorizations dedicated to unpacking the relation between looking and power, as well as the use of visual technologies within the realm of the imaginary—and as a means to produce desire.[4] Considering the relation between looking and power, vis-à-vis the representation of black bodies, there has not been a significant intracultural dialogue about the perpetuation and proliferation of what could be characterized as antiblack images by artists of African descent. Nor has there been a conversation about how black cultural producers' self-position within the logics of antiblackness in the United States. If there is one central component of Walker's work, it is that she has weaponized satire to broach these difficult issues, igniting a debate that is in much need of reinvigoration.

I tend to view Slavoj Žižek's dirty joke about Christ as operating much like Walker's imagery; that is, I see her artwork as essentially dirty jokes about slavery. There is a perceived earnestness in the interpretation of Walker's work that tends to overlook the presence of satire, an element that lies very much on the surface of her production. This characteristic, which is really an expressive mode, has been present even in interviews, her personal biographical accounts, and commentaries. To a certain degree, this element of her creativity and public persona has produced much controversy. The first time I encountered Walker's work was in her 1997 exhibition "Upon My Many Masters" at the San Francisco Museum of Modern Art (SFMOMA). The most significant piece in the exhibition, a sweeping wall installation titled *The End of Uncle Tom and the Grand Allegorical Tableau of Eva in Heaven*, filled much of the gallery space, engulfing viewers in a

1.1   Kara Walker, Detail from *The End of Uncle Tom and the Grand Allegorical Tableau of Eva in Heaven*, 1995. Cut paper on wall. Installation dimensions variable; approx. 156 × 420 inches (396.2 × 1066.8 cm). Courtesy of Sikkema Jenkins & Co., New York.

bacchanalian display of depravity. The initial experience of viewing this work was jarring, as Walker's imagery was both intensely violent and sexual: yet what stood out most prominently was the artist's engagement with the antebellum plantation. All of the images contained a certain narrative opacity, or perhaps muddiness, that rendered her motivations somewhat unclear. That seeming ambivalence around one's moral interpretation of slavery was puzzling for viewers. And Walker appeared to be making fun of her audience: chiding the popular historical memory of slavery—a history that is rife with cliché, stereotype, and romanticism.

The imagery in *The End of Uncle Tom and the Grand Allegorical Tableau of Eva in Heaven* was disturbing in its self-conscious abjection: a slave girl being sodomized by what appears to be an elderly white male slave owner, while his sword penetrates the belly of a small child on the ground; meanwhile, three slave women and a child suckle each other's breasts. In another section of the tableau, a small slave girl casually defecates, leaving a trail of feces.

A reference to Harriet Beecher Stowe's 1852 novel *Uncle Tom's Cabin*, Walker's installation, upon more careful viewing, contained more heady and astute references. Scholar Gwendolyn DuBois Shaw aptly described the nuances of *The End of Uncle Tom*, unpacking the cleverness of its literary references invoking "the restaging of an apocryphal episode from Harriett Beecher Stowe's 1852 sentimental novel *Uncle Tom's Cabin*" but also "piles of excrement, children being sexually assaulted, and babies being murdered, elements that didn't fit in with my memory of the book."[5]

The form of Walker's work during this early stage of her career is now widely known: cutout silhouettes made of stark black paper that are adhered to the gallery walls. The formal dexterity and precision of Walker's craft are indeed a marvel to behold. Since the late 1990s, the artist has added drawing and video to her oeuvre, though the cutouts have remained a staple—as has the subject matter. In the wake of her ascendancy, slavery has emerged as *the* leitmotif of black art and visual culture discourse in the United States. Walker's success and the fearlessness of her representational sign system legitimated the subject of slavery, a phenomenon that emerged simultaneously with the rising interest in lynching photography.[6] Art historian Debra Willis's work on the often-neglected history of African American photography was transformative and encouraged scholars to critically explore the vast archives of photographs of black subjects—most notably, the fraught images of antiblack violence.[7] The relationship between slavery and satire (vis-à-vis post-blackness) in Walker's production is my interest here—primarily because it is what her work *does*, not what it depicts, that defines its lasting significance. There is an operation at work: an ideological slight of hand that is in dialogue with racial appropriates and the dogmas of historical memory. This dimension of Walker's conceptual approach—the ideological troubling—is often missed in critical interpretations of her production. For example, writer Kevin Young suggests, "Whatever we feel about Walker's work, she isn't kidding—or rather, her joke is a serious one, skewering the unstated, presumptuous, and unseemly desires of race, racism, and even the artist herself."[8]

Young characterizes Walker's critique as less satirical and more in earnest in its very pointed and visceral indictment of American racism. I argue, however, that in her cynicism, Walker's engagement with slavery is both a joke and in earnest at the same time: a contradiction, or perhaps a conundrum. For some, her blasphemous satire offends precisely because it is read as more of an exercise in detachment than a sincere take on America's history of abuse. Adding fuel to the fire, the artist (particularly in the early stages of her career) made statements that expressed ambivalence toward her blackness. For that reason, Walker has always been accused by the older generation of having a cavalier, mocking, and disrespectful attitude toward her own history, and part of the backlash has been directed toward the self-loathing the artist articulates in regard to her own identity. On several notable occasions, Walker has spoken openly about her ambivalence toward her African American identity and has articulated a kind of passive complicity with the incestuous and sadomasochistic mechanisms of American racism. In a 1996 interview with New York art critic Jerry Saltz, Walker once notoriously stated that "all black people in America want to be slaves a little bit."[9] Walker has made other inflammatory statements over the years, comments seemingly designed to poke fun at certain black folks—particularly those who, in their essentialist attitudes, wield black victimization as a form of cultural currency.

Gwendolyn DuBois Shaw recounts Walker's recollections of her childhood in Atlanta, where she speaks of being ostracized by other African American children because they perceived her California accent to be too white:

> Surrounded by the legacy of the Jim Crow laws and the *Gone With the Wind* mystique that Atlanta self-cultivates, the teenage Walker viewed her life as though it were being led in a minstrel show, one that she had accidentally fallen into. She began seeing her racial identity as something that was lived and performed on a daily basis in a sort of "pageant" in which she was a willing participant. Her experience of this pageant, which she has likened to a continual reenactment of the Civil War era in the present day, became a metaphor for her contact with the unknown. In reflection of these teenage experiences, much of her art has been a search to discover exactly what *her* role might be within this unbidden drama.[10]

Shaw's observations are correct in that they aptly characterize a budding satirical impulse in Walker: a cynicism that ultimately endeavored to upset the dictates of racial obligation. The artist's entry into the international art world produced a violent rupture and a departure from respectability. The most infamous response to Walker was by Betye Saar, the respected African American conceptual artist. Born in 1926, Saar is a much-revered elder stateswoman in the arena of black American art, as well as a noted commentator on the history of antiblack racism. It is now a well-known story, but Saar launched a letter-writing campaign against Walker in the wake of the younger artist having been awarded the MacArthur Fellowship in 1997. Saar found it offensive that such an inexperienced artist could be given a distinction often awarded to individuals much farther along in their careers: "How do young persons just a few years out of school get a show in a major museum? The whole art establishment picked their work up and put it at the head of the class. This is the danger, not the artists themselves. This is like closet racism. It relieves them of the responsibility to show other artists. Here we are at the end of the millennium seeing work that is derogatory and racist."[11] Saar further states: "I have nothing against Walker except that I think she is young and foolish. . . . Kara is selling us down the river."[12] It has been pointed out by Shaw and many other commentators, including myself, that there is a contradictory dimension to Saar's critique of Walker, namely that the elder artist was at one time a racial provocateur herself, producing iconic works that used a biting wit (not to mention the playful resurrection of racial caricatures) to skewer the representational intricacies of antiblackness in the United States.

My reading of this contradiction lies in satire itself: a conceptual strategy employed by Walker (and many of her post–civil rights contemporaries), yet absent within Saar's more politically earnest indictment of white racism. Put more bluntly, Saar critiques the dominant culture. Walker, on the other hand, ridicules and critiques everyone. It is a risky approach and one that has garnered the artist a fair share of haters among the black middle class. As Shaw explains, Walker found herself "disowned by some members of her race because she spoke the unspeakable. By both inhabiting and purveying an interracial, post-Negritude encounter for her spectator, Walker is the 'bad girl' who rejects the role that her community would have her assume. Her lack of solidarity with the aims of a specific segment of the African-American middle class makes her a traitor to their cause of assimilationist integration."[13]

Shaw's blunt assessment of Walker's intervention, along with the response to it, is extremely significant to black art discourse, particularly because it broaches the uncomfortable topic of black cultural norms and their intracultural policing—which take the form of certain (often unspoken) expectations and behavioral and representational codes. The sacrosanct nature of black solidarity among the middle class is in many ways Walker's foil, yet she simultaneously challenges a specific set of demands placed on the African American artist: that they produce phantasmagorical images of blackness that traffic in racial stereotypes and the comic folly of African Americans. Walker resolves this expectation through her use of satire. She turns that expectation back onto the viewers, ridiculing their fetishistic and racialized desires while simultaneously critiquing her own complicity with this embattled relation.

American art historian Tanya Sheehan asked the important question "Where do we look for race?"[14] According to Sheehan's account, historians of American art in the second half of the twentieth century—particularly those concerned with the visual representation of race and identity—repeatedly returned to this question. In her assessment of this trend, scholars addressed this important query by turning their intellectual attention toward the black body—or more specifically, to racialized blackness. Sheehan's model is a useful exemplar of a methodological problem in American art discourse regarding the fetishization of difference. Too often, scholars of art history and visual culture perpetuate a series of clichéd positions around difference—while not attending oppositionally (as the Slovenian philosopher Slavoj Žižek suggests) to the structural barriers that prevent equity from occurring.

The historian is correct that during this period, especially during the identity debates of the 1980s and early '90s, and within museum exhibitions and institutional art discourses, there was a rising interest in contemplating the black body within the field of representation. These exhibitions, as Sheehan reminds us, were accompanied by published catalogs with a robust body of new scholarship exploring racial representation in the works of American artists like Thomas Eakins, John Singleton Copley, and Winslow Homer, as well as African American artists from the Harlem Renaissance to the era of multiculturalism.[15] In our contemporary moment, black artists must always contend with the cultural demand for authentic images of blackness. Their identity must always be on display: reified and tangible in its sincerity—a portal into the darkest regions of alterity.[16] African American artists know all too well that they produce their work in a culture where blackness (as Sheehan asserts) functions as a representational shorthand for discussions of race. The art of Kara Walker resists this expectation. Its social role is to be forever locked in a state of perpetual disobedience. It is an Otherness that stands beyond: unacknowledged and always transgressing—even while glaringly present and visible. What I am suggesting here is that there are differences that *need* to go unrecognized: always disobeying and forever outside of legitimate social existence. That is their social role: to be outsiders, to be a resplendent spectacle of unknowable difference, authentic and real in its mysterious marginalia. Walker is that disobedient subject, standing defiantly outside of social convention—and always transgressing.

LIBERAL TOLERANCE AND SOCIAL SYMBOLISM

A range of intellectuals—most notably Slavoj Žižek, as well as philosopher Wendy Brown and British-Australian scholar Sara Ahmed, have influenced my recent writings on liberal tolerance in the discourses of visual culture. In his meditations on the contradictions of liberalism, Žižek posed an important query:

> Why are today so many problems perceived as problems of intolerance, not as problems of inequality, exploitation, injustice? Why is the proposed remedy tolerance, not emancipation, political struggle, even armed struggle? The immediate answer is the liberal multiculturalist's basic ideological operation: the "culturalization of politics"—political differences, differences conditioned by political inequality, economic exploitation, etc., are naturalized/neutralized into "cultural" differences, different "ways of life," which are something given, something that cannot be overcome, but merely "tolerated."[17]

In the above quotation, Žižek locates what he characterizes as a liberal cliché: the facile identification with the Other as public performance, while either upholding or failing to challenge official structures of inequality. He has also termed this the *culturalization of politics*—the performance of political sentiment as cultural posturing.[18] If we define culture as the cumulative beliefs, values, attitudes, and meanings of a given society, the *culturalization* of politics suggests that antihegemonic sentiments have become just that: a collective set of cultivated behaviors and expressed attitudes that perform a kind of pleasing facsimile of political feeling. Within institutions, antiracism and antihomophobia (for example) have become a bureaucratically procedural and routinized form of political correctness.

In keeping with this notion, we must continually question our so-called liberal and progressive discourses—particularly, and most urgently, the multicultural justice to which they claim a commitment. Along those lines, there is a need to challenge the genteel, hushed political correctness of liberalism's bureaucratic approach to "diversity." The term *diversity* has become a kind of twenty-first-century symbol for the evils of institutionalized political correctness and the patronizing culture of trigger warnings, safe spaces, polite speech, tokenism, racial fetishism, and symbolic philanthropic gestures. If there is a politically correct expressiveness within the realm of American art history, it manifests itself in both intellectual and representational engagements with the visualization of *blackness*. In certain respects, blackness (as *the* subject of representation) has emerged as a kind of liberal cliché that allows for the performance of politically correct liberal sentiment.

DEREK CONRAD MURRAY

Philosopher Wendy Brown takes on the politically leftist adherence to the cultural and institutional logics of tolerance, which form the basis for current conceptions of liberalism. Brown argues that while tolerance is uncritically associated with modern Western culture, regulation and marginalization rest at its core: that to tolerate is not to affirm, but to conditionally allow the presence of the unwanted—a set of cultural and institutional practices she has termed "mannered racialism."[19] Therefore, liberal tolerance both sustains and is invested in the marginality of certain subjects, and ultimately consolidates the power of the dominant. What is at stake here is the realization that liberal tolerance "produces, organizes, and marks subjects."[20] I have taken up the problems of liberal tolerance specifically because they profoundly inform how cultural production is assessed, valued, and devalued. Along those lines, art produced by socially defined minorities, as well as the cultural production of a range of *Others* (whose work is dedicated to contesting the presence of inequity), is marginalized in the histories and institutional structures of the arts.

Liberal tolerance is fundamentally about saying the right things: polite speech, trigger warnings, antihomophobic and antiracist declarations, tokenism, symbolic events, and so on. However, my argument here (which is informed by Žižek and Brown) is that the institutional rhetoric of diversity often functions as a politically correct means to overtly disseminate the values of exclusion and management. Read through the logic of Brown's critique specifically, diversity means: Yes, "our" institution discriminates. It regulates access to the institution and stringently controls a certain constituency's ability to thrive. On the other hand, our discrimination is a polite one: it is rooted in tolerance and symbolic decency and manners. Under diversity, minorities may be demeaned or subordinated; yet they will be spared *homophobia*, *transphobia*, or *racism* (i.e., irrational brutal outbursts, physical violence, threats, etc.). Therefore structural bigotry (and its attendant forms of violence) is always something that occurs beyond the borders of liberal institutions and their stated values.

Sara Ahmed characterizes the function of "diversity work" within liberal institutions as generating the "right image" and fixing the wrong one, which improperly places the focus on correcting perceptions rather than eliminating structural inequities.[21] But that same "diversity work of perception" (the image game) is at play in disciplinary research methods as well, where the presence of difference (both institutionally and representationally) is treated as an unwanted guest that is tolerated—and as Ahmed articulates, "They are temporary residents in someone else's home. . . . [T]hey are welcomed *on condition* they return that hospitality by integrating into a common organizational culture, or by 'being' diverse, and allowing institutions to celebrate their diversity."[22]

The black body in the milieu of institutionally dominant art history functions as one of its ultimate and most typifying reductions: the social symbol par excellence. My argument here is that "social symbolism" is diversity's ultimate product: the reduction of difference as a legible and reducible imago. Put more bluntly, liberal tolerance produces an *ideal subject*, and it is this subject with which we must continually contend.

I have utilized Žižek's writings as an exemplar that has meaningfully taken up the structural logics of tolerance in liberal intellectual thought. Like Wendy Brown, Žižek's approach locates contradictions within liberal progressiveness that position difference in the role of social victimhood in both *discourse and representation*, only to fail these constituencies in larger efforts to bring about equitable change. If considered through the lens of Žižek's and Brown's critique of liberal tolerance, in defending itself, American visual culture ultimately conceals its "innermost obscene secret": that within its institutional and representational frameworks and value systems are rituals and habits that marginalize, stereotype, and distort.[23] And according to Žižek, it is precisely this "obscene underground of habits" that is most difficult to change.[24] What takes the place of this change is a symbolic, liberalist, intellectual engagement with the representation of difference.[25]

In the past ten years, I have dedicated scholarly attention to the representation of blackness in contemporary African American art. My recent emphasis has been on the controversial term *post-black*—which in my formulation is an effort on the part of primarily (but not exclusively) queer artists to reimagine racialized blackness in a manner that grants them recognition. The discourse on post-black is a divisive intracultural debate about the heteropatriarchal norms and value systems within historical constructions of African American identity. In many respects, this inward turn is a response to three conflicting phenomena: (1) the enduring intracultural presence of homophobia and the black respectability politics that protects it; (2) the increasingly objectifying and fetishistic interest in the black body as both *subject* and *object*; and (3) the persistent marginalization of black people in the United States, which is glaringly evident in all aspects of society. The so-called post-black artist satirically engages with this troubling relation, as they contend conceptually with the representation of blackness, against the cultural reality of continued racial disparity.

I will not elaborate here on the specifics of post-black's emergence and ensuing debates, but I will say that I see another related term, *liquid blackness*

DEREK CONRAD MURRAY

(coined by scholar Alessandra Raengo), as doing something very similar, which is attempting to deeply expand and complicate what blackness is—and to explore the complexities of its expressiveness as residing in materiality and form. I discuss post-black not only in terms of its gender and sexual connotations and politics—but also as a type of in-betweenness, a liminal space of becoming that gestures toward the indefinable. Therefore, I see "post-black" and "liquid blackness" as decidedly post–civil rights phenomena that demark cultural positions beyond belongingness and, in many respects, embrace a condition of illegibility. I tend to think of post-black and liquid blackness as *operations* rather than categorizations or rigid definitions. Rather than attempt to remove blackness from the ideologically overdetermined black body, these notions explore its expressiveness as an affective material presence—as something that isn't simply visual but also something we can feel and smell, something that *exudes*: a presence that embodies the horror of detachment that Julia Kristeva so effectively allegorizes in her theory of abjection. In my recent writing on blackness and formalism in abstract painting, I consider the materiality of blackness as an operation that expresses itself as a kind of excremental form or base materialism. Abjection is particularly crucial to any understanding of Kara Walker's work, because as Shaw suggests, "her carnivalesque vision of an abject world consumed by violence and perverse sexuality flies in the face of the black bourgeoisie."[26] However, I argue that baseness, perversity, and the grotesque lie at the heart of racial satire because its primary function is to upset the coherence and binary-based logics of race.

The tableaux of Kara Walker rest on a fault line between the material and formal pleasures of blackness and the obscenity of historical and present-day racism. That tension is often characterized as deeply personal, suggesting that Walker's works are, in fact, always self-portraits. They represent an individual's conflicted and often perverse engagement with race. What has so often upset certain black viewers is the artist's admission that she finds a pleasure in the racial melodrama, that it conjures certain desires in her. In his critical breakdown of Walker's Negress alter ego, art historian Darby English suggests that within the artist's work can be found a struggle to comply with accepted dogmas around the historical memory of slavery.[27] English characterizes Walker's immersion into the legacies of slavery as being as much about desire as it is about suffering. It would seem that for Walker, the history of slavery is mired in fantasy, and racial abjection is among its many obscene pleasures. English's explication of Walker's personal fantasy suggests that her work is perhaps less about the past than it is a personal engagement with the psychosocial intimacies of a black female artist's conflicted relationship to her identity.[28] And this personal dimension of her work, as the scholar explicates, is always concerned with challenging the demands of racial obligation. English is correct in his pointed suggestion that to transgress racial obligation is to become a pariah of sorts and to be thrust violently into a social death. However, Walker's disobedience gleefully serves up the stereotypes and caricatures that the left-leaning art world so voraciously desires. This, of course, is a contradiction, but it is also a sign of good satire. Walker both upsets and rejects the stifling nature of racial obligation, simultaneously giving the art world what it wants: to be ridiculed and chastised, while enjoying the spectacles of abject blackness.

Scholar Darryl Dickson-Carr has written the most comprehensive volume dedicated to exploring African American satire. Titled *African-American Satire* (2001), Dickson-Carr explores the use of satire in the history of black literature—a device that (in its wielding of racial caricatures) has often been misinterpreted as an embrace of harmful stereotypes. Satire's intent, as Dickson-Carr suggests, is to push beyond mere entertainment; its primary purpose is to act as an invaluable mode of social and political critique. Yet some critics may deem this same mode a threat when the "wrong" parties are satirized, which happens fairly often. Without a doubt, satire tends to be "politically incorrect." It is iconoclastic and frequently offensive on a personal and political level.[29] My assertion, vis-à-vis the writings of Dickson-Carr, is that Walker's depictions of slavery can be interpretively unraveled only via an engagement *with* satire: that within their unique form of representational troubling resides a mix of absurd fantasy with what are often (and wrongly) perceived to be historical truths. What Walker creates are not realistic depictions of American history; they are, on the contrary, perverse meditations on an obscene chapter of history, a time that it is perhaps better understood via myth than by fact. We see this satirical approach across the artist's oeuvre and in works like *Consume* (1998), a depiction of two figures in black silhouette: a slave girl (the mythical Negress) and a young boy with ethnically European features.

The girl stands gracefully like a dancer, her back arched at attention to such an extreme that her midsection protrudes forward. She appears to be nude, with the exception of a decorative skirt and high-heeled shoes, which are clearly too large for her adolescent feet. The skirt, despite being rendered in silhouette, is reminiscent of the American-born French entertainer Josephine Baker's iconic banana skirt—yet what is most incendiary about Walker's composition is the physical relation between the two subjects. The boy, whose body is dwarfed by the girl, stands at attention in front of her: arms behind his back, as he sucks on a phallic-like appendage jetting forward from the girl's

1.2   Kara Walker, *Consume*, 1998. Cut paper on wall. 69 × 32 inches
(175.3 × 81.3 cm). Courtesy of Sikkema Jenkins & Co., New York.

skirt. Simultaneously, the Negress suckles her own upturned breast. The conjoining of the figures is sexually absurd, alluding to a range of fraught subjects—pedophilia, sexual abuse, and gender nonconformity—yet it also speaks to the grotesque, violent, and cyclical nature of racism. For Walker, racism thrives through a mix of forced submission and willing complicity: it is a process of simultaneous devouring, each participant taking turns enacting the role of abuser and abused. It is precisely Walker's holistic and satirical approach to slavery, and her suggestion that fantasy, desire, and most importantly, *complicity* are deeply enmeshed in the logics of American racism that have created the most trouble. We see this surface throughout her work, including *Successes* (1998), another silhouette work rendered with black paper.

Similar to *Consume*, the work depicts a Negress girl performing what appears to be fellatio on a white slave master. Despite the rather obscene legibility of the image, there are some visual cues that render it more complex. The phallus appears to protrude from the abdomen (not the crotch) of the male figure and into the mouth of the hunched-over girl, seeming to pass through her body and ultimately jet out of her bowels like a tail. The odd positioning of the girl on all fours echoes the male figure, whose legs look bestial, like those of a wolf. The animalistic physicality of both figures, combined with the overt and pornographic depiction of sex, conveys the baseness and degradation of the racial melodrama—albeit with a satirical cheekiness that intentionally vulgarizes the ideologically genteel vision of the noble, suffering black subject in the face of white hatred. This cyclical violence and desire, the carnality and lust to both dominate and submit, bristles from these works. They indict, just as, through fantasy and desire, they express a need for complicity.

In many respects, Walker's art slips the noose of social symbolism, even while trafficking in narrative and representational clichés around slavery. This representational paradox (the slippage between humanistic portrayal and stereotype) speaks to the notion of blackness as social symbolism, an object- and commodity-based logic that is also extremely ideological. What do black people represent to the dominant culture? This is an important question, if we are to come to any kind of understanding around the images that depict us in popular visual culture. Social symbolism is fundamentally a use value: it expresses a culturally constructed need to substantiate a set of economic relations—an economic status quo in which African Americans are inherently and irrecoverably the underclass. This is the social role of blackness—and therefore the *culture* that blackness creates is believed to issue from pathology and struggle: black music, black style and swagger, black art, black athleticism are fetishized and appropriated for their commodity value, their sense of cool, their authenticity, and their *realness*. "Everything

1.3 Kara Walker, *Successes*, 1998. Cut paper on wall. 61 × 65 inches
(154.9 × 165.1 cm). Courtesy of Sikkema Jenkins & Co., New York.

but the burden" is what writer Greg Tate has termed this phenomenon: the
notion that the so-called dominant culture wants everything from black folks
except the burden of marginalization and social discrimination—*and especially the trauma.*

On the other hand, it's true that much transcendent thought and action
have been produced as a result of the expression of pain. We see this across
identities and histories—but in regard to African American culture, I'm not
speaking of the often-fetishized noble, suffering black subject, the social

symbol that sentiment is projected onto. I'm thinking more about abstract feeling and form, movement and materiality—a very nebulous and unarticulated expressiveness that exudes what we call "blackness" or soul. We know it when we feel and experience it, when it's stirred in us, but nonetheless it often evades legibility: what is tangible and what can be articulated. I'm not suggesting that we separate black affect and sentience from pain. Rather I'm searching for a form of black expressiveness that transcends stilted ideological narratives and symbolic representations rooted in stereotype—one that slips the noose of social symbolism.

That post-ness or liquidity, whatever you call it, is that seeping and elusive black formlessness that slips through the cracks of your reductions (i.e., the sentiment that masks the contempt). That is where the humanity resides: in the black hole, the interstice that only formlessness allows. Perhaps it is only in the embrace of this operation that we might escape diversity: the image game, the politically correct house of mirrors where looking discriminatory is a far worse violation than discrimination itself. Kara Walker's satirical art, as troublesome as it is, *enjoys the wounds* of slavery (to borrow from Žižek's raunchy and caustic joke), yet not in the manner that the Slovenian philosopher suggests. Rather, Walker's reveling in the pleasures of black abjection is not simply a means to serve up a racialized spectacle to the highest bidder: it also manages to upset the logics of racial obligation and the mannered essentialisms that stifle criticality. Therefore, it would be careless to ignore Walker's irreverent post-blackness, dismissing it as the musing of a self-hating Negro; within her conceptual and aesthetic troubling is a desire to push the discourses of black representation beyond the clutches of both racial obligation and respectability politics.

Despite ongoing critiques around racial misrepresentation and the need for diversity, the everyday realities of racial/ethnic binaries and hierarchies show little sign of erosion. It appears that the race-ing of black bodies and the institutional logics of *diversity* rampant in American intellectual culture will continually disallow visual producers and scholars the freedom to visualize and theorize an expanded understanding of identity—and will simultaneously reinforce the conditions upon which blackness functions as a politically correct shorthand for well-meaning, tolerance-based discussions of race. This enduring challenge in American cultural production underlines the schizophrenic dependency on displacing responsibility for creating substantive structural change—in favor of implementing a disciplinary culture based upon the often-troubling rhetorics, procedures, and representational regimes of tolerance.

1 Slavoj Žižek, "There Is a Nicely Vulgar Joke about Christ," in *Žižek's Jokes: (Did you hear the one about Hegel and negation?)*, ed. Audun Mortensen (Cambridge: MIT Press, 2014), 9.

2 Nicole Fleetwood, *Troubling Vision: Performance, Visuality, and Blackness* (Chicago: University of Chicago Press, 2011), 16.

3 Fleetwood, *Troubling Vision*, 17.

4 Christian Metz, *The Imaginary Signifier: Psychoanalysis and the Cinema* (Bloomington: Indiana University Press, 1986).

5 Gwendolyn DuBois Shaw, "Introduction," in *Seeing the Unspeakable: The Art of Kara Walker* (Durham: Duke University Press, 2004), 4.

6 For writings on lynching photographs and visual culture research on slavery, see James Allen, *Without Sanctuary: Lynching Photography in America* (New York: Twin Palms, 2000); Dora Apel and Shawn Michelle Smith, *Lynching Photographs* (Berkeley: University of California Press, 2008); Ken Gonzalez-Day, *Lynching in the West: 1850–1935* (Durham: Duke University Press, 2006); Dora Apel, *Imagery of Lynching: Black Men, White Women, and the Mob* (New Brunswick: Rutgers University Press, 2004); Amy Louise Wood, *Lynching and Spectacle: Witnessing Racial Violence in America, 1890–1940* (Chapel Hill: University of North Carolina Press, 2011); Huey Copeland, *Bound to Appear: Art, Slavery and the Site of Blackness in Multicultural America* (Chicago: University of Chicago Press, 2013); Sarah Lewis, *Vision and Justice: Aperture 223* (New York: Aperture Foundation, 2016).

7 Deborah Willis, *Reflections in Black: A History of Black Photographers 1840 to the Present* (New York: W. W. Norton, 2002); Deborah Willis, *Posing Beauty: African American Images from the 1890s to the Present* (New York: W. W. Norton, 2009); Deborah Willis, *Black: A Celebration of a Culture* (New York: Skyhorse, 2014).

8 Kevin Young, "Miss Pipi's Blue Tale," in *Kara Walker: Dust Jackets for the Niggerati* (New York: Gregory and Miller, 2013), 45.

9 Holland Cotter, "A Nightmare View of Antebellum Life That Sets Off Sparks," *New York Times*, May 9, 2003. Cotter's 2003 review makes reference to Jerry Saltz's 1996 interview with Kara Walker, "Ill-Will and Desire," *Flash Art: The International Art Review* 191 (November/December 1996): 82–86.

10 Gwendolyn DuBois Shaw, "Tracing Race and Representation," in *Seeing the Unspeakable: The Art of Kara Walker* (Durham: Duke University Press, 2004), 12.

11 Gwendolyn Dubois Shaw, "Censorship and Reception," in *Seeing the Unspeakable: The Art of Kara Walker* (Durham: Duke University Press, 2004), 115.

12 Shaw, "Censorship and Reception," 115.

13 Shaw, "Censorship and Reception," 121.

14 Tanya Sheehan, "A Time and Place: Rethinking Race in American Art History," in *A Companion to American Art*, ed. John Davis, Jennifer A. Greenhill, and Jason D. LaFountain (New York: Wiley-Blackwell, 2015), 49.

15 Sheehan, "A Time and Place," 49.

16 Sonia Boyce and Manthia Diawara, "The Art of Identity," *Transition*, no. 55 (1992): 194–95.

17 Slavoj Žižek, "Tolerance as an Ideological Category," *Critical Inquiry* 34, no. 4 (2008): 660.

18 Žižek, "Tolerance as an Ideological Category," 660.

19 Wendy Brown, "Tolerance as a Discourse of Depoliticization," in *Regulating Aversion: Tolerance in the Age of Identity and Empire* (Princeton, NJ: Princeton University Press, 2008), 1.

20 Wendy Brown, "Tolerance as a Discourse of Power," in *Regulating Aversion: Tolerance in the Age of Identity and Empire* (Princeton: Princeton University Press, 2008), 29.

21 Sara Ahmed, "Institutional Life," in *On Being Included: Racism and Diversity in Institutional Life* (Durham: Duke University Press, 2012), 34.

22 Ahmed, "Institutional Life," 43.

23 Žižek, "Tolerance as an Ideological Category," 682.

24 Žižek, "Tolerance as an Ideological Category," 682.

25 Žižek, "Tolerance as an Ideological Category," 660.

26 Shaw, "Censorship and Reception," 123.

27 Darby English, "This Is Not about the Past: Silhouettes in the Work of Kara Walker," in *Kara Walker: Narratives of a Negress* (Cambridge, MA: MIT Press, 2003), 143.

28 English, "This Is Not about the Past," 144.

29 Darryl Dickson-Carr, "Introduction," in *African-American Satire: The Sacredly Profane Novel* (Columbia: University of Missouri Press, 2001), 5.

CHAPTER TWO

THREE-FIFTHS OF A BLACK LIFE MATTERS TOO

Four Neo-Slave Novels from the Year Postracial
Definitively Stopped Being a Thing

DEREK C. MAUS

ALTHOUGH 2016 WAS SURELY A MOMENTOUS YEAR FOR THE AFRICAN American community, it is hard—if not impossible—to argue that it was a particularly good one. In most years, the untimely deaths of such cultural icons as Prince and Muhammad Ali—alongside those of Bobby Hutcherson, Bill Nunn, Billy Paul, Afeni Shakur, Nate Thurmond, and Maurice White—would have served as sufficiently damning testimony by themselves, but 2016 also marked the constitutionally mandated conclusion of Barack Obama's presidency. Donald Trump's election at the end of a campaign that exposed—and more importantly, capitalized on—the deep and abiding racial hostilities that remain in American society delivered a coup de grâce to any remaining optimism that Obama's election (and reelection) heralded the disappearance of institutionalized white supremacy.

Eight years earlier, cultural commentators from across the political spectrum had optimistically (naively? disingenuously?) declared that Obama's election had eradicated racial divisions in American society, or at least rendered them irrelevant. While doing so, many of them also interchanged the terms *postracial* and *post-black*, a misuse with profound ramifications. The pushback against a supposedly "postracial America" began almost immediately,[1] and the sad litany of racial violence that marred the later years of Obama's presidency seemingly justified the "studied demythologization of post-Blackness" undertaken by the contributors to *The Trouble with Post-Blackness* (2015), a collection edited by Houston A. Baker and K. Merinda Simmons.[2] Many (though not all) of the essays in that collection reproduce the synonymy of *post-black* and *postracial*. For example, Erin Aubry Kaplan begins her essay by dismissing *any* potential distinction between the two terms: "Post-black, post-racial, whatever one wants to call it, in the early twenty-first century the political and cultural powers that be are declaring blackness has outlived its usefulness in American life and must be retired along with typewriters and telephone landlines."[3] Similarly, Greg Thomas asserts that James Baldwin's views on blackness have been "placed on mute by new-millennial 'post-racial' and 'post-Black' illusionists."[4] Although both of these essays (and the collection as a whole) present thoughtful counter-arguments to particular theorizations of post-blackness—primarily the one found in Touré's *Who's Afraid of Post-Blackness?* (2011)—they also undercut their claims in implying that these two terms are semiotically identical. This is a straw man that Touré himself vehemently rebuffs from the outset of his book: "Let me be clear: Post-Black does not mean 'post-racial.' Post-racial posits that race does not exist or that we're somehow beyond race and suggests colorblindness: It's a bankrupt concept that reflects a naïve understanding of race in America."[5] This crucial passage is not among the dozens of quotations from *Who's Afraid of Post-Blackness?* that appear in *The Trouble with Post-Blackness.*

The essays in the collection also eschew (again, with a few exceptions) discussion of other extant formulations of post-blackness—for example, those of Thelma Golden, Glenn Ligon, Paul C. Taylor, and Ytasha Womack—while "strik[ing] at the certainty of those who insist that life, liberty, and the pursuit of happiness are now independent of skin color and race in America" (as the book's back cover proclaims).[6] Despite Simmons's introductory assertion that "this volume is not about Touré," the remainder of *The Trouble with Post-Blackness* disproportionately attacks a questionably abridged version of his ideas instead of engaging meaningfully with other important contributions to "the implications of a 'post-black' rhetorical schema."[7] Such a narrow critical aperture exacerbates the problem that Womack identifies in her *Post Black: How a New Generation Is Redefining African American Identity* (2010): "Politicians, organizations, business leaders, social advocates, average citizens, and the like are heavily vested in the perception of who African Americans *used* to be. How we were defined fifty, twenty-five, even ten years ago. There are those invested in who we *should* be. But there's very little understanding of who we *are.*"[8]

The complete exclusion of the closely related concept of the post-soul aesthetic from *The Trouble with Post-Blackness* helps explain why so many of its essays treat post-blackness as though it were what Michelle Elam elsewhere calls a "total eclipse of blackness as we know it."[9] Both Kaplan and Thomas, for example, invoke reductively literal interpretations of the *post-* prefix to justify their claims that post-blackness seeks to "retire" or "mute" either prominent black voices such as James Baldwin or blackness altogether.[10] In the introduction to his essay collection *Flyboy 2* (2016) Greg Tate asserts that "our Black lives, creative acts, political plots, and trans-African legacies *been* mattering HERE for a good long while."[11] In doing so, he makes clear his position that intrinsic elements of contemporary black identity did not arise ex nihilo in 2008 (or 1986, or 1964, or 1925, or 1903). This point is particularly salient for me because of Tate's role in post-soul's origination. His 1986 essay "Cult-Nats Meet Freaky Deaky" described an emerging post-soul aesthetic without yet naming it (which Nelson George did in 1992): "The '80s are witnessing the maturation of a postnationalist black arts movement, one more Afrocentric and cosmopolitan than anything that's come before. . . . These are artists for whom black consciousness and artistic freedom are not mutually exclusive but complementary, for whom 'black culture' signifies a multicultural tradition of expressive practices."[12] Nothing in Tate's description "retire[s]" or "mute[s]" the "black consciousness" that "c[a]me before," in fact presaging what Touré and Trey Ellis and Mark Anthony Neal (and other post-black theorists) would later write.[13] The very title of Tate's essay implies that this new coterie of black artists "meet[s]" readily and willingly—just not deferentially—with their aesthetic ancestors.

I aim to harmonize some of the dissonance surrounding post-blackness by using Tate and several other critical voices associated with the post-soul aesthetic to analyze four novels that were published in 2016 within eighty days of each other: Natashia Déon's *Grace* (May 16), Yaa Gyasi's *Homegoing* (June 7), Ben H. Winters's *Underground Airlines* (July 5), and Colson Whitehead's *The Underground Railroad* (August 2). Although none of them explicitly addresses Trump's presidency—which was still deemed unlikely by most prognosticators in the summer of that tumultuous year—these thematically linked novels all arrived in the midst of his campaign's use of white supremacist rhetoric to entreat voters to "Make America Great Again." Using the post-soul aesthetic to concurrently examine their fictionalizations of the historical institution of slavery illuminates how and why its version of post-blackness can function as a liberating ethos in such an era of emboldened antiblack racism.

THE POST-SOUL AESTHETIC AND BLACK POST-BLACKNESS

A valuable foundation for my process is laid by Margo Natalie Crawford's contribution to *The Trouble with Post-Blackness*, which stands out for its engagement with a wide range of post-black theorists.[14] Although she demurs that "post-blackness is stuck in a misunderstanding of black aesthetic movement,"[15] Crawford also attempts to ameliorate this problem by positing what she calls "black post-blackness":

> Any progressive use of "post-black" will have to avoid the taming of the threat of "black." . . . Some of the texts and visual images that some will want to tag "post-black" deserve the less market-able names such as "post-Black Arts" and "black post-black." . . . One of the best ways to fight this distortion is to refuse to accept the dominant culture industry's marketing of the "new" and to refuse to accept that twenty-first-century African American cul-tural productions are necessarily removed from the earlier move-ments of black self-determination.[16]

I contend that the post-soul aesthetic allows for precisely such a retained connection to an ineffaceably black aspect of the past (i.e., slavery and its legacy), while also recognizing that the depiction of that past in these four novels is distinctively influenced by the cultural peculiarities of what Larry Wilmore called, during his commentary on the 2016 presidential election, "the Unblackening" of America.[17]

Whereas Déon and Gyasi tell mostly realistic—albeit formally unorthodox—stories of slavery's effects and legacies, Winters and Whitehead bend histori-cal factuality to their authorial will in approaching those same topics along more idiosyncratic vectors. All four books share tropes of characterization and plot with autobiographical slave narratives like those of Olaudah Equiano (1789), Frederick Douglass (1845, 1855), and Harriet Jacobs (1861), as well as with such contemporary touchstones as Alex Haley's *Roots* (1976), Octavia Butler's *Kindred* (1979), and Toni Morrison's *Beloved* (1987). As such, they belong in the lineage of the neo-slave narrative subgenre that Ashraf H. A. Rushdy delineated in 1999. He claimed that such works "develop arguments about how contemporary racial identity after Black Power should be medi-ated through a reconstruction of the first form in which African American subjectivity was articulated—the slave narrative. . . . [T]hey ask what it means for a postmodern author to negotiate and reconstruct what is essentially a premodern form."[18] The neo-slave novels of 2016, though, transcend this chiefly metanarrative process of "negotiat[ion] and reconstruct[ion]," per-forming new and timely historiographic work, as Salamishah Tillet noted in a collective review in early 2017: "These narratives are not only evidence of the long arm of slavery extending into our present. They also tackle the limits and possibilities of our present moment itself. Against our current back-drop . . . the question of freedom—who is, isn't, and never was free—has taken on increasing urgency."[19]

Not only do the four novels under consideration here *not* present slavery as a bygone aberration in the nation's history; they identify both it and its ongoing repercussions as the inevitable byproduct of what Whitehead's dia-bolical slavecatcher Ridgeway celebrates as "destiny by divine prescription—the American imperative."[20] That "imperative" suffuses the nativist and (white-)nationalist discourse that metastasized in the years leading up to 2016.

Déon, Gyasi, Winters, and Whitehead all produced books that were pub-lished in an American society that would soon find itself embroiled in con-stant public shouting matches over the ostensible treason of black athletes kneeling during the national anthem to protest police brutality, Trump's identification of white supremacists marching in Virginia as "very fine peo-ple," and the continuing monumentalization of men who took up arms against the United States to defend slavery. A substantial and empowered subset of Americans still embraces what Tillet calls "a civic culture that for-gets or casts itself in contradiction to the lives and contributions of enslaved African Americans."[21] Regardless of the intentions of their respective authors, all four novels became enmeshed in the fraught and superficial racial dis-courses of America in 2016 and beyond; it is for this reason that I believe it is valuable to examine them in the context of the post-soul aesthetic, a meta-discourse that challenges Americans' ignorance—willful or otherwise—regarding slavery and its relationship to black identity in the twenty-first century. Before discussing the four novels, I will first provide a brief overview of some of the characteristics of the post-soul aesthetic that are most directly pertinent to them, particularly the ludic and historiographic impulses within them that subvert and recast myriad received notions about blackness and its signification.

Bertram D. Ashe contends that growing up after civil rights only *"qualifies one to be a post-soul artist—it does not automatically make* an artist's work post-soul."[22] Rather than seeing it as an inherent characteristic imposed upon a generation by historical events—e.g., the passage of the Civil Rights Act, Obama's election—Ashe links the post-soul aesthetic to conscious and potentially iconoclastic ventures into (self-)representation that are bound up with a sequential (i.e., post-*something*) cultural context:

> The chief difference between the Civil Rights movement and ear-lier and this post–Civil Rights movement era is the black artists'

relationship to the idea of freedom. . . . Many would argue, with justification, that we are still not yet "free"—that we are not even close. But a chief landmark was obtained postbellum: we gained freedom over our bodies. . . . And the struggles during the movement era, violent and nonviolent, during which many lives were affected or lost, created the ambiguous, legally free, land of quasi-opportunity that is the US today. . . . As a result, today's black artists, who have grown up in this squishy, hazy, post–Civil Rights movement era of sometimes-real, sometimes-imagined freedom, are exploring blackness from within contexts markedly different from their forebears.[23]

Ashe's reference to "sometimes-real, sometimes-imagined freedom" resonates loudly in 2016, when the extent to which black lives matter in the United States became as unclear as it had been in decades. His observation also undergirds Tillet's contention that the four novels under consideration here collectively "show that the concept of freedom is flawed, because historically it has always been more available to some groups than to others, with some groups having something close to 'perfect' freedom at the expense of others made unfree."[24] Such an observation does not invalidate the efforts and achievements of African Americans who have fought for individual and collective freedom; it does, however, decentralize freedom as the requisite value of black identity, substituting the not-quite-synonymous idea of liberation from representational boundaries, regardless of their origins.

Ashe coined the term *blaxploration* to describe post-soul's tendency to "trouble blackness . . . in ways that depart significantly from previous—and necessary—preoccupations with struggling for political freedom, or with any attempt to establish and sustain a coherent black identity." While disrupting extant epistemologies of blackness, "post-soul 'blaxploration' acts as much on behalf of black people as traditional explorers acted on behalf of whatever nation or people they represented. As such, these post-soul artists maintain a dogged allegiance to their communities, however non-essentialized and gorged with critiques said allegiance might be."[25] Blaxploration parallels what Tate has alternately called the "open[ing] up of the entire 'text of blackness' for fun and games"[26] and "the structuring and stylizing of the bloody improvisational moment."[27] For Tate, black artists' instances of "most visible, visceral, and profound impact on the modern world have been those in which we can freely repurpose our experiences, our wagging tongues, our fun."[28] This freedom to "repurpose" involves neither a demand for legal standing nor a validation of collective achievement; it is inherently personal and idiosyncratic, although it also remains communally dependent on "our experiences" and a preexisting "text of blackness" as the raw materials for its "fun and games."

Like Ashe and Tate, Mark Anthony Neal also recognizes the post-soul aesthetic through its improvisational excursions away from collective understandings of history: "For many within the post-soul generation, the Montgomery bus boycott is representative of a small number of communal memories, such as the March on Washington in 1963 and the assassination of Martin Luther King Jr., that propel their own perceptions and understanding of that moment. . . . [P]ost-soul strategies . . . willingly 'bastardize' black history and culture to create alternative meanings."[29] These "alternative meanings" ultimately cohere into what Neal describes as "a radical reimagining of the contemporary African-American experience, attempting to liberate contemporary interpretations of that experience from sensibilities that were formalized and institutionalized during earlier social paradigms."[30]

Whitehead noted that *The Underground Railroad* arose from childhood puzzlement: "I think I'm not alone in that when I first heard about it, when I was in the fourth or fifth grade, I envisioned a subway beneath the Earth."[31] Although such a grade-school context may seem like a relatively benign example of a "formalized and institutionalized" sensibility, a later comment from the same interview reveals the shortcomings of the black history curricula in the schools he attended: "One day we did a section on slavery and Lincoln, and Lincoln comes and frees the slaves and that's all we talked about. And then a couple of years later, maybe there was something about 'separate but equal,' and then Martin Luther King comes, and everything is fine."[32] Déon describes a similarly simplistic experience: "In elementary school, I learned that the Emancipation Proclamation was a happy day for slaves, not the reality of three million people set free in the middle of one of the bloodiest wars in American history. . . . THREE MILLION innocent people without weapons or a place to go were expected to walk across battlefields to their 'freedom.'"[33]

Although such severely limited information hardly creates a rich soil for nuanced understanding of slavery's legacy, its gaps certainly provide ample artistic opportunity for an unfettered imagination. The alternately "blax-plored," "repurposed," or "bastardized" history found in the post-soul slave novels of 2016 is *not* intended just to fill in the factual blanks left by grossly insufficient formal educational processes, though; as Whitehead notes, "My philosophy is that I'm not sticking to the facts of American history, but I'm sticking to the truth."[34] Although hers is perhaps the least "post-soul" of these four novels, even Déon speaks in both historiographic and metanarrative terms about writing fiction in order to address the "sanitized history that I had come to believe as truth as an American. . . . Some part of me is trying to make sense of this history, these facts, and the versions we've told ourselves." She considers her novel part of a call to her fellow American citizens "to look back on ourselves . . . honestly. See the truth of who we've been."[35]

Although neither Whitehead nor Déon is calling for an end to Juneteenth celebrations, they both recognize that simply providing more tangible facts about the underground railroad or the reality of freed slaves' struggles in the aftermath of emancipation is not sufficient to overcome what Gyasi calls the impulse to "look away when something like this [the horrors of slavery] is happening."[36] Such impulses create the historical blind spots that both allow simplistic narratives like "and then Martin Luther King [or Barack Obama] comes, and everything is fine" to thrive and prevent a meaningful assessment of how and why present-day white supremacy evolved from the same ideology that justified slavery in the past. In addition to a fictional representation of slavery's terrible reality, these post-soul neo-slave novels also provide continuous metacommentary on how this representation relates to the here and now. Whereas such linkages between past and present were present in such earlier neo-slave novels as *Kindred* and *Beloved*, they are far more foregrounded because of the liberties taken by Déon, Gyasi, Winters, and Whitehead with both literary structure and historical factuality.

Neal's use of such language as "radical reimagining" and "liberat[ion] from [institutionalized] sensibilities" foreshadows Tillet's claim that "contemporary black writers and artists do not disaggregate slavery from the narrative of American democracy. . . . [They] foreground slavery as the mnemonic property of the entire nation."[37] What ideally results from this counterhistorical approach is a "democratic discourse [that] not only works as a corrective against monolithic cult-like narratives of an uncritical (white) patriotism, but also serves as a discourse of patriotism based on dissent, criticality, and inclusion."[38] In this way, the intensely self-aware historiographic and metanarrative aspects of the post-soul aesthetic are deployed not only to achieve personal liberation from external aesthetic constraints, but also to productively complexify "the processes by which contemporary Americans . . . construct, maintain, and reinforce various aspects of both their individual and collective identities."[39] Tillet asserts that post–civil rights artists—not all of whom are necessarily "post-soul" artists—use depictions of slavery to contest and to complicate semantically impoverished cultural narratives (what she calls "civic myths") related to blackness.[40] The blaxploration that takes place in each of the four neo-slave novels from 2016 reveals a black post-black/post-soul sensibility that simultaneously subverts a pair of odiously intertwined civic myths: the resurgent white supremacist rhetoric of recent years and the overly sunny assertions of racism's demise in the wake of Obama's election.

NATASHIA DÉON'S *GRACE*: RADICALLY REIMAGINING THE MEMORY OF SLAVERY

Grace intertwines episodes from the life of a runaway slave named Naomi with those of her daughter Josephine (Josey) in a time frame that extends from 1838 to the earliest years of Reconstruction. The book is narrated entirely from Naomi's perspective, but Déon complicates the ontology of that fact in the opening chapter by having her killed by slavecatchers moments after giving birth to Josey. The scenes of the book that recount Naomi's life depict her attempts to flee the plantation in Tallassee, Alabama, on which she has lived since birth. Naomi runs because she has killed her monstrous master, who rapes her after murdering both her sister Hazel's fiancé and her mother. Her understandable confusion about what to do or where to go emphasizes the complete lack of freedom that results from her violent act of resistance: "Where I'm gon' go, Hazel?" When her sister tells her she must run north, Naomi doesn't even know which direction that is. Hazel's response invokes a familiar trope of slave narratives, the North Star as the guide to freedom: "Follow the star like I showed you. Go only in the night." After some hesitation, she eventually takes her sister's advice, but the North Star does not lead her to freedom; instead, she settles 150 miles east-northeast of Tallassee in Conyers, Georgia, where she is eventually caught and killed several years later. Her immediate verbal response—"I cain't do this no more"[41]—to her sister's advice, though, foreshadows the final words of the book, when Naomi *does* achieve a more metaphysical form of liberation.[42]

Naomi reveals the complex subjectivity of her personal narrative when she informs the reader that she, like "all of us the dead," re-experiences the past in "flashes . . . [that] come and go, and choose what day of my life to show to me and I ain't got a say in it. . . . It's more than just seeing the moment, it's taking part in the memory as if it were happening again." Despite this vividness, she nevertheless reduces the significance of these "flashes" to "just your old life repeating itself and repeating itself and repeating itself,"[43] which parallels Déon's assertion that contemporary Americans "tell ourselves these stories [about slavery]. Retell them. Only taking full responsibility for our sanitized version, telling ourselves it was bad, misinterpreted at best, but not that bad."[44] In contrast, the sections of the book that focus on Josey's life—and, concurrently, Naomi's afterlife—seem more under Naomi's narrative control, suggesting that they empower her in a way that simply reliving the harrowing brutality of her own life does not. She demonstrates this control through a pair of metafictional questions posed when she moves forward in time to describe a scene twelve years after her death in 1848: "Where do we start when we tell the stories of our loved ones? On the day they were born or the day they mattered?"[45] The narrative tensions between these two strands of Naomi's story allude to Déon's overarching theme about how different retellings of the past change its effect on the present: "It don't matter that I was a nigga. Or a slave. What matters is that I had a daughter, who had daughters, and they had theirs."[46] Déon's use of the verb *matter* in both of these passages reverberates forward to 2016, when a more public assertion of the validity of black lives was under way.

The resolution of the novel offers two scenes that suggest radically different ways of "taking part in the memory as if it's happening again." In the fourth-to-last chapter, Josey and her family are threatened by the appearance of a marauding band of men still wearing their "faded grey uniforms" and meting out their skewed version of justice for a perceived act of miscegenation four years after the end of the Civil War.[47] Josey's light-skinned appearance—the result of her mixed-race heritage—causes one of the soldiers to assume that her black husband is using the racial leniency of Reconstruction to take advantage of a white woman when he sees them "kissing and hugging up on each other," a sure sign to him that "everything's all gone to hell."[48] The following chapter—tellingly titled "Judgment"—intertwines the book's two lifelines/timelines, simultaneously relating how Naomi was flushed out of hiding, tracked down, and ultimately killed in 1848, and how Josey's husband was saved at the last moment from execution at the hands the unreconstructed Confederates. The common element in both stories is a man referred to as Bobby Lee in 1848 and as General Robert L. Smith in 1869. In the earlier timeline, he is a member of posse that murders Naomi in retribution for the killing of her master, whereas in the later one he uses his status as a former Confederate general to pacify the men who still acknowledge his legally defunct authority.[49] His speech seems equally directed toward the vigilantes of 1869 as those defending the institutionalized Confederate symbols that remain throughout the United States of 2016: "All of us were ready to die for this great nation. . . . Lives marked with courage and bravery. We're all owed respect. . . . There's a good sum offered for you and your men on account of the marauding y'all did in Virginia. The peaceful end is to turn yourself in now. Give folks who still believe in you a chance to call you heroes, too."[50] Déon uses a fictional Confederate general named Robert Lee to call for a collective process of truth and reconciliation (in the political sense) over the memory of the Civil War and its central issue, slavery.[51] Such a process would presumably involve acknowledgment of his own active role in Naomi's death, a synecdoche for the inhumane acts committed by "this great nation" that are not mitigated by his lofty oratory.

The second portion of the book's resolution concerns Naomi's only successful intercession in her daughter's life. Years earlier, she had watched helplessly as Josey was raped by George Graham, the debauched brother of the white woman who initially raised Josey after Naomi's death. When George again threatens Josey while she is hiding from the soldiers, Naomi applies her imperfect understanding of how to interact with the physical world—at the cost of grievous suffering and dissolution. She gained this knowledge earlier in the book from a slave named Bessie, the only person in the book aware of her presence (a fact Naomi cannot explain). Although Bessie counsels Naomi that "revenge ain't for you to do," Naomi responds that she must "count the cost" for herself and decides to "thrust [her]self inside Josey" in order to "fill her lungs, make her breathe, [and] make her grab the stone" with which she bludgeons George to death. Her consciousness—and her narrative voice—fade out as the chapter ends: "I cain't see no more. I cain't hear. I cai."[52]

The final chapter inscribes Naomi's sacrifice as an act of loving righteousness and maternal vengeance that is justified not only by George's refusal to recognize Josey's emancipation but also by Bobby Lee's more radical command to submit himself to justice. Both of these concluding scenes enable the survival of black characters explicitly through the termination—legal or corporeal—of an embodied white supremacy. Naomi tells the reader at the start of both the first and last chapters that she has been dead since "before you were born, before your mother was born, 'fore your grandmother."[53] Nevertheless, she still has both the means and seemingly the need to tell this version of her and Josey's interconnected stories. It is only after retelling her story—and seemingly revising its ending by interceding on Josey's behalf at the very moment in which it seemed Naomi's fate might befall her as well—that she is released from the uncontrollable "flashes" of her own history into an afterlife in which a star *does* guide her to a reunion with her dead mother.[54] Her process is less of Morrison's "rememory" and more of Neal's "radical reimagining," though both are at root strategies for liberation from a story of the past that offers only more trauma in the present.

YAA GYASI'S *HOMEGOING*: A "CLEARER,
YET STILL IMPERFECT" SENSE OF HERITAGE

Homegoing is likewise narratively bifurcated and multigenerational in scope. The two strands of its story originate in eighteenth-century Ghana with a pair of half sisters who never meet one another, despite briefly—and ironically—inhabiting the same gruesomely emblematic building. Effia grows up among the Fante people but is eventually married (partly through subterfuge on the part of her mean-spirited stepmother) to James Collins, the governor of the English slave castle near her home village. Esi grows up as the daughter of an influential man in an Asante village but is eventually captured by the Fante and sold into slavery in America. She departs her homeland via the same castle that is overseen by Effia's husband, with whom Esi briefly interacts before undergoing the Middle Passage. Although Effia's life is certainly not an easy one, she nevertheless manages to carve out a comfortable existence with Collins, despite the scorn of his white coworkers and her relative exile from her home village. As a result, her lineage initially enjoys a measure of status and privilege that stems from their direct complicity in the very slave trade that sundered Esi from everyone and everything she had known in the world. The fates of the two half sisters are simultaneously fused and riven in ways that neither of them could ever know.

This curiously coupled dichotomy—initially symbolized by Effia's magnificent lodgings in the castle directly atop the fetid dungeon in which Esi awaited transport via slave ship—to some extent holds for much of the novel, as Effia's progeny attempt to navigate the maelstrom of European colonialism in Africa, while Esi's struggle first as slaves and later as second-class citizens of a racist United States. The twelve subsequent chapters focus alternately on one descendant of each half sister through six successive generations, with the final chapter bringing the two strands together as Marjorie and Marcus, the respective great-great-great-great-grandchildren of Effia and Esi, meet in present-day California and fall in love. The novel ultimately comes full circle in both genealogy and geography, ending on the beach in Ghana near the slave castle in which much of the opening chapters is set. As Marcus feels overwhelmed by the weight of both the personal and communal history signified by the castle's *"Door of No Return,"*[55] Marjorie calms his anxiety by giving him a familial heirloom—a black stone—that dates all the way back to their common (though unknown to either of them) ancestor Maame, the mother of both Esi and Effia.

The novel's fourteen focalized black characters include both scoundrels and sages, both the magisterial and the marginalized; the chorus of their not-always-harmonious voices becomes an act of blaxplorative historiography of the "three centuries" that Countee Cullen described as "remov[ing]" contemporary African Americans from the "scenes [their] fathers loved" in his 1925 poem "Heritage."[56] Gyasi's sprawling overview builds a cultural bridge back to West Africa but does so without nostalgia, refusing to romanticize the significance of such a connection even as she asserts its unmistakable existence. As such, her novel has far more in common with Saidiya Hartman's history/memoir, *Lose Your Mother: A Journey along the Atlantic Slave Route* (2006), than with *Roots*. Gyasi revealed her historiographic intentions in an interview, stating that she "was more interested in kind of getting to look at the ways that slavery and colonialism changed really subtly over a very long period of time. . . . I wanted to talk about how the moments that we are dealing with in the present didn't just appear out of nowhere. They are connected to every single moment in time that came before, tracing back to this huge thing in the 18th century."[57] Like Womack, Gyasi's interest in the African past is intended to illuminate the present—to find out "who we *are*" more than who we "used to be"[58]—and to allow her to explore the answer not to Cullen's incantatory question "Spicy grove, cinnamon tree / What does Africa mean to me?"[59] but rather to "this broad question of what it means to be black in America."[60]

Whatever her answer to that latter question may be, Gyasi makes it clear that it is not a definitive one. She presents numerous characters whose lack of knowledge—sometimes the product of willful ignorance—about their familial past causes them great suffering, frequently in the form of haunting visions and dreams. However, she also depicts other characters whose reconstructive curiosity about that past offers some palliation. Yaw, a history teacher in the Gold Coast at the time of Kwame Nkrumah's ascendance, lays out a strategy for his students in the late 1940s and, by extension, for Gyasi's reader: "We believe the one who has power. He is the one who gets to write the story. So when you study history, you must ask yourself, Whose story am I missing? Whose voice was suppressed so that this voice could come forth? Once you have figured that out, you must find that story too. From there you get a clearer, yet still imperfect, picture."[61] Although not all of the fourteen focalized characters represent stories that are "missing" or "suppressed," most of them do. Gyasi's novel reconstructs fictionally an example of the sort of African American familial histories that slavery and other forms of cultural marginalization have rendered unrecoverable. The black stone that Marjorie gives to Marcus serves as the metaphor for a "clearer, yet still imperfect" shared heritage. The stone *does* bond them, even if only the time-traveling reader knows how and why. Gyasi can imaginatively restore—at least partly—through historical fiction what conventional history has effaced.

BEN H. WINTERS'S *UNDERGROUND AIRLINES*:
NO COMPROMISES, NO SATISFACTION

Underground Airlines employs tropes taken from both detective fiction and science fiction in telling the story of an African American man named Victor. He collaborates with the US Marshals Service to return runaways under the Fugitive Persons Act to the "Hard Four" southern states—Louisiana, Alabama, Mississippi, and a unified Carolina—in which slavery is still legal in this alternate-history version of the contemporary United States.[62] The morality of Victor's tale is complicated by the fact that he is himself an escaped "Person Bound to Labor," as slaves are euphemistically called.[63] Victor had been recaptured by the marshals six years prior to the start of the novel's timeline. He participates in the recapture of more than two hundred other runaways after striking a deal with a mysterious government agent named Bridge, who becomes his handler: "I pursued my cases efficiently and effectively, and as long as I did that, my own past remained buried. I remained in the North and free. Give and take. Negotiation and conciliation. Compromise."[64]

Winters's word choice alludes to the historical role of compromise in perpetuating slavery. The antebellum history of the United States is replete with deals—e.g., the Three-Fifths Compromise of 1787, the Missouri Compromise of 1820, or the Compromise of 1850—that reinforced slavery's legal status in the South in exchange for national stability and cohesion. The novel's epigraph is taken from Winters's fictional Crittenden Compromise, which forestalled the Civil War by making slavery perpetually legal where it already existed. The law that constantly threatens Victor with a return to bondage is also the result of such a political compromise. The obvious difference between these grand political gestures and Victor's cooperation with the marshals is that his is a Hobson's choice. He can do the bidding of his white captors and enjoy a limited freedom that is subject to revocation at any moment, or he can return to slavery; neither option offers anything near genuine liberation, but he nevertheless articulates a lesser benefit: "That's the problem with doing the devil's work. It can be pretty satisfying now and again."[65]

Victor becomes involved in an unusual case centered on Father Barton, the leader of an Indianapolis-based cell of the novel's eponymous network of abolitionists, and Jackdaw, a runaway from a gigantic slave-owning garment corporation in Alabama. In the course of his pursuit of Jackdaw, he discovers grotesque corruption and hypocrisy, perhaps best exemplified by the widespread violation of the Clean Hands law. Intended as a complete prohibition on the "possession, sale, or consumption of slave-made goods," Victor describes this law as a superficial "article of faith," a "consolation" and a "comfort" for those in the "Righteous North."[66] He also notes that its legality is upheld by the Supreme Court not because of sympathy with the enslaved but rather because "wearing clothing that had been plantation-picked and plantation-sewn did grave harm to the people" who wore such clothes, a satirical reference to the historical brand of abolitionism that objected more to the moral injuries that slavery inflicted on slaveowners than to the physical and mental depredations suffered by slaves.[67] After he discovers evidence that corporations—specifically, the one from which Jackdaw escaped—and the federal government have been colluding to skirt the law's strictures, Victor becomes less willing to continue obfuscating his reality (and by extension, that of the nation as a whole) in order to retain the provisional form of quasi-freedom he is afforded by his compromise. Winters makes clear the ethics of such continued compromise in another fictional source used as an epigraph to the novel's final section, quoting from the Reverend Kevin Shortley's book *On the Urgent Necessities*: "Compromise is not the worst of sins, but it is the busiest. The only one we're all doing, twenty-four hours a day. Seven days a week."[68]

The subversion of amoral (and/or immoral) compromises, unearned satisfaction, and "conscience-soothing balms" like the Clean Hands law, lies at the heart of the novel's particular expression of post-blackness. As a white writer, Winters does not himself seek to (re)define blackness; instead, he critiques the ways subjugation to white Americans' demands constrains—literally and figuratively—African Americans as well as the ineffectuality of efforts to dismantle those demands. As Winters explains in an interview, "Surely it isn't the responsibility of African Americans to end racism against African Americans, as if they are the perpetrators instead of the victims. . . . As if it is the responsibility of the African American community of artists and authors to deal with and think about this, process it, and to heal it. As opposed to it being the responsibility of all of us."[69] Winters echoes Baldwin's observation that "the sloppy and fatuous nature of American good will can never be relied upon to resolve hard problems" in suggesting that bigotry is perpetuated in part by self-servingly "satisfying" half-measures from its opponents: "Declaring hatred for slavery was easy for a man like Father Barton; not only easy, but useful, gratifying—*satisfying*. And of course its cold and terrible grip could never fall on him directly."[70] The title of Winters's book explicitly (re)names—and in doing so, respectfully "bastardizes"—a touchstone of both white and black abolitionist virtue, while its resolution suggests that eliminating both rhetorical and institutional white supremacy requires still greater effort. As Martha, Victor's most dedicated white ally in the book, notes, slavery's legacy remains pervasive in the United States: "People think it's far away, but it's not. It's here. It's everywhere. Clouding over everything. Hanging over everything."[71] There could hardly be a more clear-cut warning for anyone still believing America had become post-racial just because it elected a black president.

COLSON WHITEHEAD'S *THE UNDERGROUND RAILROAD*: THE LIMITS OF BLACK FREEDOM

Finally, Whitehead's *The Underground Railroad* combines aspects of the techniques of each of the previous three books—*Grace's* narrative fragmentation, *Homegoing's* multigenerational episodicity, and *Underground Airlines's* overt manipulation of history—in constructing what became the most critically heralded neo-slave novel of the twenty-first century. Although most of the novel follows the progress of an escaped slave named Cora, it opens with a section detailing the life of her grandmother Ajarry, who (like Esi in *Homegoing*) had been kidnapped into slavery from the Gold Coast. Furthermore, Cora feels abandoned by her mother, Mabel, who seems to have successfully escaped from the Randall plantation several years prior to the opening of the novel's action. With the help of the underground railroad—made literal as a subterranean "marvel to be proud of"[72]—Cora escapes from the Georgia plantation where she has lived and travels through a series of states—South Carolina, North Carolina, Tennessee, and Indiana—in what Whitehead described in an interview as being "sort of like *Gulliver's Travels*. . . . [T]he book is being rebooted every sixty pages as she enters a new state that presents an alternative view of American history of what might had happened if we had gone differently."[73] Using a narrative structure that hearkens back to his *John Henry Days* (2001), Whitehead alternates chapters delineating Cora's experiences in these states with shorter chapters that provide detailed exposition—often going back decades before Cora's birth—for various characters who figure directly or indirectly in Cora's life. The individuals depicted in these chapters include Ridgeway, the slavecatcher who obsessively pursues both Cora and her mother; Stevens, the doctor who wants to implement a mandatory sterilization program for freed slaves in seemingly benevolent South Carolina; Ethel, a nominal abolitionist who reluctantly takes Cora into her house in genocidally racist North Carolina; Caesar, the slave with whom Cora escapes from Georgia; and finally, Mabel, Cora's mother.

The book generally juxtaposes a series of cultural narratives that consider what place—if any—blackness might occupy in a country that gives legal authority over freedom and slavery (and thus, life and death) to men like Ridgeway, who defines the American spirit as "the one that called us from the Old World to the New, to conquer and build and civilize. And destroy what needs to be destroyed. To lift up the lesser races. If not lift up, subjugate. And if not subjugate, exterminate."[74] None of the "alternative views of American history" that Cora encounters in South Carolina, North Carolina, and Tennessee remove the inherent white supremacy of Ridgeway's perspective, but the community that Cora finds on Valentine's farm in Indiana near the end of the book initially seems to offer a different path predicated on black agency and black self-determination. A pivotal scene set there involves a debate between a high-minded abolitionist orator named Elijah Lander and a former slave named Mingo, who wants to exclude those refugees "who do not have the character we do" from the community. Lander's rebuttal of Mingo's starkly exclusionary argument not only invokes elements of "the entire interracial abolitionist movement"[75] but also advances a fundamentally liberated identity for his nineteenth-century listeners that doubles as an invocation of black post-blackness for readers in 2016: "We are not one people but many different people. How can one person speak for this great, beautiful race—which is not one race, but many, with a million desires and hopes and wishes for ourselves and our children? . . . For we are Africans in America. Something new in the history of the world, without models for what we will become. . . . Color must suffice. It has brought us to this night, this discussion, and it will take us into the future."[76]

Lander's words set the community on "the verge of some new order, on the verge of clasping reason to disorder, of putting all the lessons of their history to bear on the future."[77] This idealism is shattered almost immediately, though, as a mob that includes Ridgeway bursts into the hall, shoots both Lander and Cora's lover, and burns the entire farm to the ground. The omniscient narrator notes that Sybil, one of the massacre's survivors, maintained until her death decades later that "Mingo was the informer . . . [who] told constables that the farm harbored fugitives and provided the particulars for a successful ambush."[78] Even though this assertion is no more validated by the narrator than any of the competing ones recounted immediately thereafter, it adds yet another potential layer of disillusionment through the prospect of self-destructive black collusion with the forces embodying Ridgeway's racist "American spirit." Although Cora manages to escape from Ridgeway's clutches yet again—leaving him bleeding and raving on the platform of a station of the literalized underground railroad—her freedom remains, as it has throughout the book, "a thing that shifted as you looked at it, the way a forest is dense with trees up close but from outside, from the empty meadow, you see its true limits."[79] Her departure to the west as part of an apparently segregated wagon train only promises the potential continuation of her life/journey, not a definitive movement toward the kind of truly liberated black community that Lander envisioned.

Regardless of the significant differences in their authors' backgrounds, each of the novels considered herein offer black post-black/post-soul strategies for countering the civic myths surrounding the role of slavery in shaping the contemporary social landscape of the United States. Déon formulates an opportunity for racial reconciliation that is predicated on a forthright acknowledgment of the hard truths of a brutal past. Gyasi offers her readers an enriched, but far from prescriptive, sense of communal black identity by reconstructing a black family history that remains inaccessible through conventional narrations of slavery and its effect. Winters issues a challenge (mostly) to white readers to give up the satisfaction of #staywoke hashtags and similarly glib gestures of "solidarity or empathy or guilt"[80] that might blind them to the scope of racism's continuation in American culture. Whitehead provides some hope that escape from the gruesome brutality of the past is possible, but is not so optimistic as to suggest that Lander's dream of a country in which "we rise and fall as one, one colored family living next door to one white family" is any more achievable than the dream that Martin Luther King Jr. famously expressed.[81] Such radical developments remain sadly absent from both his novel and America in 2016.

NOTES

1 For example, less than a year after Obama's election, Roopali Mukherjee called for a concerted scholarly effort "geared to illuminating ruptures as well as continuities that constitute the 'post' in 'postracial.'" She contended that "the idea of the 'end of race' deserves a careful regard. . . . Indeed, the task ahead . . . is not to decipher if race matters anymore but rather to illuminate how race matters differently within the cultural valences of this moment." See Roopali Mukerjee, "Racial Politics (in the United States)." *Social Text* 27, no. 3 (Fall 2009): 219–22.

2 Houston A. Baker, "Conclusion: Why the Lega Mask Has Many Mouths and Multiple Eyes," in *The Trouble with Post-Blackness*, ed. Houston A. Baker and K. Merinda Simmons (New York: Columbia University Press, 2015), 252.

3 Erin Aubry Kaplan, "The Long Road Home," in Baker and Simmons, *The Trouble with Post-Blackness*, 189

4 Greg Thomas, "African Diasporic Blackness Out of Line: Trouble for 'Post-Black' ~~African~~ Americanism," in Baker and Simmons, *The Trouble with Post-Blackness*, 75.

5 Touré, *Who's Afraid of Post-Blackness? What It Means to Be Black Now* (New York: Free Press, 2011), 12.

6 See Thelma Golden, "Introduction," in *Freestyle* (New York: Studio Museum in Harlem, 2001), 14–15; Huey Copeland, "Post/Black/Atlantic: A Conversation with Thelma Golden and Glenn Ligon," in *Afro Modern: Journeys through the Black Atlantic*, ed. Tanya Barson and Peter Gorschlüter (Liverpool: Tate Liverpool, 2010), 76–81; Paul C. Taylor, "Post-Black, Old Black," *African American Review* 41, no. 4 (Winter 2007): 625–40; Ytasha L. Womack, *Post Black: How a New Generation Is Redefining African American Identity* (Chicago: Lawrence Hill Books, 2010).

7 K. Merinda Simmons, "Introduction: The Dubious Stage of Post-Blackness—Performing Otherness, Conserving Dominance," in Baker and Simmons, *The Trouble with Post-Blackness*, 1, 2.

8 Womack, *Post Black*, 22. Italics in original.

9 Michelle Elam, *The Souls of Mixed Folk: Race, Politics, and Aesthetics in the New Millennium* (Stanford, CA: Stanford University Press, 2011), 21.

10 I wholeheartedly concur with William Maxwell's assertion that "James Baldwin, buried on 8 December 1987, often looks like today's most vital and beloved new African American author. . . . [T]he impression that Baldwin's work has returned to preeminence, unbowed and unwrinkled, reflects its ubiquity in the imagination of Black Lives Matter." William L. Maxwell, "Born-Again, Seen-Again James Baldwin: Post-Postracial Criticism and the Literary History of Black Lives Matter," *American Literary History* 28, no. 4 (Winter 2016), 812–13.

11 Greg Tate, "Introduction: Lust, of All Things (Black)," in *Flyboy 2: The Greg Tate Reader* (Durham: Duke University Press, 2016), 6. Italics and capitalization in original.

12 Greg Tate, "Cult-Nats Meet Freaky Deke," in *Flyboy in the Buttermilk* (New York: Simon and Schuster, 1992), 200, 207.

13 See Touré, *Who's Afraid of Post-Blackness?*, 23; Trey Ellis, "The New Black Aesthetic," *Callaloo* 38, no. 1 (Winter 1989), 237; Mark Anthony Neal, *Soul Babies: Black Popular Culture and the Post-Soul Aesthetic* (New York: Routledge, 2002), 3.

14 For example, she addresses not only Touré's book but also Golden's introduction to the Studio Museum's 2001 *Freestyle* show, Darby English's *How to See a Work of Art in Total Darkness* (2010), and Kenneth W. Warren's *What Was African American Literature?* (2011). Crawford eventually expanded her essay into a book-length study titled *Black Post-Blackness: The Black Arts Movement and Twenty-First-Century Aesthetics* (Urbana: University of Illinois Press, 2017).

15 Margo Natalie Crawford, "'What Was *Is*': The Time and Space of Entanglement Erased by Post-Blackness," in Baker and Simmons, *The Trouble with Post-Blackness*, 23.

16 Crawford, "'What Was *Is*,'" 29–31.

17 See Juana Summers, "Larry Wilmore for President: Keeping It 100 on 2016," *Mashable*, last modified October 2, 2015, https://mashable.com/2015/10/02/larry-wilmore-nightly-show-interview/.

18 Ashraf H. A. Rushdy, *Neo-slave Narratives: Studies in the Social Logic of a Literary Form* (New York: Oxford University Press, 1999), 7.

19 Tillet, "Free Is and Free Ain't."

20 Colson Whitehead, *The Underground Railroad* (New York: Doubleday, 2016), 222.

21 Salamishah Tillet, *Sites of Slavery: Citizenship and Racial Democracy in the Post-Civil Rights Imagination* (Durham: Duke University Press, 2012), 6.

22 Bertram D. Ashe, "Theorizing the Post-Soul Aesthetic: An Introduction," *African American Review* 41, no. 4 (2007), 621. Italics in original. See also Neal, *Soul Babies*, 22.

23 Ashe, "Theorizing the Post-Soul Aesthetic," 619.

24 Salamishah Tillet, "Free Is and Free Ain't," *Public Books*, last modified February 10, 2017, www.publicbooks.org/free-is-and-free-aint.

25 Ashe, "Theorizing the Post-Soul Aesthetic," 614.

26 Tate, "Cult-Nats Meet Freaky Deke," 200.

27 Tate, "Introduction: Lust, of All Things (Black)," 2.

28 Tate, "Introduction: Lust, of All Things (Black)," 2.

29 Neal, *Soul Babies*, 21–22.

30 Neal, *Soul Babies*, 3.

31 Michael Cohen, "#ScribdChat with Colson Whitehead," *Literally* (blog), *Scribd*, October 12, 2016, http://literally.scribd.com/home/2016/10/12/scribdchat-with-colson-whitehead.

32 Cohen, "#ScribdChat with Colson Whitehead."

33 Natashia Déon, "Red-Faced and Shaking," *Powell's Books Blog* (blog), June 8, 2016, www.powells.com/post/original-essays/redfaced-and-shaking. Emphasis in original.

34 Tanvi Misra, "Making a Real Underground Railroad," *Citylab*, last modified August 23, 2016, https://www.citylab.com/transportation/2016/08/colson-whitehead-underground-railroad-nyc-slavery/496586/.

35 Déon, "Red-Faced and Shaking."

36 Leah Mirakor, "More at Stake Here Than Beauty: An Interview with Yaa Gyasi," *Los Angeles Review of Books*, September 24, 2016.

37 Tillet, *Sites of Slavery*, 11.

38 Tillet, *Sites of Slavery*, 12.

39 Derek C. Maus, *Understanding Colson Whitehead* (Columbia: University of South Carolina Press, 2015), 7.

40 Tillet, *Sites of Slavery*, 6.

41 Whether or not Déon intended it, the echo of Eric Garner's tragic final words—"I can't breathe"—is hard not to hear at this juncture, especially since the phrase featured in several high-profile protests around the time she was working on the novel.

42 Natashia Déon, *Grace* (Berkeley, CA: Counterpoint, 2016), 30.

43 Déon, *Grace*, 33.

44 Déon, "Red-Faced and Shaking."

45 Déon, *Grace*, 37.

46 Déon, *Grace*, 1.

47 Déon, *Grace*, 365.

48 Déon, *Grace*, 367.

49 Earlier in the book, we are also told that he saves the newborn Josey—perhaps because of grief at the loss of his own young daughter—and passes her along to a sympathetic white woman to raise as her own.

50 Déon, *Grace*, 393.

51 See Priscilla B. Hayner, *Unspeakable Truths: Transitional Justice and the Challenge of Truth Commissions* (New York: Routledge, 2011).

52 Déon, *Grace*, 399.

53 Déon, *Grace*, 1, 401.

54 Déon, *Grace*, 401–2.

55 Yaa Gyasi, *Homegoing* (New York: Alfred A. Knopf, 2016), 299. Italics in original.

56 Countee Cullen, "Heritage," in *Collected Poems by Countee Cullen*, ed. Major Jackson (New York: Library of America, 2013), line 7.

57 Isaac Chotiner, "I Was Thinking about Blackness in America," *Slate*, June 6, 2016.

58 Womack, *Post Black*, 22.

59 Cullen, "Heritage," lines 9–10.

60 Chotiner, "I Was Thinking about Blackness in America."

61 Gyasi, *Homegoing*, 226–27.

62 Ben H. Winters, *Underground Airlines* (New York: Mulholland Books, 2016), 20, 12.

63 Winters, *Underground Airlines*, 19.

64 Winters, *Underground Airlines*, 21.

65 Winters, *Underground Airlines*, 32.

66 Winters, *Underground Airlines*, 190–91.

67 Winters, *Underground Airlines*, 191.

68 Winters, *Underground Airlines*, 297.

69 Stephanie Klein, "The Rumpus Interview with Ben H. Winters," *The Rumpus*, last modified July 8, 2016, http://therumpus.net/2016/07/the-rumpus-interview-with-ben-h-winters/.

70 James Baldwin, *The Fire Next Time* (New York: Dial Press, 1963). 101; Winters, *Underground Airlines*, 11. Italics in original.

71 Winters, *Underground Airlines*, 113.

72 Whitehead, *The Underground Railroad*, 168.

73 Cohen, "#ScribdChat with Colson Whitehead."

74 Whitehead, *The Underground Railroad*, 221–22.

75 Manisha Sinha, "The Underground Railroad in Art and History: A Review of Colson Whitehead's Novel," *Muster* (blog), *Journal of the Civil War Era*, November 29, 2016, https://journalofthecivilwarera.org/2016/11/under ground-railroad-art-history-review-colson-whiteheads-novel/.

76 Whitehead, *The Underground Railroad*, 286.

77 Whitehead, *The Underground Railroad*, 286–87.

78 Whitehead, *The Underground Railroad*, 279.

79 Whitehead, *The Underground Railroad*, 186.

80 Winters, *Underground Airlines*, 113.

81 Whitehead, *The Underground Railroad*, 286.

CHAPTER THREE

WHISPERING RACISM IN A POSTRACIAL WORLD

Slavery and Post-Blackness in Paul Beatty's The Sellout

CAMERON LEADER-PICONE

THE SELLOUT CATAPULTED PAUL BEATTY TO A NEW LEVEL OF FAME
following its Man Booker Prize win in 2016. Prior to that award, Beatty had
been a respected but iconoclastic novelist and poet. His highest-profile work,
his debut novel *The White Boy Shuffle*, was published in 1996, and he published only two other novels in the two decades prior to *The Sellout*. Though
The White Boy Shuffle is now a staple of college syllabi and has been analyzed
by many scholars (including this one) as a key text of post-soul culture, Beatty's other novels have been comparatively understudied. *The Sellout* is a deliberately provocative novel that, like Beatty's other works, skewers major public
figures and attacks what are often seen as sacrosanct ideas or narratives.
Indeed, upon winning the Booker Prize, many news stories highlighted how
its controversial subject matter led eighteen British publishers to turn down
the manuscript before a small publisher bought it, making it eligible for the
award.[1] The novel's plot is relatively simple. The narrator—the titular "Sellout," also called BonBon, and whose last name is Me—is the homeschooled
son of a professor of "Liberation Psychology," who experiments on him.[2] In
the course of the novel, he loses his father to police violence, enslaves Hominy
Jenkins—Buckwheat's understudy from *The Little Rascals*—and reinstitutes
segregation in his fictional Southern California hometown before being put
on trial for his crimes at the Supreme Court.

Because Beatty's plot centers the revival of slavery and segregation, it may
appear strange to analyze the novel in terms of post-blackness, a concept that
has been critiqued as unrealistically optimistic.[3] Reviving slavery in particular, as the original structure of juridical exclusion from the state, suggests a

novel operating in an afropessimist mode in which the fundamental, and perpetual, unfreedom of the black subject lies at the center of the nation and modernity more broadly.[4] However, while Beatty critiques American progress narratives, his prescription for liberation is individualistic and highlights the ultimate targets of his satire: discourses of authenticity. In this, Beatty echoes the central strains of post-blackness, which challenge not racialization itself but rather the responsibilities and expectations read through racialization, particularly in relation to the black artist. Beatty's novel, then, underscores Derek Conrad Murray's claim in another of this book's chapters that "satire upends a compulsory politics of racial fidelity" and is thus central to any discussion of post-black art.

Over the last two decades, post-blackness has migrated from a tentatively forwarded descriptor of a new generation of young black visual artists by Studio Museum of Harlem curator Thelma Golden to a much broader generational or era-labeling term. Among scholars, much of the push back against post-blackness derives from the fiction writer and journalist Touré's expansion of the term in his 2011 book *Who's Afraid of Post-Blackness?*[5] In that book's introduction, Touré acknowledges Golden's initial definition of the term and explains that his intent is to use it as a way to normatively describe a new era of African American identity. Like Touré, Ytasha Womack, author of *Post-Black: How a New Generation Is Redefining African American Identity* (2010), takes black Americans' relative increase in economic mobility as evidence that black identity has shifted, and must shift, to resist prescriptive accounts of what it means to be black. In other words, post-blackness in the broad sense refers to resistance to discourses of authenticity and a normative emphasis on the agency of the individual in relation to racial performance. Derek Conrad Murray links post-blackness in visual art with a broader questioning of how blackness has failed to account for the diversity of black people, particularly with regard to queer identity and gender performance. As he explains, "If post-black represents a threat, it is to the hegemony of hetero-patriarchal expressions of blackness that, in their essentialist logics and racial nostalgia, relegate African-American identity to a series of limiting scripts."[6]

Murray's use of the term hearkens back to Golden's initial definitional context. For Golden, the new generation of post-black artists to which she refers were not "post-black" as a modifier of "art," but more post–"black art," referring to the aesthetic traditions of the Black Arts Movement. Rather than proffering a definitive declaration, Golden's definition is tentative and, importantly, embedded within humor. She seeks to emphasize how the artists she chose for the exhibit do "work" that "speaks to an individual freedom that is a result of this transitional moment in the quest to define ongoing changes in the evolution of African-American art and ultimately to ongoing redefinition of blackness in contemporary culture."[7] The "ideological and chronological dimensions and repercussions" of the term to which she refers foreground post-black art as an assertion of freedom for artists who, while recognizing the limitations of structural racism, seek a new aesthetic grammar through which to represent blackness.[8] While Beatty quite vocally resists the implicit progress narrative he reads into the various "post-expressions" he disdains, his work aligns with Golden's definition of an aesthetic movement that prizes the idiosyncratic as a means of plumbing necessary and difficult truths about race and racism in contemporary American society.[9]

Indeed, Beatty's very resistance to locating his works within the broader tradition of African American literature—he describes himself as "trying to look beyond expectations of what a black book is supposed to be"[10]—typifies post era rejection of aesthetic mandates rooted in either market expectations or intraracial claims of authenticity. Analyzing the work of Percival Everett, Rolland Murray describes Everett's interrogation of black literature's "incorporation" into mainstream academic and publishing institutions.[11] Similar to Everett, Beatty responds to this institutionalization by challenging reader expectations of what African American literature can and should look like as a way to clear space for self-definition. As in his other novels, Beatty valorizes his protagonists as figures capable of recognizing and naming the toxicity of American racism even as he indicts them for their complicity in it. While *The Sellout* circulated, and was awarded, as a provocation in which the main character brings back slavery, its ultimate targets are the market forces, state actors, legal structures, and intracommunity claims that restrict the freedom of black people.

LEGAL FICTION(S)

At its heart, Beatty's novel interrogates race as what Karla Holloway calls a "legal fiction." As Holloway explains, the development of black literature parallels the broader contestation over personhood and citizenship: "One might argue that African America's literary history paralleled African Americans' own history of personhood, in which the first task was to prove that we were fully human rather than the fractional persons the Constitution declared us to be."[12] Rather than seeking to write himself into personhood, either by demonstrating a capacity for reason or for creativity or by highlighting the paradox inherent in the contradiction between America's stated ideals and their actual history, Beatty makes clear that blackness itself is a label designating a lack of personhood, leading him to seek selfhood and meaning outside of its reactionary boundaries. The endpoint of Beatty's portrait of a "new" blackness is not as simplistic as the statement that "blackness is passé" in his previous novel, *Slumberland* (2008), would superficially suggest.[13] Instead, Beatty seeks to move beyond the versions of blackness connected to either incorporation into the state or the market in favor of a blackness that doesn't "giv[e] a fuck" and that "doesn't sell."[14]

Beatty frames the novel with a Supreme Court case ostensibly about the narrator's revival of slavery. Though it is a "legal fiction," Beatty is not particularly interested in statutes or actual legal questions. As such, it is unclear what exactly the Supreme Court will rule on in the narrator's case. Not that it matters, as the Supreme Court never does rule in the text of the novel. Instead, Beatty makes clear that the Supreme Court case represents the long-standing question of black people's legal personhood. Early on, the narrator positions himself this way:

> It's a trip being the latest in the long line of landmark race-related cases. I suppose the constitutional scholars and cultural paleontologists will argue over my place on the historical timeline. Carbon-date my pipe and determine whether I'm a direct descendent of Dred Scott, that colored conundrum who, as a slave living in a free state, was man enough for his wife and kids, man enough to sue his master for his freedom, but not man enough for the Constitution, because in the eyes of the Court he was simply property: a black biped "with no rights the white man was bound to respect."[15]

This quote pivots on the clearest jurisprudential statement of blackness and noncitizenship, Chief Justice Roger Taney's ruling in *Dred Scott*.[16] Black people's struggle for freedom and equal citizenship responds to the categorical exclusion voiced by Taney. Abolitionists and later civil rights advocates sought to bring black people under the umbrella of legal personhood, to reverse Taney's words to say that black people not only do have rights that the white man is bound to respect but that those rights have been violated and thus require some form of legal sanction in order to be respected. The Supreme Court, in this history, serves as the well-trodden battleground across which such a claim has been fought for over and over again.

Beatty's novel rehearses the highlights of the battles that played out in front of the court following the post–Civil War amendments designed to repair this constitutional exclusion: *Plessy v. Ferguson*'s declaration that separate was equal as long as adequate resources were provided for black people; *Brown v. Board*'s overturning of *Plessy* through the ruling that legal separation inherently marks black people as inferior, harming their psyches. Beatty even invokes 2 Live Crew's challenging of obscenity laws. The purpose of this legal history is twofold. On the one hand, the narrator's supposed actions offend the post–civil rights legal fiction of color-blind constitutionalism. As critical race theorists have explained, the landscape of post-*Brown* legal precedent has sought formal equality rather than "substantive personhood."[17] Under color-blind constitutionalism, the post–Civil War amendments repaired the original text's discriminatory structure, and the hundred-year battle over equal rights produced or necessitated not equality but instead the absence of discrimination.[18] That such color-blind constitutionalism is belied by both history and ongoing structural racism generates Beatty's ironic plot in which the narrator's revival of slavery and segregation gives offense based not on existing racial hierarchies but instead on his violation of this legal illusion.

On the other hand, the legal history that Beatty traces here excludes the narrator from a genealogy of struggle. From the abolitionist lawyers who helped Scott make his claims, to the civil rights attorneys who used Homer Plessy's removal from a white train car as a test case, to the NAACP Legal Defense Fund that successfully argued *Brown*, the history of Supreme Court litigation has arguably been the most successful battleground in the efforts of black people to be recognized as citizens. The narrator's actions directly violate the collective responsibility imposed by that struggle: it is this history that he sells out. His revival of slavery and segregation mocks claims of progress and rejects arguments for even a thin politics of respectability. Both color-blind constitutionalists and civil rights activists claim to represent the nation's stated values and make their claims based on the authority of those values. Beatty's narrator cuts through this to assert his own authorship and authority. In his dismissal that it will be a project of scholars and "cultural paleontologists" to properly assess his role in American legal history, he exempts himself from a responsibility within that history either to the rights enumerated in the Constitution or those who seek to see those rights fully realized through substantive equality.

The novel's setting in Dickens, California, connects the dispute over black legal personhood with semiotic arguments over truth. Dickens is a thinly veiled stand-in for Compton.[19] As with his debut novel, *The White Boy Shuffle*, Beatty presents a Los Angeles metropolitan area that is both diverse and extremely segregated. Like Compton, Dickens began as an agricultural refuge for white people south of downtown Los Angeles, where the earliest version of the area's black community clustered. One of the core elements of Cheryl Harris's canonical argument about legal personhood, which claims that "whiteness" functions as a property right, is that whiteness confers material value.[20] The histories of Compton and Dickens typify the connection between this materiality and the philosophy of individual liberty underlying private property rights. For developers like Griffith Dickenson Compton, property ownership confers citizenship through an agrarian ideal in which self-ownership, as a condition of democratic participation, requires land. Quite obviously, this association between property ownership, self-sufficiency, and citizenship functions as the obverse of the enslaved's lack of legal person-hood, as they are denied even ownership of their own bodies. This contradic-tion motivates the narrator's humorous introduction of himself: "I grew up on a farm in the inner city."[21] The implicit contrast here between "farm" and "inner city" elucidates a cultural imaginary in which not only is the rural marked as white, but the exclusive right of whites to self-ownership is pre-sumed. The inner city that Beatty invokes is the province of cultural stereo-types of black gangsterism and poverty, stereotypes that contrast with farm imagery used to construct the image of a white American heartland.

Beatty's fictional Compton functions as an inverted utopia, a black (w)hole within which society's marginalized are disappeared.[22] Drawing on his under-graduate studies in psychology at Boston University, Beatty parallels the idea of legal personhood with the existential development of the self. For the narrator, that means his identity is fundamentally wrapped up in the two formative influences on his personality, his father and Dickens, both of which disappear early in the novel. His father is murdered by the Los Angeles Police Department for questioning their authority, and Dickens is removed from the map in a modern redlining scheme through which surrounding property values are propped up by acting as if the urban ghetto in the area does not exist. These "disappearances," then, underscore the insidiousness of struc-tural racism and state violence. In both cases, the power of the government violates the rights of black people, relegating them to second-class citizenship and denying their right of redress. Rejecting police requests to return his father's body to their custody, the narrator finds a paradoxical freedom as a product of the legal "no place" of Dickens, taking the body and planting it on his farm. The return of the body to the literal soil of Dickens conjoins the idea of lineal descent and citizenship in the land (jus soli). That citizenship, however, is in Dickens, not the United States, cementing the now quite literal claim that "Dickens was me," a play on the narrator's last name. In other words, the novel's Supreme Court framing is ultimately a feint. The reader gains no resolution to the legality of the narrator's actions or the consequences he faces. What drives the plot, rather, is his attempt to get Dickens back on the map.

Early in the novel, appearing in front of the Supreme Court, Beatty's version of Clarence Thomas stares at the narrator with a glare, demanding, "Where you from, fool?"[23] The justice's gaze prompts the narrator's figurative response of "Nowhere," the literal consequence of Dickens's unmapping. The community's erasure provides the context for the enslavement of Dickens's most famous resident, Hominy Jenkins. Beatty's characterization of Hominy typifies the novel's complex relationship to the most abject stereotypes. Despite harboring some exceptionally grotesque minstrel scenes, *The Little Rascals* offered what Julia Lee explains was "an unusual fantasy of interracial friendship" through which black performers such as Billie Thomas, who played Buckwheat, became famous and were even celebrated by the black press.[24] Hominy is a caricature but a remarkably nuanced one. Those who would reject him as the avatar of America's racist id miss the freedom he locates in his own acting. His marginalization parallels Dickens's own. As the narrator explains, Hominy "had the misfortune of being born in Dickens, California, and in America Hominy is no source of pride: he's a Living National Embarrassment. A mark of shame on the African-American legacy, something to be eradicated, stricken from the racial record, like the hambone, Amos 'n' Andy, Dave Chappelle's meltdown, and people who say 'Valentine's Day.'"[25] The slippage in this description between the "misfortune" of being born in Dickens and being a national embarrassment combines the two such that Dickens itself becomes a national embarrassment, a version of the grotesque stereotyping that defined Hominy's acting. Here, Beatty invokes the construction of the "ghetto" produced by the 1980s crack epidemic, gangsta rap, film, and television that has turned South Central Los Angeles into a floating signifier of a certain kind of inner-city gang territory.[26] For both Hominy and South Central Los Angeles, the narratives constructed through the circulating media images fail to account for the lived experience of the people being stereotyped. Thus, while Hominy is a minstrel archetype in one regard, he also represents a fallen figure whose greatest legacy—the thing he takes most pride in—has been relegated to the dustbin of racist history.

It is in this context that the narrator "enslaves" Hominy. I put *enslaves* in scare quotes because Beatty offers a performance of slavery rather than its actuality. Hominy seems to desire abjection. When the narrator saves Hominy from an act of self-lynching, Hominy asks him to "cut my penis off and stuff it in my mouth,"[27] reenacting the most grotesque racism from American history. His life saved, Hominy actually asks to be enslaved, saying, "I'm a slave.

That's who I am. It's the role I was born to play. A slave who also happens to be an actor."[28] These words resonate on two levels during the scene. On the one hand, his minstrel past does represent the popular cultural extension of the role of "the slave." In a sense, he has been playing the slave his entire life, and it is only in this moment that he claims it as his own. On the other hand, in asking the narrator to make him chattel, he reconstructs a play-acting version of slavery that they perform. Indeed, the narrator's acting ability in this regard lags Hominy's. He must be prodded into beating Hominy before offloading the responsibility to a local dominatrix who charges him extra to perform the attendant racial abuse. He is unable to force Hominy to do any labor, and is even unable to manumit his slave when he tries. Orlando Patterson argued in his canonical *Slavery and Social Death* that the state of enslavement constitutes a social death that is actually an extreme form of dishonor. The other dominant characteristics, such as natal alienation, in which the enslaved is divorced from any lineage and not allowed to inherit or pass on name or property, arise from this state of social dishonor.[29] Beatty's instantiation of slavery plays as a comic version of Patterson's definition. Jenkins appears sui generis, a fully alive stereotype desiring only further abjection. As his statement that "I'm a slave" implies, his dishonor precedes his enslaved status through his role as the archetypal minstrel. Both the narrator and Hominy, in fact, already exist in a state of dishonor, marginalized in a community literally wiped off the map. Connecting enslavement with the commodification and performance of blackness as well as the capacity of government policy to render whole populations outside of society's protection, Beatty questions the validity of the canonical American historical narrative of progress from slavery to freedom.

Indeed, not only does Hominy get to play out erotic fantasies of abjection, but he gains a paradoxical freedom in submission. Declaring in a paraphrase of libertarian philosopher Robert Nozick that "true freedom is having the right to be a slave,"[30] Hominy rejects the narrator's authority to free him.[31] In a scatological performance of slavery, the narrator attempts to write a manumission note for Hominy:

> "To Whom It May Concern," the contract read. "With this deed I
> hereby emancipate, manumit, set free, permanently discharge, and
> dismiss my slave Hominy Jenkins, who's been in my service for
> the past three weeks. Said Hominy is of medium build, complex-
> ion, and intelligence. To all who read this, Hominy Jenkins is now
> a free man of color. Witness my hand on this day, October 17th,

the year of 1838." The ruse didn't work. Hominy simply pulled down his pants, shit on my geraniums, and wiped his ass with his freedom, then handed it back to me.[32]

In this moment, the narrator attempts to negotiate the tension between the performance of slavery in which he participates and his desire to evade the weight of its violent history. The grotesque parody of real documents objectifies Hominy even as it aestheticizes the narrator's attempt to distance himself from slavery by dating the contract historically. Hominy's actions, by contrast, explode the narrator's pretensions. The bodily action of wiping his ass with manumission papers mocks history's sanitization and asserts his agency over his own performance.

These simulacra of historical oppression multiply across the text. The narrator overturns bans on segregation in public accommodations with a sign designating the front of Los Angeles County buses for white people. He mocks *Brown v. Board* by erecting a construction site for a magnet school offering a high-quality education for white children. For Beatty, these signifiers of segregation and slavery organize reality not through the weight of state coercion or power, but rather through the definitional effect they have on those who give them weight. What these simulacra offer the post–civil rights inhabitants of Dickens is an order and certainty that they lack. One of the first labors the narrator undertakes with the enslaved Hominy is the redrawing of Dickens's borders. As the narrator claims, "What are cities really, besides signs and arbitrary boundaries."[33] In this short line, Beatty voices a broader semiotic argument. Boundaries give meaning to both what is included and what is excluded. In doing so, they generate individual and group interests, prompting people to guard their interests or seek provision of others. In the case of school segregation, the presence of an arbitrary signifier of privilege—the white magnet school—motivates achievement on the part of the already segregated black and Latinx school in Dickens. Those achievements then activate status envy and ethnonationalism among white parents, who demand entry to the school from which they have systematically withdrawn support for decades.

The power of such arbitrary and capricious boundaries works even on those aware of their falsity. The narrator, for example, explains his own subordination to the power of the line he himself drew to recreate the borders of Dickens: "I have to confess that, in the days after I painted it, I, too, was hesitant to cross the line, because the jagged way it surrounded the remnants of the city reminded me of the chalk outline that police had needlessly drawn around my father's body. But I did like the line's artifice. The implication of solidarity and community it represented. And while I hadn't quite reestablished Dickens, I had managed to quarantine it. And community-cum-leper colony wasn't a bad start."[34] Linking the city boundary with his father's murder at the hands of the state highlights how boundaries typically gain their weight through state power. The murder of black people at the hands of police reveals the architecture of a broader caste system through which differential forms of citizenship are reproduced, a process of rendering, as Lisa Cacho argues, parts of the population "legally illegible" and thus "ineligible for personhood."[35] The governmentality of post–civil rights American neoliberalism allocates resources and exerts violence to indicate whose lives are protected and whose lives are disposable, a logic centered by the phrase *Black Lives Matter*. Drawing the boundary asserts the legitimacy of the community contained within those lines and demands their recognition. At the same time, the line drawn by the narrator is not just artificial but also somewhat meaningless absent the enforcement power the state claims. Though drawing the line is a communal action—as the narrator explains, when he stops painting in the evening, others start to fill in the line themselves—it expresses only the self-definitional agency of those within its boundaries. In other words, the line in the street is both a mapping and an extension of the ongoing process of unmapping. It reasserts Dickens as place but does so by acceding to the organizing logic of white supremacy that led to its erasure. The line on the street joins Hominy and the narrator's placing of signs on the freeway voicing the larger social forces that led to exclusion: "WATCH OUT FOR FALLING HOME PRICES and CAUTION—BLACK ON BLACK CRIME AHEAD."[36] The invocation of these stereotypes does not subvert their power or undermine their effect, but the explicitness names the boundaries for what they are.

As indicated by the scene in which the narrator resegregates public transportation as a gift for Hominy's birthday, Beatty wants mainly to unveil the ongoing forces of segregation, rather than point toward their demise: "Grandfather of the post-racial civil rights movement known as 'The Standstill,' he sat in the front of the bus, on the edge of his aisle seat, giving each new rider the once-over. Unfortunately for him, Dickens is a community as black as Asian hair, as brown as James, and after forty-five minutes of standing-room-only, all-minority ridership, the closest he got to a white person was the dreadlocked woman who got on at Poinsettia Avenue toting a rolled up yoga mat."[37] The instantiation of this new post– (anti–) civil rights movement lacks the idealism of past struggle. It not only does not seek to make claims based on American original principles, but it seeks to reinforce existing hierarchies precisely to indicate their power. The problem, however, is that Los Angeles in particular and American society more generally are already so intensely segregated that there is no one for Hominy to give his seat up for. The ultimate joke, then, for Beatty is that the segregation the sign seemingly imposes was there all along. As with the early Supreme Court scenes, the anger produced by such explicitness only responds to the voicing of what is already reality rather than the underlying reality itself. In other words, Beatty reveals how a superficial race-neutrality pervades the post–civil rights order. If the struggle of the civil rights movement sought substantive equality for black people and full citizenship within the state, Beatty suggests that its primary effect was the concealment of ongoing exclusion. Under this logic, the narrator's crime of whispering racism in a postracial world is the voicing itself.

UNMITIGATED BLACKNESS

The broader framing of the novel in terms of the Supreme Court reveals its ultimate irony. Black people have sought redress by appealing to the nation's ideals through the judicial system for centuries, only to meet with frustration and incomplete progress. It is through this lens, then, that one can understand Beatty's post-black liberation philosophy. Beatty connects the legal struggle for the recognition of black people as full citizens with the construction of racial identity to parody how feelings of obligation rooted in a history of black struggle for civil rights and equality lead to alienation. Sitting in the courtroom, the narrator attempts to summon the sense of racial filiation— "I make one last attempt to be at one with my people"[38]—that he has so egregiously violated through his indifference by visualizing civil rights era newsreel images in his head. In this case, however, the images fragment, collapsing under the weight of what is demanded of them:

> The film inside my head begins to skip and sputter. The sound cuts out, and the protesters falling like dominoes in Selma, Alabama, begin to look like Keystone Negroes slipping en masse on an affirmative-action banana peel and tumbling to the street, a tangled mess of legs and dreams akimbo. The marchers on Washington become civil rights zombies, one hundred thousand strong, somnambulating lockstep onto the mall, stretching out their stiff needy fingers for their pound of flesh. The head zombie looks exhausted from being raised from the dead every time someone wants to make a point about what black people should and shouldn't do, can and cannot have.[39]

Rather than revealing a noble history of struggle, the newsreel transforms to show an awful necromancy in which the activists of the past are summoned to stand in for any discussion of black history or the black experience with their actions divested of meaning and intent. Beatty's awful divestiture of political empowerment orphans his narrator. Washing his hands of the collective responsibility assigned to racial identity and shrugging off the supposed burden of representing the race as a whole, the narrator questions the validity of the arbitrary signs and boundaries that make up blackness as a signifier.

As the action moves into the courtroom at the end of the novel, a fictional liberal justice distills the novel's core thematic concern, which is blackness itself: "What we must not fail to remember is that 'separate but equal' was struck down, not on any moral grounds, but on the basis that the Court found that separate can never be equal. . . . *Me v. the United States of America* demands a more fundamental examination of what we mean by 'separate,' by 'equal,' by 'black.' So let's get down to the nitty gritty—what do we mean by 'black'?"[40] In *Brown*, the court relied on psychological evidence derived from the "doll tests" of Kenneth and Mamie Clark. In those tests, the Clarks demonstrated that even very young children, of all races, perceive and act upon the social preference for whiteness and the denigration of blackness. Based on this evidence, the court concluded that separate facilities carry an inherent inequality and social stigma, and that not even material equality can redeem them. As the fictional justice explains, this is not a moral claim as to the rightness or wrongness of segregation but rather an instrumental one. Beatty's novel implicitly responds: formal legal equality does not produce substantive equality. Indeed, it only masks ongoing exclusion in the superficial language of civil rights, and that language is itself arbitrary.

In other words, for Beatty, blackness encompasses its own signs and boundaries used to create an artificial group identity. This is Beatty's post-blackness, not a progressive claim as to change having occurred or occurring in the near future, but instead a relationality to the world's already fallen state that offers just a bit more freedom than the alternative. Because Beatty resorts to a psychological explanation of hierarchy and oppression, placing state coercion in the service of human indecency rather than as its originator, he locates that freedom outside of the state in the mind of the individual. The "unmitigated blackness" he celebrates has as its defining characteristic not giving a fuck, a freedom that he acknowledges requires embracing the meaninglessness of its effect: "There should be a Stage IV of black identity—Unmitigated Blackness. I'm not sure what Unmitigated Blackness is, but whatever it is, it doesn't sell. On the surface Unmitigated Blackness is a seeming unwillingness to succeed. . . . Unmitigated Blackness is coming to the realization that as fucked up and meaningless as it all is, sometimes it's the nihilism that makes life worth living."[41] To care about how one's blackness operates within the social structures that give it meaning is to accede to external logics, and thus to relinquish one's freedom. There may not be justice in Beatty's vision, but there is the only recognition that is possible, that of the self. In other words, refusing to mitigate one's blackness is a process of truth telling, but one that lacks the assumption that its product will be societal change. Embracing the meaninglessness of the identity performance removes the constrictions of authenticity and empowers the individual.

In line with this idea, late in *The Sellout*, the novel's narrator claims that his real crime is that of telling uncomfortable truths: "Well, I've whispered 'Racism' in a post-racial world."[42] The ambiguity of even the possibility of his case's resolvability before the Supreme Court only reinforces Beatty's rejection of any legalistic reparation for American racism and the progress narrative that such an investment in legal structures implies. In its place, Beatty leaves the reader with only the position of the cynical individual observer marveling at a nation gone mad. Indeed, the novel ends with the signal moment of postracialism in all its ridiculous glory. In this "closure" chapter, Barack Obama, or, as Beatty labels him, "the black dude," has just been elected. Foy Cheshire, the cynical, hustling academic turned public intellectual who functions as the narrator's main antagonist throughout the novel, celebrates, waving an American flag. The narrator questions Cheshire's actions, to which Foy replies "that he felt like the country, the United States of America, had finally paid off its debts."[43] Similarly, following the election, newsrooms and websites across the country came out with take after take arguing that the election of a black man to the presidency revealed that the nation had reached, or would soon reach, a postracial era.[44] Cheshire's words hammer home this point: the debt has been paid. The past is now just the past. Replying to Cheshire's naive optimism, Beatty's narrator is incredulous. American history is a parade of violence and exploitation rooted in genocide and slavery, the narrator suggests; its debts can never be paid. He stands, gazing upon a nation that seems to have lost its mind as Beatty offers "closure" that is not closure at all.

Importantly, Beatty rejects the idea that the product of such truth telling should be the return to a romanticized group identity. Instead, he embraces an individualism that lends his novel its post-blackness by positioning this observer as a lone individual, not as part of any broader collective. In doing so, *The Sellout* reveals its continuity with Beatty's past work. As an interview with Beatty notes, his novels contain recurrent scenes in which individual and group identities are put in conflict and deconstructed.[45] In *The White Boy Shuffle*, it is the moment when his friend Nick Scoby tells Gunnar Kaufman, about to head off to the newly elite Boston University, to "stay black, nigger."[46] In *The Sellout*, that moment occurs in the novel's final scene before the thematically linked coda involving the first black president. The narrator and Marpessa, his girlfriend, go to a comedy show that rehearses a cathartic riff on Black Arts Movement fiction in which the comedian on stage performs an inverted version of Dave Chappelle's breakdown, shouting at white audience members for laughing at his jokes and driving them from the club.[47] The narrator appreciates the reactionary anger of the comedian, reveling in the power derived from policing the boundaries of who can and should appreciate black cultural expression. In the final moments, however, he reflects on something he doesn't challenge the comedian about: "I wish I'd stood up to the man and asked him a question: 'So what exactly is *our thing*?"[48] As with the phrase "stay black" in *The White Boy Shuffle*, the comedian's words presume the boundaries of authentic blackness and black expression. There is power in drawing such lines. Just as the novel traces the narrator's successful attempt to get Dickens back on the map, recognition generates community. Community, however, is not, for Beatty, something redemptive or inherently valuable, as psychologically necessary as it is. Instead, recognition interpellates, imposing its logic on those within its gaze, including the narrator. Freedom, for Beatty, can only be found in the post-black individualism of the novel's final question as to whether there is any "our" at all.

The novel's overriding irony can also be found in the demographic reality of the fictional Dickens, and Compton itself, which generates the novel's ultimate joke. Dickens, the model of blackness as popular cultural caricature, a place that serves throughout the novel as an example of blackness and the black community, is not really black at all: "If they'd just taken their racial blinders off for one second, they'd realize [Dickens] was no longer black but predominantly Latino."[49] Beatty's novel insists on the need to remove such "racial blinders" generally, even as it anatomizes a post–civil rights America in which doing so remains seemingly impossible.

NOTES

1 Paul Beatty, "Turned Down 18 Times. Then Paul Beatty Won the Booker . . . ," interview by Charlotte Higgins, *Guardian*, October 26, 2016.

2 Prof. Me's "Liberation Psychology" reflects the influence of William E. Cross's "The Negro-to-Black Conversion Experience," which Beatty cites in the novel's acknowledgments. That essay also provides Beatty with the structure of

"stages" of blackness at the end of the novel. William E. Cross, Jr., "The Negro-to-Black Conversion Experience," *Black World* 20 (1971): 13–27.

3 K. Merinda Simmons and Houston A. Baker Jr., *The Trouble with Post-Blackness* (New York: Columbia University Press, 2015).

4 Afropessimism builds on Orlando Patterson's *Slavery and Social Death* (1982) to theorize the legal status of the enslaved as property as an ontological state of nonbeing. For a (much) more detailed introduction to the work of key theorists, such as Frank Wilderson III, Jared Sexton, and Saidiya Hartman, see *Afro-pessimism: An Introduction* (Minneapolis: Racked and Dispatched, 2017).

5 Academic volumes such as *The Trouble with Post-Blackness* have rebutted Touré's use of the term by questioning both the validity of the progress narrative he claims and his book's silence on the necessity of deconstructing whiteness either alongside or as a precondition to any notion of the "post-black."

6 Derek Conrad Murray, *Queering Post-Black Art: Artists Transforming African-American Identity after Civil Rights* (New York: I. B. Tauris, 2016), 3.

7 Thelma Golden, "Introduction: Post . . . ," in *Freestyle*, ed. Thelma Golden and Hamza Walker (New York: Studio Museum of Harlem, 2001), 15.

8 Golden, "Introduction: Post . . . ," 14.

9 Paul Beatty, "An Interview with Paul Beatty," interview by Frédéric Sylvanise, *Transatlantica* 2 (2013), https://journals.openedition.org/transatlantica/6709.

10 Kate Kellaway, "Paul Beatty: 'Heartbreak Is Part of Doing Anything You Want to Do,'" interview with Paul Beatty, *Guardian*, June 11, 2017.

11 Rolland Murray, "Not Being and Blackness: Percival Everett and the Uncanny Forms of Racial Incorporation," *American Literary History* 29, no. 4 (2017): 731.

12 Karla F. C. Holloway, *Legal Fictions: Constituting Race, Composing Literature* (Durham: Duke University Press, 2014), x.

13 Paul Beatty, *Slumberland* (New York: Bloomsbury, 2008), 4.

14 Paul Beatty, *The Sellout* (New York: Farrar, Straus and Giroux, 2015), 277.

15 Beatty, *The Sellout*, 8–9.

16 Don Fehrenbacher, *The Dred Scott Case: Its Significance in American Law and Politics* (New York: Oxford University Press, 1978). The novel provides a brief summary of what was at issue in that landmark decision. Dred Scott traveled north to Illinois and what is now Minnesota with his owner. Slavery was prohibited by law in both Illinois and the Wisconsin Territory. Scott lived for a long time in free territory—time enough to get married and to start a family. Left by his owner in the Wisconsin Territory, Scott lived for a time without the presence of his master before being summoned back to the South. As Fehrenbacher explains, "In the beginning, [*Dred Scott*] posed a fairly simple legal problem for which precedent seemed to provide a ready-made solution. At each stage of litigation, however, new and bigger issues were injected into the case. Thus it grew steadily more complex and in the end became critically important to the entire nation" (6).

17 Holloway, *Legal Fictions*, xii.

18 Neil Gotanda, "A Critique of 'Our Constitution Is Color-Blind,'" *Stanford Law Review* 44, no. 1 (November 1991): 1–68. The reference to the Constitution as "color-blind" actually comes from Justice Harlan's dissent in *Plessy*, in which he argues that the majority's decision is wrong precisely because it violates the equal protection of the law, the principle contained in the Fourteenth Amendment's overturning of *Dred Scott*. As Gotanda explains, "Color-blind constitutionalism is meant to educate the American public by demonstrating the 'proper' attitude towards race: the end of color-blind constitutionalism is a racially assimilated society in which race is irrelevant" (53). Gotanda critiques color-blind constitutionalism for its reliance on thinking about race only in terms of "formal race"—the designation of race as a descriptor. He argues for the failure of this idea given that "the color-blind ideal of the future society has been exhausted since the implementation of *Brown v. Board of Education* and its progeny" (54).

19 Evelyn McDonnell, "Don't Call 'The Sellout' a Ghetto Pastoral," *Los Angeles Review of Books*, May 7, 2015. McDonnell explains that this is a reference to both "the actual founder of Compton, Griffith Dickenson Compton, and to the father of social realist novels, Charles Dickens." Beatty might also be thinking of Dickens's writings on slavery contained in *American Notes*, in which he details the horrors of slavery and its evil. At one point, Dickens refers to the "monstrous absurdity" of one of the stories he relates, a phrase that well describes Beatty's own tonal register. Charles Dickens, *American Notes for General Circulation*, Project Gutenberg (1850; repr., London: Chapman and Hall, 1913).

20 Cheryl Harris, "Whiteness as Property," *Harvard Law Review* 106, no. 8 (June 1993): 1707–91. As Harris explains, "Only white possession and occupation of land was validated as a basis for property rights" (1716), an inheritance that traces its way through American law to protect a material interest in whiteness and reify black disadvantage.

21 Beatty, *The Sellout*, 27.

22 Houston A. Baker Jr., *Blues, Ideology, and Afro-American Literature: A Vernacular Theory* (Chicago: University of Chicago Press, 1984), 113–99. I refer here to Baker's theorizing of the underground as a space that allows black protagonists to come to a full sense of self prior to returning to society. See Baker, *Blues, Ideology, and Afro-American Literature*, chapter 3.

23 Beatty, *The Sellout*, 22.

24 Julia Lee, *Our Gang: A Racial History of the Little Rascals* (Minneapolis: University of Minnesota Press, 2015), xx.

25 Beatty, *The Sellout*, 76.

26 For a discussion of hip-hop and the cultural construction of the image of South Central Los Angeles, see Robin Kelley, *Race Rebels: Culture, Politics, and the Black Working Class* (New York: Free Press, 1994), 183–227; and Murray Forman, *The 'Hood Comes First: Race, Space, and Place in Rap and*

Hip-Hop (Middletown, CT: Wesleyan University Press, 2002), 193–98. I will note, in particular, the resonance between Beatty's image of his narrator drawing a line around Dickens to reinstate its borders and the NWA video for "Straight Outta Compton." In that video, the viewer sees a map of Los Angeles, Compton's borders marked in red, a figurative boundary between the nation and the frontier, the border between two sovereign nations. Framing their most famous song, "Fuck the Police," NWA positions the city of Compton as an occupied territory, an ongoing war zone. Claiming this sovereignty, NWA puts the police on trial, claiming the authority to review and judge their actions.

27 Beatty, *The Sellout*, 74.

28 Beatty, *The Sellout*, 77.

29 Orlando Patterson, *Slavery and Social Death: A Comparative Study* (Cambridge, MA: Harvard University Press, 1982). Patterson offers the following preliminary definition of slavery: "*Slavery is the permanent, violent domination of natally alienated and generally dishonored persons*" (13, italics in original).

30 Beatty, *The Sellout*, 83.

31 Robert Nozick, *Anarchy, State, and Utopia* (Oxford: Blackwell, 1974), 331.

32 Beatty, *The Sellout*, 82.

33 Beatty, *The Sellout*, 87.

34 Beatty, *The Sellout*, 109.

35 Lisa Cacho, *Social Death: Racialized Rightlessness and the Criminalization of the Unprotected* (New York: New York University Press, 2012), 6.

36 Beatty, *The Sellout*, 89.

37 Beatty, *The Sellout*, 127.

38 Beatty, *The Sellout*, 18.

39 Beatty, *The Sellout*, 19.

40 Beatty, *The Sellout*, 274.

41 Beatty, *The Sellout*, 277. "Unmitigated Blackness" is the final stage of blackness in the narrator's explanation at the end of the novel. The concept of there being progressively more free stages of blackness derives from Cross, who describes five stages, culminating in an "internalization-commitment" that promotes self-actualization alongside a commitment to "pro-black" culture and politics. For more, see Cross, "The Negro-to-Black Conversion Experience," 22–27.

42 Beatty, *The Sellout*, 262.

43 Beatty, *The Sellout*, 289.

44 Catherine Squires, *The Post-Racial Mystique: Media and Race in the Twenty-First Century* (New York: New York University Press, 2014), 17–64.

45 Chris Jackson, "Our Thing: An Interview with Paul Beatty," *Paris Review*, May 7, 2015.

46 Paul Beatty, *The White Boy Shuffle* (New York: Picador, 1996), 155.

47 See, for example, Henry Dumas, "Will the Circle Be Unbroken?," in *Echo Tree: The Collected Short Fiction of Henry Dumas*, ed. Eugene B. Redmond (Minneapolis, MN: Coffee House Press, 2003), 105–11. In Dumas's story, the performance by a saxophonist playing an "afrohorn" kills several white audience members who refuse to heed warnings that the performance is not for them.

48 Beatty, *The Sellout*, 288.

49 Beatty, *The Sellout*, 93; Emily Straus, *Death of a Suburban Dream: Race and Schools in Compton, California* (Philadelphia: University of Pennsylvania Press, 2014). As Straus explains in her history of Compton and its school system, the city's reputation as a black city derives from its presence in the popular imaginary but also from efforts by local black political leaders to dilute Latino vote power: "By 2011 Latinos comprised two-thirds of Compton's population, but no Latino held elected city office" (227).

CHAPTER FOUR

GETTING GRAPHIC WITH *KINDRED*

The Neo-Slave Narrative of the Black Lives Matter Movement

MOLLIE GODFREY

AS AN EARLY WORK IN THE GENRE OF NEO-SLAVE NARRATIVES, OCTAVIA Butler's *Kindred* (1979) uses the trope of time travel to draw together two disparate moments and spaces in American history: the antebellum south and the novel's present day in 1976 California. In 2017, with the publication of a graphic novel adaptation of *Kindred* by Damian Duffy and John Jennings, Butler's effort to make the past freshly available was reborn for an even newer generation of readers. This retelling is a sign of growing interest in the graphic novel among consumers, academics, and educators. Many examples of this booming genre are explicitly geared toward younger audiences, including a number of adaptations of serious nonfiction such as Kyle Baker's *Nat Turner* (2006), Andrew Helfer's *Malcolm X* (2006), and John Lewis's *March* (2016). Unlike these examples, however, the graphic adaptation of *Kindred* retells a narrative already positioned as a kind of retelling. Just as Butler's text brought the "neo" to the "slave narrative" by making use of storytelling modes opened up by the genre of speculative fiction, the graphic adaptation aims once again to "make . . . the old new" by making use of storytelling modes opened up by the genre of the graphic novel.[1]

Considered together, the two versions of *Kindred* raise questions about how their aesthetic innovations—the speculative novel's use of time travel and the graphic novel's use of juxtaposed images—speak to the political concerns of their respective moments of retelling. If Butler's text uses speculative fiction's openness to the trope of time travel to bring past forms of black women's resistance to life for black militants of the 1960s and '70s, as is often argued, how and why does the graphic novel form renew and rewrite this project for the young activists of our own era: a generation coming of age surrounded by images of violence and brutality against black people, and by the gender and class politics of Black Lives Matter (BLM)?[2] How do the trope of time travel and the use of juxtaposed images, respectively, speak to efforts in each moment to contest or redefine notions of black collectivity and resistance? And what do the interests and formal innovations of these two versions of *Kindred* tell us about the relationship between these two historical moments?

This chapter argues that these two versions of *Kindred* reflect evolving efforts to articulate models of black collectivity and resistance in response to the post–civil rights rise of color blindness as a strategy for concealing the operation of systemic racism. In the original novel, the trope of time travel is used to reevaluate the concept of endurance. For many Black Power activists and intellectuals, endurance signified little more than submission to ongoing white tyranny.[3] The original *Kindred*, in contrast, uses a historically contextualized understanding of endurance not only to challenge exclusive visions of black collectivity but also to insist—as Audre Lorde, Kimberlé Crenshaw, and Patricia Hill Collins would do in the decade to follow—that combatting color-blind racism, to use Eduardo Bonilla-Silva's term, requires intersectional feminism.[4] The graphic adaptation builds on this framework by examining the value of evidence in an era defined less by its commitment to exclusive notions of black collectivity than by its commitment to post-Obama "post-racialism."[5] Pushing back against this fantasy, many Black Lives Matter activists have taken to social media to provide evidence of antiblack racism, even as other activists have grown weary and skeptical of such efforts.[6] The adaptation of *Kindred* reconsiders the value of evidence by highlighting the ways images can be juxtaposed to contest both masculinist and color-blind narratives. In the novel, these juxtapositions take a range of forms: from centering white racism over white innocence; to demanding witnesses rather than spectators of antiblack violence; to highlighting both differences and connections in the experience of racism across space and time. Taken together, these novels posit endurance, evidence, and the novels themselves as part of a larger effort to enable diverse communities of black people to develop an intersectional black consciousness and to speak to one another not only about the violence of America's racial past but also about the violence of its "postracial"—or what Michael Tesler calls its "most-racial"—present.[7]

Examining these two versions of *Kindred* in relation to the political needs of their moments of production also reveals their relationship to two transitional moments in the rise and subsequent transformation of what has been called the post-soul or post-black aesthetic. Mark Anthony Neal defines this aesthetic as a post–civil rights and post–Black Power "reimagining of the contemporary African American experience, attempting to liberate contemporary interpretations of that experience from sensibilities that were formalized and institutionalized during earlier social paradigms"—especially those sensibilities that "deny . . . a full range of black identities."[8] Although Neal insists that the respectability politics of earlier generations were as limiting as were the "patriarchal and heterosexist" tendencies of the Black Power movement, key post-black manifestos, such as Trey Ellis's "The New Black Aesthetic" (1989) and Thelma Golden's introduction to the *Freestyle* catalog (2001), present the post-black aesthetic as a post–Black Arts aesthetic that grows out of and explodes the unifying strategies of black nationalism.[9] The original *Kindred*, as part of the genre of neo-slave narratives that arose during and immediately after the rise of the Black Arts Movement (BAM), is also part of this larger shift toward the pluralizing gestures of post-blackness. As Ashraf Rushdy argues, neo-slave narratives "engage in an extended dialogue with their own moment of origins in the late sixties and early seventies . . . [including] the meaning of Black Power."[10] For A. Timothy Spaulding, this means that many neo-slave narratives bring together "the political ideology of black nationalism . . . and the deconstructive project of postmodernism," but he adds that this nexus must be understood as equally intersecting with early black feminist efforts "to recover the literary tradition of black women writers that black nationalism had ignored" and thus complicating unified notions of black identity by "arguing that any view of black identity must examine the interaction of race, class, gender, and sexuality."[11] Because many neo-slave narratives, including *Kindred*, were written by black women, drew on developing black feminist theory, and emphasized black female perspectives, looking to this text and this genre as a key moment in the transition from the Black Aesthetic to the post-black aesthetic illuminates the role played by black feminism in that transition.[12]

The more recent graphic retelling of *Kindred* occupies another transformative moment in the post-black aesthetic, away from the post–Black Power need to articulate a plurality of black identities and interests, and toward the BLM-era need to reassert black collectivity without sacrificing the commitment to plurality, intersectionality, and inclusion upon which black feminists, black queer folk, and others insist. As the BLM website puts it, "Our network centers those who have been marginalized within Black Liberation Movements."[13] While this platform connects to Ellis's refusal "to deny or suppress any part of our complicated and sometimes contradictory cultural baggage to please either white people or black," the renewed political urgency of this more recent moment also marks a departure from Ellis's claim that, for post-black writers, "racism is a hard and little-changing constant that neither surprises nor enrages."[14] Rather, as Soyica Diggs Colbert argues, the post-Ferguson era is animated by rage, which has become an important response to the "invisible and routine forms of racism" that "serve as a primary mechanism for securing racial hierarchies."[15] As Colbert puts it, "Every day and in the midst of crisis, black rage acknowledges the limits of black citizenship and enables the cultivation of black political collectivity by uniting individuals through a shared feeling"; it is a direct response to the "invisible forms of racism" that "slowly eat away at black subjects."[16] Brittney Cooper similarly names this feeling "eloquent rage," which she describes as a black feminist renewal of Audre Lorde's post–Black Arts work, elaborated in "The Uses of Anger: Women Responding to Racism," for the post-Obama era.[17] In the murky space between the intersectional openness of post-blackness and the invisible racism of postracialism, black rage emerges, for Colbert, as "a collective feeling that organizes a social group invested in resisting quotidian forms of racial violence," a group brought together by the feeling of rage rather than by nationalist or exclusionary notions of identity and unity.[18] The graphic adaptation of *Kindred* speaks directly to this need to make evident invisible forms of racism in order to foster a new sense of black collectivity, one that harnesses both the political urgency and the intersectionality of prior generations of black feminism.

ENDURING TIME IN *KINDRED* (1979)

The original *Kindred*'s reevaluation of endurance is connected to the neo-slave narrative's negotiation of time. In the post–civil rights era, both white conservatives and black nationalists posited a temporal break between their ideologies and those of a prior era. For white conservatives, it became useful to present the civil rights movement as a major break in America's racist history and to present themselves as representatives of this newly color-blind America, even as they continued to support policies that negatively impacted African Americans.[19] Black nationalists, by contrast, insisted that America had not dramatically changed as a result of civil rights. However, they did argue that the black community and black individuals had changed—transformed by Black Power and the Black Aesthetic from "a Negro" into "an African American or black man."[20] In the Black Arts imagination, slavery often acted both as a symbol of persistent racism in America, such as the slave ship / subway car doomed never to make port in Amiri Baraka's *Dutchman* (1964), and as a symbol of prior black submission to their literal and cultural enslavement, as when Baraka claimed that he had "literally changed into a blacker being" by "discarding [his] 'slave name' and embracing blackness."[21] In black nationalist ideology, submission and enslavement were also often feminized, as when Malcolm X criticized integrationist sit-ins by saying "an old woman can sit . . . but it takes a man to stand."[22] The neo-slave narrative intervenes in both conservative and black nationalist characterizations of the past by recovering not only the black perspectives marginalized by white historiography but also those perspectives marginalized by black nationalist historiography. In clear dialogue with the black feminist recovery of black female voices in works by Toni Cade Bambara, Alice Walker, Paule Marshall, Audre Lorde, Barbara Christian, and others, many neo-slave narratives extend the black nationalist recovery of black history, while simultaneously challenging Black Power's masculinist self-presentation as a break with a submissive—and often feminized—past.[23]

Butler's *Kindred* complicates Black Power's dismissal of feminized forms of submission. In the novel, an African American woman named Dana finds herself pulled back in time to save the life of her white slave-owning ancestor, Rufus, able to return to her present day only when she feels her own life is at risk. Much of the novel explores Dana's failure to understand slavery—a failure linked to the inadequacy of books and the inadequacies of Dana's contemporaries.[24] Thanks to time travel, however, Dana becomes, like Frederick Douglass before her, both "a witness and a participant" in the institutions of slavery: from the physical violence of whipping, rape, and the slave trade to the psychological violence through which enslaving and enslavement became a way of life for white and black Americans.[25] However, whereas Douglass would go on to describe "how a slave was made a man," Dana's story follows a reverse course, explaining how a man—or, in Dana's case, a woman—could be made a slave.[26] *Kindred*'s many resonances with Douglass's work also shore up Butler's critique of her contemporary moment. After all, Douglass's famous 1857 claim that "the limits of tyrants are prescribed by the endurance of those whom they oppress" was famously adopted as a slogan of the Black Power movement by Stokely Carmichael, who quoted the line in his own speeches to describe Black Power's need to break with the past.[27] It is this claim—that endurance only maintains the black community's submission to enslavement—that *Kindred* directly interrogates.

With a protagonist who is literally pulled back in time by the needs of her slave master ancestor, *Kindred* challenges those strains of Black Arts and Black Power ideology that emphasize the Black Power moment as a break with the past. Rather than insisting upon a formal and temporal break with passive, submissive, or assimilative forms of black resistance, *Kindred* purposely blends the new with the old, the "neo" with the "slave narrative," and

Dana's fate in the present with her ancestors' fates in the past. Dana's experience of being physically tied to her own history also forces her to reevaluate the various actors in that history, most notably Aunt Sarah, who is described as "the kind of woman who would be held in contempt during the militant nineteen sixties . . . the handkerchief head, the female Uncle Tom."[28] At first, Dana looks down on her too—comforted by this sense of "moral superiority"—until Rufus comes back "with what was left of Alice" after Alice's attempted escape.[29] Face-to-face with the physical consequences of refusing to submit to one's tyrant, Dana begins to doubt whether 1960s radicals truly understand the structural realities that made self-defense untenable for so many enslaved people—and especially for enslaved women. The same could be argued of Dana's ancestor Alice, who becomes the unwilling mother of Rufus's children. As Angelyn Mitchell puts it, all of the "choices" Alice has in the face of Rufus's advances have "devastating consequences"; considered in the context of these structural realities, her choice to submit "her body but not her spirit" could be understood as a "strategy of resistance."[30]

Dana's experience of being tied to the past forces her to reevaluate not only her relationship to black liberation politics but also her understanding of female empowerment and female sexual autonomy. At the outset, Dana is positioned as a liberated woman by the standards of the nineteenth century and the present: in the past, she shocks her ancestors because she dresses "like a man"; in the present, she shocks her husband, Kevin, when she refuses to do his typing for him.[31] Compared to Alice, who is frequently described as Dana's mirror image, Dana often seems like the more advantaged and liberated version of the two, but her relative freedom is slowly revealed to be just as tenuous as Alice's. They both begin the novel as free black women—Dana free in the present and Alice free in the past—who are nevertheless yoked back into slavery over the course of the novel by forces beyond their control. On the surface, Alice seems to take the path of endurance to her own detriment, submitting to Rufus's sexual demands and eventually killing herself. Dana, in contrast, seems to take the path of self-defense to her own freedom, resisting Rufus's sexual demands to the point of killing him and freeing herself. However, Dana is all too aware how easily she could have made the other choice: "I realized how easy it would be . . . to . . . forgive him even this . . . in spite of all my talk. But it would be so hard to raise the knife. . . . So hard to kill."[32] She also fears that her choice of self-defense was the more selfish one, coming at the cost of the safety of many of her friends: "Now I said simply, 'Self-defense.' . . . 'But the cost . . . Nigel's children, Sarah, all the others.'"[33] Dana's self-doubt suggests that—in the context of past forms of structural inequality—endurance and submission are driven not by individual weakness but rather by an investment in the collective health of black communities. In this way, the novel troubles the black nationalist association of the principle of self-defense with the development of self-reliant black communities, pointing to ways in which the structures of enslavement complicate easy characterizations of submission and resistance.

This troubling of the Black Power mantras of self-defense and self-reliance shows that, for *Kindred*, black nationalist claims to have liberated oneself from past forms of submission problematically decontextualize the past. This critique seems especially important when considered in relation to the moment of *Kindred*'s composition, in the aftermath of the Nixon presidency and just before the ascendency of Ronald Reagan. As Keeanga-Yamahtta Taylor explains, this is the era in which conservatives began to wield "color-blindness" as a tool "to resist the growing acceptance of 'institutional racism' as the central explanation for Black inequality" and to shift the blame from white institutions to black moral failures: "Downplaying race meant, once again, emphasizing culture and morality as important to understanding Black progress."[34] Claiming not to see race became a way of not seeing history, or its effects, and thus shoring up conservative representations of the persistent effects of structural racism as evidence of black moral failures.[35] In the context of this emerging logic, Black Power's willingness to use the submissiveness of enslaved people as a reverse symbol for their own more manly form of resistance could be read as similarly shifting the blame from structural inequities to black moral failures. The trope of time travel in Butler's *Kindred* not only echoes the positive reevaluation of black female ancestors we see in other black feminist writing of this period, but it does this in order to better assert what Black Power advocates such as Stokely Carmichael would elsewhere acknowledge was the necessity of historical and structural knowledge in the fight against antiblack institutions.[36] Like subsequent black feminist writing by Audre Lorde, Kimberlé Crenshaw, and Patricia Hill Collins, *Kindred* suggests that an intersectional understanding of the past and the present better equips us to address structural racism.

IMAGES AS EVIDENCE IN *KINDRED* (2017)

With the emergence of BLM, the operations of structural racism have reached heightened public consciousness. Popular books and films such as Michelle Alexander's *New Jim Crow: Mass Incarceration in the Age of Colorblindness* (2010) and Ava DuVernay's *13th* (2016) trace the current policing of black communities and individuals to a long history of racial oppression, while demonstrating the intimate connection between that history and putatively color-blind institutional practices that disproportionately affect communities of color. Similarly, BLM activists have combatted the illusions of color blindness rooted in the Nixon and Reagan eras by flooding social media with tangible evidence of racial injustice—from the everyday violence of #LivingWhileBlack to videos of police violence that recall the images of whipping, lynching, and police brutality that circulated during prior eras of unrest.[37] As Taylor puts it, "The advent of social media has almost erased the lag between when an incident happens and when the public becomes aware of it. Where the mainstream media have typically downplayed or even ignored public claims of police corruption and abuse, the proliferation of smartphones fitted with voice and video recorders has given the general public the ability to record these incidents and share them far and wide on a variety of social media platforms."[38]

The democratization of visual documentation and dissemination means that BLM activists now have unprecedented control over the images that circulate regarding racial injustice, and they can use these tools to combat dominant narratives that endorse color blindness and black moral failure. In the popular press, black victims of police brutality are routinely identified using either mug shots or "thug" shots that seem to suggest they deserved their deaths, whereas white perpetrators are usually identified with "respectable" school portraits or family photos. BLM activists use social media to call out and counter these mainstream narratives—for example, juxtaposing the image circulated in the press of police-shooting victim Michael Brown flashing hand signs with Brown's graduation photo, or juxtaposing the suited school portrait that the press used to identify Stanford rapist Brock Turner with Turner's mug shot. Such juxtapositions deliberately contest dominant narratives that promote conservative investments in color blindness and black moral failure by pointing to the ways in which these narratives insist on black guilt and white innocence even when the black person is the victim and the white person has committed a crime. In the process, these juxtapositions reframe images originally used as evidence of white innocence to be legible as evidence of white racism.

Although *Kindred*'s graphic novel adapters, Damian Duffy and John Jennings, decided after some debate not to update Dana's contemporary moment from 1976 to 2016, their use of the graphic novel form—a form defined by its use of deliberately juxtaposed images—nevertheless shifts the story's emphasis toward the concerns of the present.[39] In a historical moment in which we are increasingly inundated with videos and images of black death, the visual is inescapably political: whereas literary works about slavery such as Edward P. Jones's *The Known World* (2003) and Colson Whitehead's *The Underground*

Railroad (2016) continue to win acclaim and awards without much controversy, visual narratives of slavery such as Steve McQueen's *12 Years a Slave* (2013) have been described as "torture porn," and Nate Parker's *The Birth of a Nation* (2016) was criticized not only for its director's personal violence against women and the film's related gender politics, but also for what was described as the film's "lazy" and "extraneous" violence.[40] Critics of these films are responding to the way these images can function as easily as evidence in the process of witnessing historical or contemporary violence as they can as a spectacle of black suffering and death that only demonstrates and perpetuates America's indifference to black suffering.[41] Nevertheless, the technological leap afforded by smartphones and social media means that it is now primarily through the production and juxtaposition of images that the criminalizing and color-blind narratives that perpetuate racial inequality are being contested. In the graphic adaptation of *Kindred*, the prologue emphasizes the importance of the image, replacing several pages of text with a single image of Dana's lost arm, juxtaposed with the words "I lost my arm on my last trip home" and the title "Prologue" (see figure 4.1). Standing alone as it does, the image initially seems to say it all about the structural pain inflicted on Dana by the past. And yet, as a "prologue" to the book that will follow, the image also implies that we will need more images to understand the relationship of that past to our future. Although an understanding of history and institutionalized structures of inequality is as important to the graphic retelling as it was to Butler, the new version redirects our attention to the value of images in developing this understanding—and to how they can be juxtaposed to witness rather than create spectacles out of antiblack violence.

Like the prologue, the whipping of Dana's ancestor, Alice's father, is similarly graphic—a primal scene in Dana's introduction to slavery that directly mirrors Frederick Douglass's infamous description of the beating of Aunt Hester, which Saidiya Hartman describes as "a primal scene" that serves as "an inaugural moment in the formation of the enslaved" while also raising questions about how we as readers "participate in such scenes" without "exacerbating the indifference to suffering that is the consequence of the benumbing spectacle."[42] Douglass navigates the tension between witnessing and participating carefully, describing Hester's beating thus: "The first of a long series of such outrages, of which I was doomed to be a witness and a participant. It struck me with awful force. It was the blood-stained gate, the entrance to the hell of slavery, through which I was about to pass. It was a most terrible spectacle. I wish I could commit to paper the feelings with which I beheld it."[43] Douglass demonstrates his role as a witness to Aunt Hester's beating by

4.1   Prologue, *Kindred* (2017), p. 7. Courtesy of John Jennings.

emphasizing its impact upon him; every time her body is struck, the meaning of the event strikes Douglass with equal force. In the graphic adaptation of *Kindred*, images are juxtaposed to emphasize precisely this relationship between the spectacle of black pain and the need to witness rather than become numb to that pain (see figure 4.2). As in Douglass's text, which challenges the reader to understand him- or herself as a similar "witness and participant" in the beating, the reader of *Kindred* is coached—this time through the juxtaposition of images—to understand that such spectacles require our witness. For every image of Alice's father being beaten, we have a corresponding image of Dana or Alice witnessing the beating. The images are arranged to align Dana with Alice as equal witnesses of this "primal scene" via identical depictions of their sobbing faces. In contrast, the face of Alice's mother appears without tears and at a different angle; she has long since passed through Douglass's "blood-stained gate." As readers of this scene, we must align ourselves with one of these witnesses—either one of the ones being newly introduced to this spectacle of violence or the one who, eyes closed, no longer needs to see evidence of the spectacle to serve as its witness.

Kindred's gender reversal of Douglass's primal scene also speaks to current concerns about what Crenshaw has called the "urgency of intersectionality."[44] The BLM hashtag was founded by three queer and trans women with the goal of centering people who had been sidelined by prior black liberation movements. And yet, as one of the #blacklivesmatter founders argues, the deaths of black men at the hands of police are centered by the media and by many BLM activists in ways that continue to obscure the experiences of black women and queer folk.[45] As Crenshaw puts it, "When you can't see a problem, you pretty much can't solve it."[46] In *Kindred*, the gendered reversal of Aunt Hester's beating speaks to the primacy given to violence against black male bodies in the images that circulate during our contemporary moment, but it also insists on including within the narrative the impact of this violence on black women. Other moments in the graphic novel—enslaved men in chains being sold away from their families for minor infractions—similarly resonate with contemporary conversations about the prison-industrial complex, though, as with the beating of Alice's father, they insist on including black women such as Dana either within or in juxtaposed frames. Considered in relation to the text as a whole, however, such images of violence against men are outliers: the primary violence in the novel is against women—against Dana, against Alice, against Sarah, against Tess—and we see it in all forms: beatings, rape, having their children taken away, being taken away, and suicide—forms that recall for a contemporary reader the

The man's body convulsed, but the only sound he made was a gasp.

But I could hear his breathing, hard and quick.

He began to moan . . .

He took several more blows with no outcry . . .

Then the man's resolve broke.

. . . low gut-wrenching sounds . . . torn from him against his will. Finally he began to scream.

I could literally smell his sweat, hear every ragged breath, every cry, every cut of the whip.

I could see his body jerking, convulsing, straining . . .

His screaming went on and on.

My stomach heaved.

4.2   The primal scene, *Kindred* (2017), pp. 42–43. Courtesy of John Jennings.

violence against black women that movements like #SayHerName show our culture routinely ignores.[47] Just as the original novel challenged the emphasis on male-centered forms of resistance in the Black Power movement, the graphic retelling uses the inclusion of images of women within the frame and within the text as evidence that challenges the emphasis on male-centered images of injustice that persists within and in response to BLM.

Black feminists insist not only on intersections but also on connections. As Angela Davis puts it, "We are still faced with the challenge of understanding the complex ways race, class, gender, sexuality, nation, and ability are intertwined—but also how we move beyond these categories to understand the interrelationships of ideas and processes that seem to be separate and unrelated. Insisting on [these] connections . . . is a feminist process."[48] Similarly, *Kindred* insists on a range of connections across time, gender, race, and class. The graphic version of the novel also makes use of a number of mirroring images that emphasize connections between characters across these lines—connections between Dana's white husband and white slave patrollers and owners, between Dana and Alice, and between Dana and Rufus.[49] While such connections are also made in the original novel, the graphic adaptation further emphasizes the ways that images are used to draw people into opposing narratives despite these underlying connections. Although Dana has access to advantages that Alice lacks, the graphic novel layers these differences on top of their visual similarities. They appear repeatedly as mirror images of each other, the only differences being their clothing and hairstyle (see figure 4.3). These juxtapositions recall BLM's similar use of juxtaposed images to refuse respectability as the only response to the criminalization of blackness—embracing images of Trayvon Martin wearing a childish smile alongside unsmiling images of Martin wearing one of the "thuggish" hoodies on which his murder was blamed.[50] Like Trayvon pictured at protests both with and without his hoodie, neither Dana nor Alice is more or less deserving of life than the other. Juxtaposing these images in this way offers evidence that their differences are not moral; they are structural.

In the moments leading up to Rufus's death, the book emphasizes Dana's similarity to him using the juxtaposition of their faces to highlight the relationship between the unjustly criminalized black pain and rage also evident in the collective response to Michael Brown's death in Ferguson (marked here by Dana's tear) and the structurally endorsed and excused white practices of racial injustice that motivated and excused Michael Brown's murder (see figure 4.4). This image, like others in the book, resonates with the imagery of superhero comics, here recalling the villain Two-Face, who represents the difficulty of separating moral rights from wrongs. And yet these images also

4.3 The urgency of intersectionality, *Kindred* (2017), p. 113. Courtesy of John Jennings.

4.4   Two-Face, *Kindred* (2017), p. 232. Courtesy of John Jennings.

work against familiar superhero narratives, as when Dana's beating by over-seers employs the familiar graphics of comic book action sequences.[51] Considered in juxtaposition with individualizing and moralizing superhero narratives like Captain America that these images recall, the graphic retelling of *Kindred* suggests that America is not so super. *Our* hero—Dana—cannot defend herself against the oppressive structures of American history.

KINDRED AND COLLECTIVITY

In the final pages of both versions of *Kindred*, the novels articulate the need for evidence and its elusiveness. The original version points to the difficulty of reconciling the present with the past: "Why did I even want to come here?" Dana asks. "To try to understand. To touch solid evidence that those people existed. To reassure yourself that you're sane," Kevin replies.[52] Made sane by this shared consciousness of the past, Dana and Kevin have become more closely connected, even as they have also become conscious of their deeper divisions. As my student John Albrite observed in conversation, Kevin—as a white man—has had the luxury of not having to give up his principles in the past, whereas Dana's structurally precarious position has forced her to reevaluate many of the principles of self-determination, self-reliance, and self-defense that she once took for granted. In the graphic version, the question of evidence further recalls recent debates over the value and limitations of images as evidence. Do these images enable us to act as witnesses, or is their power lost to the dominant narratives that make them spectacles of dehumanization?

Dana's claim that the evidence of her experience is out of reach is belied not only by the loss of her arm but also by the weight of the book in our hands. All we need do is flip back a few pages and the evidence she remembers is recorded forever in the book—much like the videos and images that circulate in the media and social media on an endless loop. Nevertheless, that evidence is refused by one reader—the farmer who now occupies the land upon which Rufus Weylin's plantation stood. In the original novel, the farmer appears in passing: "But the farmer knew nothing—or at least, said nothing."[53] In the graphic novel, he is given his own voice and his own panel, and his refusal to acknowledge the evidence of the text cannot be disentangled from his apparent hostility toward Kevin and Dana as an interracial couple, evident in the added dialogue: "Now how 'bout you and your . . . *friend* stay the hell out of my fields" (see figure 4.5). The farmer's emphasis on his ownership of these fields challenges Dana's ownership of her past; as owner of the former Weylin plantation, he claims the right to dictate the meaning of the narratives circulating about that land, and the right to deny the structural history of black exploitation and white privilege upon which that ownership is based. Kevin's supportive grip on Dana's hand in the graphic novel's final panel, coupled with his stated effort to "try to understand" and his direct gaze into Dana's eyes, all stand in contrast to the farmer's closed eyes and refusal to see. On the other side of Dana, we see her arm lost to slavery against the backdrop of the American flag—her arm as the evidence that color blindness and individualized narratives of white innocence and black moral failure want us not to see.

Both versions of *Kindred* suggest that combatting structural racism requires intersectional analysis. The original novel shows that Black Power's claim to have broken with a feminized and submissive black past only marginalizes black women and feeds into post–civil rights color-blind narratives that dehumanize and criminalize black people. The graphic adaptation draws this argument into conversation with BLM's use of juxtaposed images to address the development of these color-blind narratives in the post-Obama era. The endings of both novels point explicitly to these narratives' stubborn persistence. In the original, Dana's experience has been swept under the rug by the literal lack of historical records and the farmer's figurative refusal of historical memory. In the graphic version, the suppression of Dana's experience by the farmer is even more intentional, belying the fantasy of a postracial America. Both novels' conclusions also point to the possible failure of their own narratives, returning us to the question of whether endurance and image-based evidence are viable strategies of resistance. These failures suggest that the project of both novels is not necessarily about convincing the farmer or other hostile readers, but about forming a community around structurally conscious readers such as Dana, and even Kevin. Endurance and

4.5   "To reassure yourself that you're sane," *Kindred* (2017), p. 237.
Courtesy of John Jennings.

evidence may not be capable, in and of themselves, of overturning white
power structures, or even demonstrating that they need to be overturned.
Rather, they come together as processes that produce black collectivity and
antiracist collectivity: collectivities predicated not on sameness but on a
shared structure of feeling; collectivities that, in defiance both of the "invisible
forms of racism that slowly eat away at black subjects" and the color-blind
narratives that deny this is happening, remind black subjects that they are
sane.[54] Post-black neo-slave narratives such as these versions of *Kindred* offer
new ways of making black collectivity visible in the age of color blindness.

1 Nnedi Okorafor, introduction to *Octavia E. Butler's Kindred: A Graphic Novel Adaptation* by Damian Duffy and John Jennings (New York: Abrams, 2017), vi.

2 See, for example, Philip Miletic, "Octavia E. Butler's Response to Black Arts / Black Power Literature and Rhetoric in *Kindred*," *African American Review* 49, no. 3 (Fall 2016): 261–75.

3 See Stokely Carmichael [Kwame Turi] and Charles V. Hamilton, *Black Power: The Politics of Liberation* (1967; repr., New York: Vintage, 1992), xviii.

4 See Audre Lorde, *Sister Outsider: Essays and Speeches* (1984; repr., Berkeley, CA: Crossing Press, 2007); Kimberlé Crenshaw, "Demarginalizing the Intersection of Race and Sex: A Black Feminist Critique of Antidiscrimination Doctrine, Feminist Theory, and Antiracist Politics [1989]," in *Feminist Legal Theory: Readings in Law and Gender,* ed. Katherine T. Barlett and Roxanne Kennedy (Milton Park: Taylor and Francis, 2018); Patricia Hill Collins, *Black Feminist Thought: Knowledge, Consciousness, and the Politics of Empowerment* (1990; repr., New York: Routledge, 2002); and Eduardo Bonilla-Silva, *Racism without Racists: Color-Blind Racism and Racial Inequality in Contemporary America,* 3rd ed. (Lanham, MD: Rowman and Littlefield, 2010), 3.

5 See Daniel Schorr, "A New, 'Post-Racial' Political Era in America," *All Things Considered* (NPR), January 28, 2008.

6 See Jamil Smith, "Videos of Police Killings Are Numbing Us to the Spectacle of Black Death," *New Republic,* April 13, 2015.

7 Michael Tesler, *Post-Racial or Most-Racial? Race and Politics in the Obama Era* (Chicago: University of Chicago Press, 2016), 1.

8 Mark Anthony Neal, *Soul Babies: Black Popular Culture and the Post-Soul Aesthetic* (New York: Routledge, 2002), 3, 8.

9 Neal, *Soul Babies,* 5. See also Trey Ellis, *Platitudes and the New Black Aesthetic* (Boston: Northeastern University Press, 2003), 190–92; and Thelma Golden, "Introduction," in *Freestyle,* ed. Christine Y. Kim and Franklin Sirmins (New York: Studio Museum in Harlem, 2001), 14. For a fuller discussion of this relationship, see Margo Natalie Crawford, *Black Post-Blackness: The Black Arts Movement and Twenty-First-Century Aesthetics* (Chicago: University of Illinois Press, 2017), 11–13, which argues that "post-blackness is often stuck in a misunderstanding of the black aesthetic movement" (12). Lordi similarly argues that theorists of the post-soul aesthetic "tend to iron out the complexity of soul" by failing to consider the work of black women in that era. Emily J. Lordi, "Souls Intact: The Soul Performances of Audre Lorde, Aretha Franklin, and Nina Simone," *Women and Performance: A Journal of Feminist Theory* 26, no. 1 (2016): 66.

10 Ashraf Rushdy, *Neo-slave Narratives: Studies in the Social Logic of a Literary Form* (Oxford: Oxford University Press, 1999), 4–5.

11 A. Timothy Spaulding, *Re-forming the Past: History, the Fantastic, and the Postmodern Slave Narrative* (Columbus: Ohio State University Press, 2005), 17, 15.

12 Although Ellis (*Platitudes and the New Black Aesthetic*, 192) acknowledges neo-slave narrative writers such as Ishmael Reed and Toni Morrison as precursors to his own postmodern sensibility, both he and the Pancho Savery article upon which he draws leave the role of neo-slave narratives and of black feminism in this shift largely unacknowledged, with Savery going so far as to describe Toni Cade Bambara, Gayl Jones, Toni Morrison, Ntozake Shange, and Alice Walker as "disciples of Ralph Ellison," but not as pioneers, practitioners, and disciples of black feminism. See Pancho Savery, "The Third Plane at the Change of the Century: The Shape of African-American Literature to Come," in *Left Politics and the Literary Profession*, ed. Lennard J. Davis and M. Bella Mirabella (New York: Columbia University Press, 1990), 243.

13 See "About," *Black Lives Matter*, https://blacklivesmatter.com/about/.

14 Ellis, *Platitudes and the New Black Aesthetic*, 189, 197.

15 Soyica Diggs Colbert, "Black Rage: On Cultivating Black National Belonging," *Theatre Survey* 57, no. 3 (2016): 338, 352.

16 Colbert, "Black Rage," 337, 352.

17 Brittney Cooper, *Eloquent Rage: A Black Feminist Discovers Her Superpower* (New York: St. Martin's Press, 2018), 151–52; Audre Lorde, "The Uses of Anger: Women Responding to Racism" [1981], in *Sister Outsider: Essays and Speeches* (Berkeley: Crossing Press, 2007), 124–33.

18 Colbert, "Black Rage," 337. On the potential slippage from post-blackness to postracialism, or from post-blackness to antiblackness, see *The Trouble with Post-Blackness*, ed. Houston A. Baker and Merinda K. Simmons (New York: Columbia University Press, 2015); and Michael Eric Dyson's comments at 9:09–56 in Michael Eric Dyson and Joy Reid, "Between the Lines," *Schomburg Center*, online livestream, https://livestream.com/schomburgcenter/events /4721660/videos/112656505.

19 See Bonilla-Silva, *Racism without Racists*, 1–17.

20 Addison Gayle, "The Black Aesthetic," in *The Addison Gayle Jr. Reader*, ed. Nathaniel Norment Jr. (Urbana: University of Illinois Press, 2009), 302.

21 Amiri Baraka [LeRoi Jones], *The Autobiography of LeRoi Jones* (Chicago: Lawrence Hill Books, 1997), 376.

22 Malcolm X, "Don't Sit-in, Stand Up," *Marxist Internet Archive*, https://www .marxists.org/reference/archive/malcolm-x/index.htm.

23 On the black feminism of neo-slave narratives in general and *Kindred* in particular, see Elizabeth Ann Beaulieu, *Black Women Writers and the American Neo-Slave Narrative: Femininity Unfettered* (Westport: Greenwood Press, 1999); and Angelyn Mitchell, "Not Enough of the Past: Feminist Revisions of Octavia E. Butler's *Kindred*," *MELUS* 26, no. 3 (2001): 51–75.

24 See Octavia Butler, *Kindred* (Boston: Beacon Press, 1988), 36, 48, 117, 177.

25 Frederick Douglass, *Narrative of the Life of Frederick Douglass, an American Slave* (1845; New York: Penguin, 1986), 51. In Butler's *Kindred*, when Dana witnesses enslaved children playing slave auction, she remarks that she "never realized how easily people could be trained to accept slavery" (101). Similarly, Dana's belief that she can keep Rufus "from growing up into a red-haired version of his father" (5) proves naive.

26 Douglass, *Narrative of the Life*, 107.

27 Frederick Douglass, "The Significance of Emancipation in the West Indies," speech, Canandaigua, New York, August, 1857, 289; Carmichael, speech at Morgan State College (1967), qtd. in Rhonda Williams, "Black Women, Urban Politics, and Engendering Black Power," in *The Black Power Movement: Rethinking the Civil-Rights Black Power Era*, ed. Peniel E. Joseph (New York: Routledge, 2006), 79.

28 Butler, *Kindred*, 145.

29 Butler, *Kindred*, 145.

30 Mitchell, "Not Enough of the Past," 61.

31 Butler, *Kindred*, 60, 109.

32 Butler, *Kindred*, 260.

33 Butler, *Kindred*, 264.

34 Keeanga-Yamattha Taylor, *From #BlackLivesMatter to Black Liberation* (Chicago: Haymarket Books, 2016), 18. Of course, as figures such as Booker T. Washington demonstrate, the effort to blame racial inequities on black moral failures is not new. As W. E. B. Du Bois said, Washington's "doctrine has tended to make the whites, North and South, shift the burden of the Negro problem to the Negro's shoulders and stand aside as critical and rather pessimistic spectators." W. E. B. Du Bois, *The Souls of Black Folk* (New York: Penguin, 1996), 49.

35 Bonilla-Silva, *Racism without Racists*, 39–43; Candice Marie Jenkins, *Private Lives, Proper Relations: Regulating Black Intimacy* (Minneapolis: University of Minnesota Press, 2007), 64–70. The infamous Moynihan Report (1965), which Jenkins discusses at length, is a prime example of such conservative representations of racial inequities as the result of black moral failures. See Daniel Patrick Moynihan, *The Negro Family: The Case for National Action* (Washington, DC: US Department of Labor, 1965).

36 Carmichael helped to define institutional racism as a concept. Carmichael and Hamilton, *Black Power*, 4–5.

37 Ta-Nehisi Coates credits the technologies of smartphones and social media for the recent resurgence of black protest, which he relates to the role played by television in the civil rights movement. Hari Srenivasan, "Ta-Nehisi Coates: We Accept Violence against African-Americans as Normal," interview with Ta-Nehisi Coates, *PBS NewsHour*, July 23, 2015. Images also played a key role at other key moments of black protest, from the use of images of whipping-scarred bodies and respectable portraits by abolitionists, to the use of lynching

photographs and portraits of the black middle class that fueled the rise of the NAACP, to the images of police brutality, mob violence, Emmett Till, and peaceful, well-dressed protestors that mobilized civil rights. See Ramesh Mallipeddi, *Spectacular Suffering: Witnessing Slavery in the Eighteenth-Century British Atlantic* (Charlottesville: University of Virginia Press, 2016); Jasmine Nichol Cobb, *Picture Freedom: Remaking Black Visuality in the Early Nineteenth Century* (New York: New York University Press, 2015); Jacqueline Goldsby, *A Spectacular Secret: Lynching in American Life and Literature* (Chicago: University of Chicago Press, 2006); and Martin A. Berger, *Seeing through Race: A Reinterpretation of Civil Rights Photography* (Berkeley: University of California Press, 2011).

38 Taylor, *From #BlackLivesMatter*, 10.

39 Christian Coleman, "Octavia Butler's *Kindred* in Living Color, from Novel to Graphic Novel: A Q&A with Damian Duffy," *Beacon Broadside*, January 12, 2017; Scott McCloud, *Understanding Comics: The Invisible Art* (New York: Harper, 1993), 9.

40 Armond White, "Dud of the Week; *12 Years a Slave* Reviewed by Armond White for CityArts," *New York Film Critics Circle*, October 16, 2013, www .nyfcc.com/2013/10/3450/; Aliya S. King, "You are Not Required to Witness *The Birth of a Nation*'s Violence," *Jezebel*, October 7, 2016.

41 See Brittney Cooper, "Black Death Has Become a Cultural Spectacle: Why the Walter Scott Tragedy Won't Change White America's Mind," *Salon*, April 8, 2015.

42 Saidiya Hartman, *Scenes of Subjection: Terror, Slavery, and Self-Making in Nineteenth-Century America* (Oxford: Oxford University Press, 1997), 3–4.

43 Douglass, *Narrative of the Life*, 51.

44 Kimberlé Crenshaw, "The Urgency of Intersectionality," *TEDWomen 2016*, https://www.ted.com/talks/kimberle_crenshaw_the_urgency_of _intersectionality.

45 See Alicia Garza, "A Herstory of the #BlackLivesMatter Movement," in *Are All the Women Still White? Rethinking Race, Expanding Feminisms*, ed. Janell Hobson (Albany: State University of New York Press, 2016); Marcia Chatelain and Kaayva Asoka, "Women and Black Lives Matter," *Dissent* 62, no. 3 (2015): 54–61.

46 Crenshaw, "The Urgency of Intersectionality."

47 For example, the "tendency by the news media to cover the murders and abductions of affluent or middle-class white girls far more than those of boys, poor kids and kids of color" is an extension of the effort to blame black suffering on black moral failures: "Often the assumption is that the white girls are quote-unquote innocent victims whereas with poor children or children of color, there's some nefarious activities involved." "Missing White Girl Syndrome," *Journalism Center on Children and Families*, http://journalismcenter .org/when-a-child-dies/missing-white-girl.html.

48 Angela Davis, *Freedom Is a Constant Struggle: Ferguson, Palestine, and the Foundations of a Movement* (Chicago: Haymarket Books, 2016), 4.

49 Duffy and Jennings, *Octavia E. Butler's* Kindred, 50–51, 157, 232.

50 In Geraldo Rivera's words, speaking on *Fox News* after Trayvon Martin's death: "You dress like a thug, people are going to treat you like a thug." "Geraldo Rivera: Trayvon Martin's Hoodie Is as Much Responsible for His Death as George Zimmerman," *Fox News*, March 23, 2012.

51 Duffy and Jennings, *Octavia E. Butler's* Kindred, 49.

52 Butler, *Kindred*, 264.

53 Butler, *Kindred*, 262.

54 Colbert, "Black Rage," 352.

"STAY WOKE"

*Post-Black Filmmaking and the Afterlife of Slavery
in Jordan Peele's* Get Out

KIMBERLY NICHELE BROWN

ARGUABLY ONE OF THE MOST POIGNANT SCENES OF CONTEMPORARY
African American film history is the ending of Spike Lee's *School Daze* (1988).
Vaughn "Dap" Dunlap (Larry Fishburne) sprints onto the yard of the fictitious
historically black Mission College pointedly at the crack of dawn and loudly
beseeches his fellow classmates and black viewers alike to "wake up!"
Although *stay woke* has gained traction as a millennial phrase popularized
by the Black Lives Matter movement, permutations have existed, I would
imagine, since Europeans first set foot on the African continent. "Staying
woke" is to employ bell hooks's "oppositional gaze"[1] or to be what Manthia
Diawara calls a "resistant spectator"[2] in the face of mainstream media's scopic
regime and the racialized surveillance that constitutes African American life.
Remaining hypervigilant, being racially cognizant, and developing fluidity in
the lexicon of white supremacy are metacognitive and ocular strategies Badu-
esque "master teachers"[3] impart to their pupils. "Staying woke" is the antidote
to black complacency; its practitioners seek to rouse those laboring under
the illusion that racial parity exists. One must either "stay woke" or "wake
up" because whiteness, configured as the body snatcher, the proverbial
bogeyman, or the monstrous femme fatale populates the grotesquerie of the
US societal landscape and terrorizes the real and imaginative lives of blacks
with equal fervor.

During his 2018 acceptance speech at the Producers Guild of America
award ceremony, Jordan Peele explained that in order to create the preter-
natural atmosphere for his directorial debut, *Get Out* (2017), he had to ask

himself what really scared him: "It's not white people. . . . It's silence. *Get Out* is my protest against that."[4] Peele prioritizes the scopic pleasure of blacks while validating our fears regarding the everyday horror of white supremacy reflected in the silencing of black voices and the disavowal, on the part of antiblack or willfully ignorant whites, that racism persists.

Written during Barack Obama's presidency and released a little over three months after Donald Trump's election, Peele scripts *Get Out* in the context of near-constant reportage on state-sanctioned police violence against blacks and on violations of black civil liberties, culminating in a general malaise preceding Trump's election. Producer Sean McKittrick explains that the movie "was a response to the Obama era's post-racial-era lie. There are some aspects of the story . . . that evolved because [of] . . . how the country was devolving—Jordan started this process before Trayvon Martin."[5] For many the murder of seventeen-year-old Martin by George Zimmerman in 2012 shattered the illusion that Obama's presidency had ushered in a new era of racial equality. Concurrently, as Frank Wilderson argues, one must remember that "neoliberalism with a Black face is neither the index of a revolutionary advance nor the end of anti-blackness as a constituent element of U.S. antagonisms."[6]

Get Out offers a reassessment of "post-blackness" as one of the "latest 'post' neologisms to account for the concept of race in our present moment."[7] Therefore, I use the term *post-black* as both a generational delineator and a descriptor of Peele's filmic aesthetic.[8] Here *post-*, like Ramón Saldívar's recouping of "post-race aesthetics," is "a conceptual frame . . . that refers to the logic of something having been 'shaped as a consequence of' imperialism and racism," as in "postcolonial," rather than signaling racism's end.[9] In *Get Out*, Peele showcases post-blackness as a tool of liberation predicated on satirical and surrealist techniques as a more effective mode than social realism to combat and reflect the absurdity of our present "post-truth" moment. Additionally, in keeping with Thelma Golden's coinage, Peele's post-black aesthetic is "not so much an abandonment of political and cultural struggle as it is an 'attitude,' a critical posture."[10] Through a postmodern mode of narrative filmmaking predicated on cynicism, experimentality, a fluid media literacy, irony, and self-reflexivity, Peele takes a liberationist approach that marks a "shift from essential notions of blackness to metanarratives on blackness."[11]

Rebuking the myth of linear racial process, Peele conceives *Get Out* as an allegory for slavery: "I realized that slavery was not something of the past. . . . [I]n today's time . . . we have black men and women abducted and put in dark holes. We have our freedoms taken away. . . . I realized . . . that there were people being locked up and taken out of the world and taken from their families for holding less weed than I was smoking while I was writing this movie."[12] Essentially, Peele is describing "the afterlife of slavery." Sadiya Hartman argues, "If slavery persists as an issue in the political life of black America, it is not because of an antiquarian obsession with bygone days or the burden of a too long memory, but because black lives are still imperiled and devalued by a racial calculus and a political arithmetic that were entrenched centuries ago. This is the afterlife of slavery—skewed life chances, limited access to health and education, premature death, incarceration, and impoverishment."[13]

Through post-black filmic narratology, Peele takes auteurist license to challenge the power Hollywood asserts over the representation and spectatorship of blacks, particularly black men, by offering a filmic treatise on the precarity of black male existence as demonstrative of slavery's afterlife.

The plot hinges on Chris Washington's (Daniel Kaluuya) anxiety about meeting the parents of his white girlfriend, Rose Armitage (Allison Williams), for the first time. A macabre amalgam of *Guess Who's Coming to Dinner* (1967) and *Cocoon* (1985),[14] the film culminates in the revelation that Rose routinely lures unsuspecting blacks to her family's home to be lobotomized and used as bodily vessels for wealthy aging whites. The plot serves as a proxy for white America's protracted fear of miscegenation and yet renders such fear ironic in the face of the habitual co-option and cultural appropriation of black bodies and culture. The Coagula Order's procedure of transferring white psyches into the young and virile bodies of talented blacks, then, is Peele's way of signifying on the parasitic nature of cultural appropriation, particularly on the part of white liberals, as a new millennial reframing of slavery in the United States.

I further posit that the Sunken Place, where the black psyche is banished once the transference is complete, is the Nowhere of which Ralph Ellison's Ras the Destroyer speaks.[15] To the unnamed protagonist and Tod Clifton, Ras states, "I ask both of you, are you awake or sleeping? What is your pahst and where are you going? Never mind, take your corrupt ideology and eat out your own guts like a laughing hyena. You are nowhere, mahn. Nowhere!" (*Invisible Man* 287). The Sunken Place, then, is the geographic hinterland in this present conjuncture that replicates the political reality of the Middle Passage—a space in which blacks are stripped of agency, rendered mute and held in limbo, stuck between being and nothingness. Irrespective of class status, Peele envisions black life as characterized by its fugitive status, where blacks must always actively resist falling into the Sunken Place. As an antidote, Peele employs various conceptual metaphors for the gaze to suggest we "stay woke," or rather remain cognizant of slavery's afterlife.

If, as Paul Gilroy argues, displacement is the hallmark of black modernity, then black fugitivity as constituent of black postmodernity resonates throughout the film. Francesca T. Royster argues, "The fugitive describes the artistic impulse to escape the constraints of the objectification and social death of slavery—but also to never fully escape its embodied lesson."[16] Throughout the film, the phrase *get out* not only references the type of call-and-response expected from black audiences watching horror films but acts as the film's continual warning against possible re-enslavement.[17]

Peele's post-black aesthetic, particularly in depicting the nominal freedom and vulnerability of black men, begs a reassessment of traditional gaze theory's preoccupation with white women. Laura Mulvey argues, "The paradox of phallocentrism in all its manifestations is that it depends on the image of the castrated woman to give order and meaning to its world."[18] Jane Gaines critiques gaze theory's reliance on the radical feminist construction of "absolute patriarchy," given how black men have historically been denied the power of the gaze afforded to white men and because it "disregards the position white women occupy over Black men and women."[19] Additionally, Daniel Y. Kim explains that in *Black Skin, White Masks* Frantz Fanon found white male spectatorship of black male bodies to be analogous to how they look at women "as bodies whose alterity is signaled by the wounds of castration they bear. The black male experience . . . is one of being looked at as a body that has been castrated by the white male Other who looks—of being, in a sense, castrated by the looking itself."[20]

Although *Get Out* can be classified as androcentric, it is not phallocentric. *Get Out* is decidedly a male-centered text; however, Peele encourages an intersectional approach to theorizing a black male gaze not predicated on scopophilic desire. Rather than an oppositional approach that focuses on the "repressed gaze" of black men that bell hooks describes as being "unleashed" with the advent of television and movie screens, where black men "could 'look' at white womanhood" without fear of reprisal, Peele centers black male woundedness as elemental to Hollywood's colonial gaze.[21]

The opening scene demonstrates the paradoxical nature of black male woundedness, where "the wound is both the critical sign of the fearsome and deadly street hood prone to violent engagement, and definitive proof of the corporeal vulnerability of that very same body."[22] Andre Hayworth (Lakeith Stanfield) wanders an affluent suburb in search of the house he has been lured to under false pretenses in the middle of the night. Speaking to an unidentified woman on his cell phone, Andre alludes to his embodied woundedness:

"I feel like a sore thumb." He calls the neighborhood "creepy and confusing," which is antithetical to typical descriptions of the suburbs by whites. Andre's trepidation should be read in the context of white inhospitality to blacks depicted in fictionalized accounts like Lorraine Hansberry's *Raisin in the Sun* (1959) or in real-life examples like that of Trayvon Martin. Inevitably, a white Porsche drives up. Its radio plays an ominous tune, "Run Rabbit Run," which is the first of three songs in Peele's post-black soundscape that highlight black fugitivity. An unidentified white man wearing a medieval helmet places Andre in a sleeper hold, drags his limp body to the car, and puts him in the trunk. His capture alludes to Africans who were kidnapped from their homelands during the slave trade.[23]

The interlude inserted after Andre's abduction consists of a traveling shot of tree-lined woods; this simulates the second-person point of view designed to make the viewer feel as if she or he is watching the scenery from a moving vehicle—Peele is taking the viewer on a journey meant to suture the viewer's empathy with Chris's plight. This interlude is underscored by the haunting musical accompaniment "Sikiliza Kwa Wahenga," which is Swahili for "Listen to (Your) Ancestors," while the song's lyrics roughly translate as "Something bad is coming. Run." Peele forgoes derivative sonic tropes of black horror such as "voodoo sounds" and instead offers a post-black vibe encompassing "distinctly black voices and black musical references, so it's got some African influences, and some bluesy things going on, but in a scary way, which you never really hear."[24] In lyric and tonality, the song is indicative of what Nathaniel Mackey calls the "fugitive spirit" of black music, because, in imparting the film's overall message, it replicates the existential angst of contemporary blacks.

Functioning as Chris's literal and proverbial wake-up call and the third song of black fugitivity, Childish Gambino's (Donald Glover's rhapsodic alter ego) "Redbone" masquerades as a love song while it eerily entreats black men to be ever vigilant and never get caught "sleeping" or unawares.[25] The song plays as the next scene cuts between a montage of Chris's black-and-white photographs depicting African Americans in the inner city, a shot of Chris shaving in the mirror, and one of Rose in a bakery eyeing donuts presumably to take on their road trip.

As a successful photographer, Chris is the personification of the black male gaze as well as the proverbial poster child for a more hopeful strain of post-blackness. As Touré intones, "Post-Black means we are like Obama: rooted in but not restricted by Blackness."[26] And yet, used in the context of a horror film about the racial anxieties black men face, Gambino's 70s-inflected vocals serve as a double entendre where the American dream and white women (as his just dessert) become interchangeable symbols of both success and foreboding. Peele explains, "One fear with a black man dating a white person is that they're at risk of turning their backs on their own family and their own blackness and abandoning a piece of their identity."[27] Similarly, the opulence of Chris's apartment juxtaposed with the photographs shown in the montage hint at a potential chasm between Chris and his working-class and poor counterparts. To punctuate this idea, Chris's lathering of his face with shaving cream symbolizes whiteface, while accidently cutting his face highlights his precarious position as a black man in today's society.

Peele uses the interracial love story as a framing device that conflates the theme of family with citizenship and national belonging, thereby highlighting how America's failure to fully integrate blacks into its familial fold propagates slavery's afterlife. Stanley Kramer uses the same plot device in *Guess Who's Coming to Dinner*, where, like Chris, the black male suitor serves as the litmus test of the white parents' self-proclaimed liberalism. Even though she says she's never dated a black man before, and therefore never brought one home to meet her family, Rose is convinced that her parents will accept Chris because they are not racist and "would have voted for Obama for a third term" if it were possible. However, as an extended metaphor of slavery's afterlife, *Get Out* demonstrates succinctly how racism supersedes political party affiliations and has no geographical boundaries.

The remainder of the film takes place on the Armitage estate, which is set in the fictitious town of Lake Pontaco in upstate New York. In actuality, the real house used for the movie is located in Fairhope, Alabama. The house's antebellum architectural design and the unintentional blurring of geographical boundaries by the location scouts enables Peele to revive conventions of the American gothic that locate the South as the origin of US racism while also calling liberal white northerners to task; thus the United States as a whole is indicted for its innate racist quality.

Through the characters of Georgina (Betty Gabriel) and Walter (Marcus Henderson), black domestic workers supposedly hired to take care of Dean's aging parents, Peele evokes the master/slave dynamic of the antebellum South. Upon reaching the kitchen during the house tour he's giving Chris, Dean states, "My mother loved her kitchen, so we keep a piece of her in here." The camera then pans to Georgina, and it is later revealed that she and the groundskeeper are two of Rose's conquests—their bodies are now inhabited by Rose's grandparents, Roman (Richard Herd) and Marianne Armitage.[28] Peele lampoons the adage commonplace among white owners that the enslaved were "like one of the family." Dean explains that they "couldn't bear to let them go," once his parents died. Even though in this instance the servants *are* actually part of the family, this newly manufactured Armitage family dynamic is problematic; in creating their collective cover story, the only scenario they can concoct to explain Georgina and Walter's presence is one that reinforces black servitude.

At another point during the house tour, Dean pauses in front of an old picture of his father in a track uniform. He explains that Roman "almost got over" losing to the African American track star Jesse Owens in the qualifying round at the 1936 Olympics in Berlin. Dean muses, "What a moment. I mean, Hitler's up there with all of his Aryan race bullshit, this black dude comes along and proves him wrong in front of the entire world, amazing." Because, as the viewers learn later, Walter was once a world-class sprinter, this story offers the rationale for Roman's decision to procure Walter's body and an insight into the motives of all who belong to the Coagula Order, of which the Armitages are founding members.

The Coagula Order is a fictional white supremacist organization composed of wealthy whites who, believing they are "gods in the cocoons," kidnap gifted blacks to use their bodies as vessels for immortality.[29] The Order shares the same symbol as the process of alchemy, a butterfly emerging from a chrysalis. This allusion calls to mind the "alchemy of slavery" and the processes "by which skin tone and slavery were synthesized into race and profit."[30] The order's selection process also resembles that of slavers, who bred blacks based on physical attributes or poached Africans from specific regions to profit from their agricultural acumen. Peele uses the Coagula Order to demonstrate the easy slippage between cultural appropriation and the persistence of racialized biocapitalism in the twenty-first century.[31]

Similar to Dean's take on domestic service, Roman finesses this parasitic relationship as family symbiosis. Documentary footage of the original, white Roman Armitage is shown to Chris toward the movie's climax; here Roman explains the black host's role in the procedure as follows: "You have been chosen because of the physical advantages you've enjoyed your entire lifetime. With your natural gifts and our determination we could both be part of something greater, something perfect. The Coagula Procedure . . . Maybe one day you'll enjoy being members of the family." As if to punctuate his statement, the video ends with the entire Armitage family gathered in front of their home.

Having never known his father and having been orphaned at eleven after a hit-and-run driver struck his mother, Chris desperately longs for familial attachments. It is this longing rather than a fetish for white women that draws him to Rose and also makes him susceptible to the Coagula Order. As a psychological pre-op to the transplanting procedure, Rose's mother, Missy Armitage (Catherine Keener), uses hypnotic torture that preys on Chris's desire for familial belonging and his guilt about passively watching television rather than calling the authorities when his mother failed to return home after work; she lay dying in the rain for several hours while he ignored his instinct that something was amiss. Under the auspices of curing his smoking habit, Missy hypnotizes Chris without his consent.

In a medium close-up, the camera catches what has quickly become an iconic look of sheer terror: tears stream down Chris's face, his eyes bulge, and his face contorts upon realizing he can't move. She explains, "You are paralyzed just like that day when you did nothing, *you did nothing*. Now, sink into the floor. Sink." The camera cuts to young Chris's back as he sits on his bed watching a blurry image on television. The camera simulates Chris's sinking, suturing the younger Chris with his adult version as he dips beneath the mattress into a universe of nothingness. He is in suspended animation, falling in slow motion into the abyss. His arms flail as he watches the image of Missy sitting in her armchair until she appears to be a televised image herself. Missy explains that Chris is now in the Sunken Place.

The choice to costume Kaluuya in a gray hoodie for this scene is significant. The hoodie became a symbol worn in solidarity by millions of protestors nationwide when Trayvon Martin was murdered.[32] The Sunken Place, then, represents the necropolitics of contemporary black existence. Borrowing from the work of Susan Buck-Morss, Achille Mbembé explains that the plantation slave lived nonsynchronously with her or his owners in "an unequal relationship . . . along with the inequality of the power over life."[33] If, as the Black Lives Matter movement reveals, white privilege still entails taking black life with impunity, then the Sunken Place renders present-day black life analogous to the condition of the antebellum slave: "The slave is . . . kept alive but in a *state of injury*, in a phantomlike world of horrors and intense cruelty and profanity."[34]

Eager to confide in his best friend, Rod Williams (Lil Rel Howery), about his discomfort, Chris reports that the white people he's met thus far act as if "they haven't met a black person that doesn't work for them," while the black people seem to have "missed the Movement." Chris characterizes the masquerading blacks as such because they neglect to pass as black in any way legible to Chris; they speak in an affected manner, do not readily understand slang, dress in an unfashionable or servile manner, traverse unspoken codes of black conduct in the presence of whites, and are satisfied to replicate outmoded racialized social scripts of behavior. The blacks trapped inside actually exist in the Sunken Place and therefore serve as a metaphor for those who succumb to social alienation and marginalization rather than resisting; because of their complacency and passivity, their limited consciousness marks the internalization of the white gaze, which leaves them in a perpetual "state of injury."[35]

Although *Get Out* is replete with symbolic references that connote captivity, slavery, and imperialism, the most overt allusion to slavery's perduring existence is found in the scenes depicting the Armitages' annual picnic, which culminates in an actual slave auction. The predominately white guests arrive,[36] begin to mingle, and instead of inspecting Chris's teeth and genitals as in antebellum slave auctions to determine his suitability as a slave, guests bombard him with intrusive questions; one woman goes so far as to squeeze his chest and ask Rose if it is true that sex with a black man is better.

When Chris leaves after being overwhelmed by all of the attention, Dean holds a silent auction, thinly disguised as a bingo game, to sell Chris's body to the highest bidder. The bingo game enables Peele to make fun of white-themed pastimes, but also to highlight how white elites play games with black lives, while blacks are oftentimes oblivious to their peril. Chris is pictured in a large gold frame, with a cocky look and his trusty camera in hand, seemingly advertising his marketable skill. Although the auction is held in silence to avoid arousing Chris's suspicion, the silence also signifies on covert forms of racism in the United States as well as white silence in the face of racist oppression.

Chris's paralysis during his mother's death acts as a cautionary tale about the dangers of inaction in the face of injustice. To extrapolate, if videographers who capture acts of violence enacted by police against blacks are said to *bear witness*, a passive viewer's inactivity makes her or him complicit. It is significant, then, that the first instinct of every black person who awakens or is revived from the Sunken Place is to warn Chris that he is in imminent danger. For example, when Chris confides to Georgina, "Sometimes, when there's too many white people, I get nervous, you know?" this feeling obviously resonates. Her face reveals the internal struggle between Georgina and Marianne to gain control, thereby signaling that something is wrong. Additionally, when Chris spies through his camera's lens Andre Hayward, the man kidnapped in the opening scene, who identifies now as Logan King, he snaps a furtive picture for Rod's inspection. The flash breaks Missy's hypnotic spell. Having regained control over his body, Andre instinctively attempts to save Chris from a similar fate by frantically yelling at him to "get out."

In *Get Out*, Peele provides viewers with four potential saviors who might prevent Chris from falling prey to the Coagula Order and being enslaved in the Sunken Place: Chris himself, Rod, Jim Hudson (Stephen Root), and Rose. Chris emerges as the embodiment of a black gaze that is instinctually apprehensive of whites, which inevitably makes *Get Out* antithetical to horror films with white protagonists whose plots are driven by their naïveté. The unease Chris feels during his stay at the Armitage estate inadvertently causes him to employ *dark sousveillance*, —a term Simone Browne coined "to situate the tactics employed to render one's self out of sight" as a method to combat "antiblack surveillance."[37] Chris uses his camera to shield himself from objectification (i.e., hiding behind the lens), but he also controls the gaze. When he points his camera at the mingling white guests, he places the Armitages and their ilk under surveillance and has the potential to weaponize the gaze to his advantage.

Like Chris, his best friend Rod also represents the black male gaze, given his profession as an agent with the Transportation Security Administration (TSA). Rod's occupation as a surveillance expert and his role as the film's comic relief work in tandem. Although he is empowered by the state, viewers are prone to dismiss him as a proverbial Imhotep or black nationalist conspiracy nut. Adept at "staying woke," Rod proves to be not that far off base when he theorizes that Chris is being used as a sex slave. When he fails, predictably, to get the police to intervene, Rod models for the audience what it means to be one's brother's keeper by continuing to investigate Chris's disappearance on his own.

Jim Hudson is a blind art dealer who presents himself as Chris's ally and an admirer of his photography, labeling the other guests as ignorant: "They mean well but they have no idea what real people go through." Jim confesses to Chris that he failed as a photographer, submitting wilderness photos to *National Geographic* fourteen times "before realizing I didn't have 'the eye' for it."[38] Viewers learn that instead of being Chris's savior, Jim is actually the one purchasing Chris's body. Later, when Chris has the opportunity to ask Jim why the Order chooses blacks as surrogates, Jim replies, "Who knows, some people want to change, some people want to be stronger, faster, cooler, but please don't lump me in with that. What I want is deeper. I want your eyes, man, I want those things you see through." Jim's literal blindness, then, represents American color blindness as a "disavowal of racialized perception" that "involves distancing oneself from the social reality of racism and failing to properly acknowledge its influence on social cognition."[39]

Initially, Rose presents herself as a white ally who eschews color blindness and is becoming "woke" in her own right. After hitting a deer on the way to the estate, she stands up to the white policeman who demands to see Chris's identification even though Rose was the one driving.[40] Later in what Chris categorizes as her "racial flow," Rose compares her parents' racial microaggressions toward Chris with the racist assumptions made by the cop. Through Rose's duplicitous nature, however, Peele reverses the trope of monstrous blackness depicted in American gothic literature; instead Rose emerges as the embodiment of "monstrous-feminine whiteness"—a phrase Amy K. King coins to describe Delphine LaLaurie (Kathy Bates) in *American Horror Story: Coven.*[41] Unlike Delphine, Rose is not overtly racist or vulgar, nor is her brutality depicted as "exceptional"; on the contrary, she reveals racism to be emblematic of our nation's character and reminds viewers that covert racism is just as deadly. Rose also enables Peele to critique how some blacks see white women as harbingers of death and deceit, rather than as merely totemic symbols of success. Through her character, Peele connotes white women's historic complicity in lynching black men. For example, when Rod calls Chris hoping once again to get him on the line, Rose answers his phone and pretends not to know Chris's whereabouts. When Rod interrogates her further, Rose switches tactics and accuses Rod, who has been flirtatious with her in the past, of wanting to have sex with her. Flustered, Rod vehemently denies any interest in Rose and hangs up. Rod calls her a "fucking genius," because it is clear Rose understands that as a white woman she can easily weaponize a sexual assault allegation against a black man.

Peele uses Rose's depiction to signify on *Guess Who's Coming to Dinner* as a filmic predecessor that envisions miscegenation as the solution to racist oppression. For example, Chris and Rose, as an interracial couple, signify the hope of a postracial future. At the family's annual picnic, Kaluuya is costumed in a blue denim shirt, while Williams wears a red and white horizontal-striped sweater; when the two are filmed together, they subliminally read as the American flag. However, in rejecting interracial love as a cure for racism, Peele also forecloses the possibility of a white savior. He states cheekily, "I knew in my heart that anybody who's seeing a movie in a wide-release in America, would have to think, '*There's no way Universal Studios would allow the one good white person in this film to also be evil!*' Rose subverts that," adding, "Sometimes all white people are evil—*sometimes*—but not *all* the time." Referring to her past roles, particularly as Marnie in *Girls* (2012–17), Allison Williams explains, "We are using the thing that I was finding so sticky, to flip the bird to the audience, basically, and say 'Ha! You trusted me so much because I'm so WASP.'"[42] However, rather than finding solace in the genteel civility of WASPs through the curious mannerisms displayed by Rose, once Chris has been captured and she has dropped her mask, Peele codes WASPs as controlling and neurotic. In one of the final scenes, Rose sits in her room practicing segregation through her cereal consumption: she separates her Fruit Loops from her milk while searching through NBA draft picks for her next conquest. With pictures of her previous victims mounted behind her on the wall, Rose listens to the theme song from *Dirty Dancing* (1987), "(I've Had) The Time of My Life."

Ironically, given its connection to slavery, Chris escapes by stuffing his ears with cotton fibers he extracts from a rip in the leather chair he's tied to so as to block Missy's videotaped hypnotic suggestion. He then fakes unconsciousness and successfully catches Rose's brother Jeremy (Caleb Landry Jones) off guard when he comes to collect him for transplantation. Once free, Chris goes on a murderous rampage; he bludgeons Jeremy with a bocce ball, impales Dean on the horns of the taxidermied deer head, and skewers Missy in the eye with her own teaspoon. His weapons of choice are poetic since each item reflects that character's method of debasing or enslaving Chris.

Chris commandeers Jeremy's car and, in his haste to get away, accidently strikes Georgina/Marianne with his car, recalling Rose's earlier accident with the deer. Chris's decision to save Georgina corrects the decision he made as a child to ignore his mother's peril. Unfortunately, when she regains consciousness, Chris must contend with a livid Marianne rather than a grateful Georgina; she attacks Chris, causing him to crash into a tree. Georgina/Marianne dies in the crash. After ducking Rose's rifle blast, Chris is finally chased down and subdued by Walter/Roman. Remembering Andre/Logan's reaction to his phone's flash, Chris manages to wake Walter in the same fashion. As an act of camaraderie toward Chris, Walter continues to pretend he's Roman and asks Rose for the rifle so that he can kill Chris himself. Instead, he shoots Rose in the stomach and then turns the rifle on himself, thereby enabling Chris to overpower Rose. In their tussle for the rifle Chris ends up straddling her while romantic music plays in the background. Slipping back into the role of the doting girlfriend, Rose touches his face: "Chris, I'm so sorry. It's me, I love you, I love you, I love you." Chris nods as if in agreement, but refusing to be duped by sentimentality again, he chokes her while the music grows louder and more sinister. Collapsing the tropes of the domestic abuser with the black male rapist, this scene almost reinscribes Rose as victim. However, this is Chris's "confrontation with the abject" in the figure of Rose. The scene is designed to "eject the abject and redraw the boundaries between the human and nonhuman."[43] Rather than recoil in fear, Rose grins maniacally and seemingly urges Chris to tighten his grip, thereby revealing her true monstrous nature.

Kinitra Brooks, among others, has criticized Peele for not allowing Chris to murder Rose. Brooks argues, "The film's finale serves as one more indictment of black men's sustained inability to punish white women for their willful complicity in white supremacy."[44] Murdering Rose would blur the line between the human and nonhuman or code Chris's previous conduct as a façade of civility obfuscating his inherent monstrosity as a black man.[45] Instead, Chris frees himself from the hold Rose has on him. Once she is unmasked, Chris loosens his grip, and Rose's smile drops; at that moment, it is clear that they are both seeing each other truly for the first time. When the flashing lights of a car approach, Rose enacts the traditional performance of white feminine monstrosity—that of the proverbial white female victim. Much to her chagrin, however, the flashing lights belong to Rod's TSA vehicle rather than the police. Aisha Harris calls this moment "the final subversive trick" of the movie: "We're used to seeing black people die first . . . but Chris takes his place within the horror canon as an inverse of the Final Girl. The Final Girl is almost always a white woman (and usually a brunette) who manages to defeat the monster and save herself. . . . We're supposed to identify with her and wish for her victory."[46]

In an alternate ending, Rose retains her status as the Final Girl and Chris remains monstrous in the eyes of the state, when the actual police appear and arrest him. When Rod visits Chris in prison, he seems resigned to his fate and is unwilling to work on his defense. The last thing the audience sees is Chris retreating, clad in an orange jumpsuit and framed by white prison bars as he descends deeper into the recesses of the prison—the Sunken Place. Although perhaps a more realistic outcome, the alternate ending inadvertently assuages racist whites because the black man as "the threatening phobic object is 'contained'" and the white male viewer in particular "is returned to his safe place of identification and mastery."[47] Peele explains,

> There's lots of different sunken places. But [the film] specifically became a metaphor for the prison-industrial complex, the lack of representation of black people in film. . . . [N]o matter how hard he screams at the screen he can't get agency across. He's not represented. And that, to me, was this metaphor for the black horror audience, a very loyal fan base who comes to these movies, and we're the ones that are going to die first. So the movie for me became almost about representation within the genre.[48]

Although written with both slavery and the prison-industrial complex in mind, rather than offer an ending that would more readily highlight how disposable black life truly is, Peele chooses an ending that considers the affective needs of black audiences at this historical juncture. McKittrick explains, "We tested the movie with the original 'sad truth' ending where, when the cop shows up, it's an actual cop and Chris goes to jail. . . . [I]t was like we punched everybody in the gut. You could feel the air being sucked out of the room. The country was different. We weren't in the Obama era, we were in this new world where all the racism crept out from under the rocks again."[49]

The ending Peele ultimately chooses is a compromise between social realism and a utopian vision. Chris might inevitably end up in prison *regardless* of Rod's act of camaraderie and heroism. Therefore, Peele's choice to spare black viewers the trauma of Chris's death or incarceration is an act of cinematic resistance that can best be understood in the context of black fugitivity. Tina Campt argues that fugitivity "highlights the tense relations between acts of flights and escape, and creative practices of refusal—nimble and strategic practices that undermine the category of the dominant."[50] Chris's avoidance of a prison sentence, no matter how temporary his freedom, is Peele's way of undercutting Hollywood's tendency toward objectifying black bodies either through "racialized aesthetic framing" or "commodification."[51] Staging Chris's escape, even if momentary, is a post-black gesture toward radical hope, while the alternate ending's insistence upon realism hinders scopophilic pleasure on the part of black audiences.

Black viewers leave the theater temporarily satiated, even if we understand the similarity between Chris's precarious fugitivity and our own. Ending with Rod's admonishment, "I mean, I told you not to go in that house" and "Sikiliza Kwa Wahenga" as a nondiegetic framing device reminds black audiences that we can never get too comfortable. As he has done throughout *Get Out*, Peele beseeches us one final time to "stay woke."

NOTES

1   bell hooks, "The Oppositional Gaze: Black Female Spectators," in *Black Looks: Race and Representation* (Boston: South End, 1992), 118.

2   Manthia Diawara, "Black Spectatorship: Problems of Identification and Resistance," in *Black American Cinema* (New York: Routledge, 1993), 214.

3   Erykah Badu, "Master Teacher," on *New Amerykah Part One (4th World War)*, Universal Motown, 2008. In this song, Badu laments the difficulty of finding a utopia where "niggers" don't exist, only "master teachers." In keeping with the theme of the album, Badu envisions that those who also have a heightened racial consciousness like her will lead others in remaking America and building a "beautiful world."

4   Dino-Ray Ramos, "Jordan Peele Says It Feels Like 'We're in the Sunken Place' Right Now—PGA Awards," Deadline Hollywood, January 20, 2018, https://dead line.com/2018/01/jordan-peele-get-out-stanley-kramer-award-pga-awards -norman-lear-1202264687/.

5   Jada Yuan and Hunter Harris, "The First Great Movie of the Trump Era," *New York Magazine*, February 19, 2018, www.vulture.com/2018/02/making -get-out-jordan-peele.html.

6 Frank B. Wilderson, *Red, White and Black: Cinema and the Structure of U.S. Antagonisms* (Durham: Duke University Press, 2010), 4.

7 Richard Purcell, "Trayvon, Postblackness, and the Postrace Dilemma," *Boundary 2* 40, no. 3 (2013): 139.

8 Here I am using Mark Anthony Neal's definition of black "post-soul babies" to include monikers such as the Hip Hop Generation, the New Black Aesthetic, post-black, and post-soul—all of which roughly reference a group of artists born after the post–civil rights movement, "who came to maturity in the age of Reagonomics and experienced the change from urban industrialization to deindustrialization, from segregation to desegregation." Mark Anthony Neal, *Soul Babies: Black Popular Culture and the Post-Soul Aesthetic* (New York: Routledge, 2002), 3.

9 Ramón Saldívar, "Historical Fantasy, Speculative Realism, and Postrace Aesthetics in Contemporary American Fiction," *American Literary History* 23, no. 3 (2011): 575.

10 Purcell, "Trayvon, Postblackness, and the Postrace Dilemma," 153.

11 Neal, *Soul Babies*, 3.

12 Breanna Edwards, "*Get Out* Is an Iconic, Critically Acclaimed Film, but Writer-Director Jordan Peele 'Didn't Know It Was Ever Going to Get Made,'" *The Root*, February 8, 2018, https://thegrapevine.theroot.com/getout-is-an-iconic -critically-acclaimed-film-but-br-1822834271.

13 Saidiya V. Hartman, *Lose Your Mother: A Journey along the Atlantic Slave Route* (New York: Farrar, Straus and Giroux, 2008), 6.

14 *The Stepford Wives* (1975) and *Invasion of the Body Snatchers* (1978) are two other points of reference.

15 Ralph Ellison, *Invisible Man* (New York: Vintage Books, 1972), 366.

16 Francesca T. Royster, *Sounding like a No-No: Queer Sounds and Eccentric Acts in the Post-Soul Era* (Ann Arbor: University of Michigan Press, 2013), 12.

17 Peele states, "The whole idea of the movie is 'Get out!' — it's what we're screaming at the character on-screen." Charles Pulliam-Moore, "The Hidden Swahili Message in 'Get Out' the Country Needs to Hear," *Splinter*, March 1, 2017, https://splinternews.com/the-hidden-swahili-message-in-get-out-the-country -needs-1793858917.

18 Laura Mulvey, "Visual Pleasure and Narrative Cinema," *Screen* 16 (Autumn 1975): 6.

19 Jane Gaines, "White Privilege and Looking Relations: Race and Gender in Feminist Film Theory," *Cultural Critique* 29, no. 4 (Autumn 1986): 68.

20 Daniel Y. Kim, *Writing Manhood in Black and Yellow: Ralph Ellison, Frank Chin, and the Literary Politics of Identity* (Stanford, CA: Stanford University Press, 2005), 5.

21 bell hooks, "The Oppositional Gaze," 118.

22 Cassandra Jackson, *Violence, Visual Culture, and the Black Male Body* (New York: Routledge, 2011), 18.

23 Peele borrows the tactic of having a character fall victim to a masked villain in the opening scene from Wes Craven's *Scream* (1996). At the end of that scene, a white couple finds their babysitter, Casey Becker (Drew Barrymore), hanging from a tree in the backyard—essentially, she has been lynched. Peele's reappraisal of Craven's scene reveals that black men are more imperiled in suburban environs than their white female counterparts. See Monica Castillo, "Seven Films to Stream if You Loved 'Get Out,'" *New York Times Watching*, March 10, 2017, https://www.nytimes.com/2017/03/10/watching/get-out -movie-influences-what-to-watch.html.

24 Caity Weaver, "Jordan Peele on a Real Horror Story: Being Black in America," *GQ*, February 2017, 38.

25 "Redbone," from Gambino's studio album, *Awaken My Love*, Glassnote Records, released on November 17, 2016.

26 Touré, *Who's Afraid of Post-Blackness? What It Means to Be Black Now* (New York: Free Press, 2011), 12.

27 Mekado Murphy, "Jordan Peele Narrates a Scene from 'Get Out,'" *New York Times*, February 23, 2017.

28 The actress who plays Marianne Armitage in the stock footage is uncredited.

29 Dean Armitage uses this phrase toward the end of the movie.

30 Walter Johnson, "The Slave Trader, the White Slave, and the Politics of Racial Determination in the 1850s," *Journal of American History* 87, no. 1 (2000): 16.

31 See Olivia Banner, *Communicative Biocapitalism: The Voice of the Patient in Digital Health and the Health Humanities* (Ann Arbor: University of Michigan Press, 2017), 52.

32 See Mimie Nguyen, "The Hoodie as Sign, Screen, Expectation, and Force," *Signs* 40, no. 4 (2015): 791.

33 J. A. Mbembé and Libby Meintjes, "Necropolitics," *Public Culture* 15, no. 1 (2003): 21.

34 Mbembé and Meintjes, "Necropolitics," 21.

35 Mbembé and Meintjes, "Necropolitics," 21.

36 There is a Japanese guest present. Peele explains that the character was added to demonstrate that the Order is an international operation. See "Jordan Peele Explains Inclusion of Asian Character in 'Get Out' to Bobby Lee on Tiger-Belly Podcast," YouTube, accessed June 4, 2018, https://www.youtube.com /watch?v=OHm_IX2fMtU. Additionally, Mitchell Kuga muses that the character signifies "that anti-black racism spans continents, that even an inscrutable foreigner has access to privileged white spaces that both exclude and commodify black bodies." Mitchell Kuga, "The Asian Guy in 'Get Out' Is Just Another Tired Portrayal of Asians in Hollywood," Mic, March 6, 2017, https:// mic.com/articles/170360/the-asian-guy-in-get-out-is-just-another-tired -portrayal-of-asians-in-hollywood#.hFZGIVkJY.

37 Simone Browne, *Dark Matters: On the Surveillance of Blackness* (Durham: Duke University Press, 2015), 21.

38 The reference to *National Geographic* recalls the journal's history of often racist and unethical reportage and photography in regard to indigenous populations and people of color in general. In its March 2018 issue, *National Geographic* issued an apology for its past racist coverage and announced its intention to offer a yearlong series on racial issues starting in April as a part of "political strategy" of redress. See Susan Goldberg, "For Decades, Our Coverage Was Racist: To Rise above Our Past, We Must Acknowledge It," *National Geographic*, March 2018.

39 José Medina, *The Epistemology of Resistance: Gender and Racial Oppression, Epistemic Injustice, and Resistant Imaginations* (New York: Oxford University Press, 2013), 40.

40 Robert Jones Jr. argues that this scene is reminiscent of the one in Spike Lee's *Jungle Fever* (1991), "where Wesley Snipes's character is being accosted by police and Annabella Sciorra's character intervenes thinking she can save him if she just lets the cops know that he's with her." Son of Baldwin, "Get the Fuck Outta Here A Dialogue on Jordan Peele's Get Out," *Medium*, February 27, 2017, https://medium.com/@SonofBaldwin/get-the-fuck-outta-here-a -dialogue-on-jordan-peeles-get-out-831fef18b2b3.

41 Just as Barbara Creed coined the term *monstrous-feminine* to emphasize "the importance of gender in the construction of her monstrosity," King's added qualifier of "whiteness" offers an intersectional dimension to the figure of the monstrous woman. See Amy King, "A Monstrous(ly-Feminine) Whiteness: Gender, Genre, and the Abject Horror of the Past in American Horror Story: Coven," *Women's Studies* 46, no. 6 (2017): 557.

42 For all quotations, see Dino-Ray Ramos, "'Get Out' Director Jordan Peele on Divisiveness, Black Identity and the 'White Savior,'" *Deadline Hollywood*, October 22, 2017, http://deadline.com/2017/10/jordan-peele-get-out-film -independent-forum-keynote-speaker-diversity-inclusion-1202192699/.

43 Barbara Creed, *The Monstrous-Feminine: Film, Feminism, Psychoanalysis* (London: Routledge, 1993), 14.

44 Kinitra D. Brooks, "What Becky Gotta Do to Get Murked? White Womanhood in Jordan Peele's *Get Out*," *The Root*, March 3, 2017, https://verysmartbro thas.theroot.com/what-becky-gotta-do-to-get-murked-white-womanhood -in-j-1822522591.

45 Here I am thinking of the climactic scene in Amiri Baraka's play *The Dutchman* (1964), in which the white temptress, Lula, eventually goads the black male protagonist, Clay, into losing his temper, and then she subsequently murders him.

46 Aisha Harris, "The Most Terrifying Villain in *Get Out* Is White Womanhood," *Slate*, March 7, 2017, www.slate.com/blogs/browbeat/2017/03/07/how_get _out_positions_white_womanhood_as_the_most_horrifying_villain_of .html.

47 Kobena Mercer, *Welcome to the Jungle: New Positions in Black Cultural Studies* (New York: Routledge, 1994), 194.

48 Zack Sharf, "'Get Out': Jordan Peele Reveals the Real Meaning behind the Sunken Place," *Indie Wire*, November 30, 2017, www.indiewire.com/2017/11 /get-out-jordan-peele-explains-sunken-place-meaning-1201902567.

49 Yuan and Harris, "The First Great Movie of the Trump Era." *Vulture*, February 22, 2018.

50 Tina Campt, *Listening to Images* (Durham: Duke University Press, 2017), 50.

51 James Edward Ford, "Introduction," *Black Camera* 7, no. 1 (2015): 110.

CHAPTER SIX

THE SONG

Living with "Dixie" and the "Coon Space" of Post-Blackness

CHENJERAI KUMANYIKA, JACK HITT, AND CHRIS NEARY,
WITH AN INTRODUCTION BY BERTRAM D. ASHE

JUSTIN ROBINSON WAS THE FIRST ORIGINAL MEMBER OF THE CAROLINA Chocolate Drops to leave the band, and I always wondered why. As of this writing, the popular black string band continues to tour and record with Rhiannon Giddings as the sole original Drop left, but Robinson's departure in early 2011 always nagged at me. And then, on November 17, 2017, Gimlet Media released "The Song," an episode of the *Uncivil* podcast, and it all became disturbingly clear.

I was once mildly obsessed with the Carolina Chocolate Drops. Between September 25, 2010, and September 19, 2011, I saw them live three times, including, gratefully, driving that first time from Richmond, Virginia, to Duke University in Durham, North Carolina, to see the original trio perform. I'm no huge fan of string bands, actually, although I did enjoy their music quite a lot. No, for me it was purely theatrical; it was the thrill of watching in-the-moment post-blackness in vibrant, living color. I loved the cultural dissonance, the visual and aural tensions in play as the band joyfully played and reclaimed music that, while originally black, was now popularly viewed as deeply white, and so the insistent performance of this music by appealing young black musicians was a fascinating example of what I have referred to as "blaxploration," exploring blackness.[1] To be specific, it was an example of post-black "allusion-disruption": the Drops alluded to the popular (mis) understanding of this music as white and bluegrass and disrupted that assumption with musical excellence and historical accuracy—while providing one hell of an entertaining show all the while.[2]

Almost as intriguing as watching the Chocolate Drops themselves, though, was observing the audience. Overwhelmingly white, but with some dogged black participation as well, the cultural tensions onstage ultimately produced a "call" to which the audience displayed an equally complicated "response." What I couldn't know, however, gazing at stages in Durham and Richmond nearly a decade ago, was how that racially inflected audience response would affect Justin Robinson and would, in turn, alter and inform his view of the music he loved. As I have argued, post-blackness may well be executed "in service to the black community,"[3] but, as Malin Pereira also underlines in her contribution to this volume, it still comes with a certain cost that post-black artists sometimes have to pay. It seems to the editors of this volume that "The Song," a key episode of the *Uncivil* podcast, is a telling example of how "playing" with the combustible elements of slavery and post-blackness can sometimes have an effect on the artists themselves.

—BERTRAM D. ASHE

"THE SONG": AN *UNCIVIL* PODCAST

with Chenjerai Kumanyika and Jack Hitt [Transcript]

CHENJERAI KUMANYIKA: There are symbols of the Confederacy that still appear in popular culture, like the stars and bars flags, or the monuments to Confederate generals. But there are other remnants of the Confederacy that are still with us.

Today we're going to talk about one them. And it's one that some people might not even connect with the Confederacy.

We sent our producer Saidu Tejan-Thomas to ask people about it.

SAIDU TEJAN-THOMAS: I'm a journalist, working for a history show and—

PERSON 1: Wonderful!

ST-T: —and I was wondering if I could play you a song and just get your thought on, like, what you think about it.

[*Pause*]

ST-T: Okay, awesome.

[*Music*]

JACK HITT: Officially, this song is called "I Wish I Was in Dixie's Land," and during the Civil War, it became the unofficial anthem of the Confederacy.

This song is still heard in the South today, and so when you play it for certain folks who grew up down there you often get a reaction like this:

PERSON 5: Makes me feel good.

ST-T: Yeah?

P5: Yeah! Goes back to the roots!

ST-T: What "roots"?

P5: Well, I'm from South Carolina so it's, I mean "Down in Dixie," it's a—I mean it's a upbeat song! 'Bout the roots of everything, from everything. Not just one particular person but everybody.

JH: But of course, because of the song's tie to the Confederacy, it also provokes another, very different kind of response.

PERSON 6: It's kind of sad. When I hear that, I think about slavery and the things that my family went through when I was a little girl.

ST-T: What, what kind of things?

P6: Work, working for the—the white man. You know, being maids in their houses and farm workers, you know. I used to pick tobacco, as I—as I remember, as a child.

ST-T: But that's not a song you would play on your down time?

P6: Oh no! No. It reminds me of slavery and war.

[*Music in*]

JH: Hey, Chenj, do you remember when you first heard it?

CK: I mean, to me that song, to me, is kind of like, the anthem of white supremacy, you know. I mean, I know that it was a popular song for the Confederacy. But, you know, my first introduction to it actually was when I was little and I used to watch, like, *The Dukes of Hazzard.*

JH: What?! [*Laughs*]

CK: Yo, for like a brief period, I was, like, really into *The Dukes of Hazzard.*

[*Clip from* Dukes of Hazzard *episode*]

CK: The General Lee, you know, Daisy Duke and all that. You know, and it was like [*sings car horn melody*]. You know, I was, like, yeah, I was, like, kind of running around singing that song. And probably, I'm sure my dad saw that and was, like, very quickly, it was banned in the house. I couldn't, you know, there was no, like, there was no *Dukes of Hazzard.* This is our secret, by the way. You can't tell anyone this.

[*Music out*]

JH: So you know growing up in Charleston, SC, to me, the song was just— everywhere. It was in the ether. If you were walking down the street you might pass a—a wedding—you'd hear the song. Or if someone scored a touchdown at a football game. Hell, you'd actually hear people whistling it.

CK: In real life people actually would whistle "Dixie"?

JH: Yeah, I mean that people did—it's a catchy tune. And, you know, the song goes through, like, different periods and I think when I was growing up— it was, there was this sense that it had been kind of cleansed of its evil past. You know, almost neutered, right? I think it's one of the reasons why you can hear it in *The Dukes of Hazzard."* It would not be played in any TV show today, right? But even with that effort, the history of the song is kind of inescapable. It always manages to somehow resurface no matter what you do. I mean it's not for nothing that this song was the musical score to the pro-Klan epic *Birth of a Nation* a century ago, and only a few months ago was the name of that white nationalist gathering in Charlottesville, the Dixie Freedom Rally.

[Music in]

JH: This song has a long history in America. It's a history I thought I knew. But so far, in making this show, we've found that every aspect of the Civil War that we've looked at has had this other, hidden history.

We wondered if "Dixie" was the same.

And so I started digging into the song.

And of course, turns out the history of "Dixie" is a hot mess. And everything I thought I knew to be true . . . is wrong.

[Theme in]

CK: I'm Chenjerai Kumanyika.

JH: And I'm Jack Hitt.

CK: And this . . . is *Uncivil*.

JH: Where we ransack America's past . . .

CK: And discover that history is kind only to those who write it . . .

[Music out]

JH: So, all my life I have known three basic facts about "Dixie"—it was a Confederate anthem, it was written by a southerner, and it was written during the war.

Wrong, wrong, and wrong.

It turns out it was a pop song written by a Yankee in Manhattan *before* the war. I learned all this from Christian McWhirter, a researcher at the Lincoln Presidential Library.

CHRISTIAN MCWHIRTER: So "Dixie" is a minstrel song. Daniel Decatur Emmett—the guy who wrote it—was one of the founders of minstrelsy.

JH: Minstrelsy, of course, being:

CM: White people painting themselves up in blackface, going up on stage, and doing songs built around a caricatured image of African Americans. It's a fundamentally racist style of music. And Emmett, he was the one who came up with the idea of a minstrel troupe, that instead of having one guy in blackface on stage you'd have a whole bunch of guys. And they would all play different characters.

JH: In every minstrel show the last song was called the walk-around—the big crowd-pleasing foot-stomper with all the musicians on stage. And "Dixie" was written as one of these.

[*Music in*]

And these songs were incredibly popular with minstrel audiences in all the places where these shows were big.

JH: Where were most of these minstrel shows performed?

CM: The big cities in the North: New York, Chicago, Philadelphia, you know, Boston. They are a Northern phenomenon.

JH: That's right. "Dixie" *wasn't* born out of a Southern racist tradition. It was born out of a *Northern* racist tradition.

CM: Most of those people in that white audience thought of minstrelsy not as a caricature but as a genuine representation of what African American music in the South was like.

JH: Reporting. Journalism.

CM: Yes.

JH: So the song had a huge following in the North. But the question is, how did it become a Confederate anthem?
    Well, first, it broke out of the minstrel shows and went national.

CM: It was this huge hit in 1859, 1860. Today, it would be the number one song.

[*Music out*]

CM: The way music worked back then was not the way it works now, because there was no recorded sound. And so if there was a hit song, like, other performers would pick it up and start doing it, right? And so one of them was a guy named Jay Newcomb. And Jay Newcomb toured the South in 1860 and ends up in New Orleans, where he performs "Dixie." And all of this happens right around the time that Lincoln gets elected and the Deep South, at least, starts to secede. And so, they're, you know, they're literally ripping the Union's old anthems out of their songbooks, they're looking for a good replacement. "Well, here's this song 'Dixie.' And at least the first couple verses and chorus sure sound pro-Confederate to me, so let's start using it."

JH: The lyrics to the song *do* tell a story, but almost no one knows them; only the chorus gets sung: "In Dixieland, I'll take my stand, to live and die in Dixie."

JH: And once Confederates started using it, it went from pop song to anthem. But here's what really launched it: On February 18th, 1861, the Confederacy swore in their first president.

CM: It gets played at Jefferson Davis's inauguration in Montgomery, and that kind of gives it the unofficial, you know, seal of approval, and then it goes from there.

JH: So the anthem of the Confederate States of America was a Northern song, written in Manhattan, by a Yankee.

That's a lot to wrap your head around right there. But hold on, because none of that is right either.

[*Music*]

JH: People always debate about who wrote songs, but in the case of "Dixie" there's a really good reason to go down this rabbit hole.

First, you know that New Yorker who wrote it, Daniel Emmett? When he told his story of where the song came from, here's what he'd say:

"It was a cold and rainy afternoon in New York City when I suddenly heard the first line in my head:

'I wish I was in the land of cotton, old times there are not forgotten.' And the whole song sprang, all at once, onto paper." And that was his story.

But in Emmett's hometown in Ohio, there's another story about where this song came from, and it goes like this:

CM: So, Emmett is from Mount Vernon, Ohio. And there's an African American musical family around the same time Emmett is growing up there,
called the Snowdens. The story is that this family had this song that had
Dixie in it, and that Emmett must have heard it growing up—he committed it to memory, and you know, he's gotta write a song one night in
1859—he goes ahead and writes down the song the Snowdens taught him.

And there's good reason to believe this version is the true version.
The Snowdens were really well known. People came from *all around* to
the Snowden farm to hear their concerts. They were basically the Jackson
5 of the mid-nineteenth-century upper Ohio valley.
But besides them being famous, there's another reason Emmett might
have heard of them. The Snowdens lived next door to Emmett's
grandparents.

[*Music drop out*]

In Mount Vernon, the fact that Emmett stole this song has long been
an open secret.

CM: There's this oral tradition there that the Snowden family, uh, taught
"Dixie" to Emmett.
This is codified in the two graves. Emmett's grave, which the United
Daughters of Confederacy later put this big monument over it, saying,
you know, "The man who wrote 'Dixie.'" And then, something like a few
miles away from that in town is this grave for the Snowden family, and it
says, "They taught 'Dixie' to Emmett."

JH: "Taught," it says. The Snowdens may have written it, or other black musicians may have. In those days, especially among African Americans, there
wasn't much concern with authorship. You wrote a song and taught it to
people. And then they taught you a song.

[*Music fade up*]

The whole idea of claiming credit only starts to matter if you live in
Manhattan, where a song gets sold as sheet music and can make you
famous.

[*Music post*]

CK: Alright, Jack, so I just learned that a black family might have written "Dixie." You know, that's a thing, I mean. . . . Usually when I learn that white folks have stolen black culture, I'm glad we're finally getting our credit. But in this case, I'm not sure that I want credit for "Dixie," right? And some of it is, I don't know what to do with that. I'm not going to start playing "Dixie." I don't know, maybe I need to hear from somebody else. Like another person of color who knows more about the history. Actually, could we, would it be possible for us to find a black musician who maybe knows this history and has a different response to it?

JH: After the break, we hear from that person, a black musician who has played "Dixie"—Justin Robinson.

[*Ad break*]

CK: So before the break, we learned that "Dixie" definitely wasn't written by a Confederate Southerner, and probably wasn't even written by a white New Yorker. Most likely, it was written by a free black family in Ohio.

But even knowing this, when I listen to the song now? I just imagine slaveholders loving this song. It *still* feels like the soundtrack to white supremacy to me.

And I can't really imagine black folks wanting to sing this song or listen to it.

So when I heard there was a black musician out there performing "Dixie," I had questions.

CK: When it comes to the song "Dixie," right, like, I have a relationship to it where it, for me, is like the sonic version of the Confederate flag, right?

JUSTIN ROBINSON: [*Laughs*]

CK: There's an uncomfortability inherent with the song, and I'm just wondering if you have any of that?

JR: I don't have any from a personal level. But, like, what does it mean for a black person to be playing this song that was probably written by a black person but in the middle period has been co-opted by white supremacist ideology? That's weird! Like, that's a weird sandwich. I wanted people to sit in that, and I wanted to set it firmly on people's plates so they could regard it and have their own reactions to it.

CK: This is Justin Robinson. He's one of the founding members of the band the Carolina Chocolate Drops.

And to understand what first attracted Justin to the song "Dixie," you have to understand how he came to love this style of music in the first place. It started with the banjo.

JR: I'm from North Carolina. So the sounds of the banjo are always around, whether you want to hear them or not. Purely, it was a sonic love affair at the beginning, and then I learned more about the history later.

CK: But Justin knew the real roots of this music.

[*Music in*]

JR: The banjo comes from western Africa—Senegal, the Gambia. My ancestors may or may not have played that instrument, I don't know. And it kind of doesn't matter. To be able to hold that instrument in my hands now, knowing that this Senegalese instrument, Gambian instrument, traveled all across the ocean and is sitting in my hands in North Carolina now is kind of amazing.

CK: And it was this sense of excitement about these instruments and this music that brought Justin to the Black Banjo Gathering, a place where he knew he could meet other black musicians who loved them too.

JR: People played, and people talked, and people met each other. I knew that there was going to be a black fiddle player named Joe Thompson there, and so I wanted to go meet him.

CK: When Justin met Joe Thompson, Joe was in his eighties. And he'd been playing string music since he was a kid.

JR: He was sort of one of very few anyway who played the music traditionally, who got it from his father, and his father got it from his father, so passed down through an oral tradition.

CK: Learning the music directly from Joe had a real impact on Justin. He'd always been a fan of this style of music, but playing it with Joe made him want more.

Justin started spending every Thursday night with Joe and a couple of other musicians who he met at the banjo gathering.

JR: And we were in the country, and we were in North Carolina. And we were in a hot-ass house in April, because he's old. He *was* old at the time—you know how old people keep their houses sometimes. It was the three of us. It was me, Dom [Flemons], and Rhiannon [Giddings], and sometimes Sue Leah. And his wife would be there, and it was an all-black space, and that is the context, which is sort of its genesis . . .

[*Music out*]

CK: It was these nights in that hot Carolina house that eventually made the Chocolate Drops. They became a *band* dedicated to playing music in the black string tradition . . .

[*Music in—2–3 seconds*]

That's "Peace behind the Bridge," from the Chocolate Drops album *Genuine Negro Jig*.

[*Music out*]

Justin and the other Chocolate Drops wanted the audiences at their shows to feel the music they played as a black tradition.

And so when they thought about "Dixie" and how Daniel Emmett likely stole the song from a black band, the Snowdens, it made sense to perform it.

JR: Having that additional information about the Snowdens and about the story and all that made it a richer internal conversation, and the other members of the band would talk about—we would all talk about—its origins.

It was, you know, a contentious piece of music to be playing, certainly by black people. Yeah, 'cause probably nobody black has played it since the Snowdens, certainly not in any popular way. So yeah, we did it to be provocative.

[*Beat*]

JR: As a reclamation.

CK: A way to tell a different story about the song.

JR: I thought it was part of a larger story that we were telling. The story of how things are misappropriated, and then resold and repackaged with their original contents sort of hollowed out.

CK: Justin says he would avoid the lyrics of "Dixie" altogether, so no one sung them. They just played the instrumental music, the way they imagined the Snowdens playing it.

CK: When y'all would play this song, was there a lot of setup?

JR: Nope, I almost never said anything.

CK: Mm.

JR: I let people come to their own conclusions.

CK: So I've been to a couple of Chocolate Drops concerts. And here's what you have to know:
 A lot of times almost everybody in the audience—is white. And so I had to ask—
 I guess what I wanna ask you is—lemme ask it like this: Periodically, for whatever reasons, white folk will invite you into a coon space. And when they do that, it's never, like, "I'm going to invite you into a coon space." Do you know what I mean?

JR: You're going to have to break that down. I've never heard that term used in that particular way. What's that mean?

CK: Okay. Well, you know. [Sigh] Like to me, what I'm talking about is folks will invite you into a project that's about performing something for their pleasure. Maybe even—

JR: Oh sure. Yeah, okay—

CK: —they invite you to dehumanize yourself for profit, for their pleasure, to deepen their sense of identity. So I guess the question I'm asking *you* about this is: How do—I'm interested in what insights you have about how to navigate that.

JR: You're sort of hitting on the head what it means to be black in America or indigenous in America or sort of any other group who's having to navigate these things about how to deal with, sort of, *whiteness* and keep your own humanity at the same time—which can be complicated. Our ancestors certainly figured out how to do it, and I don't think I'm *any less smart* than they are. And so we're talking about these "coon spaces," as you call them now. As the Chocolate Drops, we have played in many such a space. Spaces that I would rather forget. It was a—it got weird, and it continued to get weirder.

CK: Is there a particular moment where you were like—that you remember where you were like, "This is really weird."

JR: Yeah. I can tell you the time. It became a little too much.

[*Music in*]

> We were in South Carolina. Now, my parents are both from South Carolina and, as most black people, have their roots in South Carolina or Virginia.

JR: We got to the festival grounds. It was a bluegrass festival in Charleston. We got into the property, I was asleep in the van, and I sat up straight. Because I didn't know, at this point, I didn't know where the gigs were—I just got in the van and shut up. And I was like, "Where *are* we?" My spirit felt wrong. And once we pulled up, I was like, "Oh!"

CK: It was a place Justin had known about since he was a kid: Boone Hall.

JR: Boone Hall is one of the first plantations that are in—that is in Charleston. A big, fancy place—like *Gone with the Wind*, a "Tara" kind of plantation.

CK: Mmm.
    And then they got on stage.

JR: And there was nothing but white people in there.
    Um, and so, that was like, "*We might be doing something wrong*." [*Laughs*] That's what I felt, in that moment. I was like, "This—the irony is not lost on me that we are at a *plantation* playing fiddle and banjo for an *all-white audience* in Charleston, South Carolina."

And I was like, this is so palatable; they love it because it makes them feel comfortable.

I walked through the crowd to go and get something to eat from one of the concession stands, and I don't know how many times I heard the n-word, like as I walked through the crowd.

It was *soul-crushing.*

[*Music*]

JR: This feels like, *not narrative disruption.* This feels like replication.

[*Music post then fade out*]

CK: This experience at Boone Hall was one of many. And it all started to affect Justin.

JR: And I became resentful of the audiences.

CK: *Mmm.*

JR: And so that—then that started to mess with *my own feeling* toward the music, which I really couldn't handle. I like the *music!* I just *do*—as a *me*—a human being—Justin Robinson; I like how the music *sounds.* So it was the . . . the . . . the *publicness* of that was messing with that love. I can't in good conscience play old-time music in public. And I haven't for quite a while. I stopped playing the music pretty much altogether.

CK: So it's heavy, listening to what happened to Justin. And just, like, the effect it had on his relationship to this music that he loved so much. Because Justin created a possibility for me to have a relationship to "Dixie," and not just "Dixie" but to that kind of music. But then when you see what happened, right, it almost, like, *confirmed* a lot of the fears that I had. But that's actually not my takeaway totally. Like, I mean, on the one hand, yeah, definitely my recommendation is, "If you're black, don't play 'Dixie' on stage in front of white people." But I feel a little bit sad. You know, Justin stopped playing the fiddle music altogether, like old-time music altogether, and I have a sense of what was lost from that, you know.

Here's the thing I think about with "Dixie," right? Here's what makes "Dixie" complicated. On one level, it's real easy just to be like, "Forget 'Dixie,' it's racist and everything." But I think about the Snowdens, and I think about that town, Mount Vernon. I mean, somebody took time to write in that gravestone, "Snowden taught 'Dixie' to Emmett." And to me that's representative of this black community that wants us to remember, and I know there's people in that community that *do* remember. And I just feel like if I say, you know, "Forget 'Dixie,'" am I betraying them in a way? And that's what makes this, like, difficult for me. And I don't, you know, I'm not sure what the answer is. I know I think for me, it's—I just have to figure out a way to sit with that discomfort.

But for Justin, he found his own solution.

JR: I just moved out to the country, which I love. It's wonderful. Ever since I've been out there, the banjo has just been speaking to me in this really particular way. Saying *"Play me, play me, play me, play me . . ."*

CK: He said sometimes he'll go out—he talked about one time he went out, and, you know, he walked out, and he has this fire pit that's like about a hundred yards from his house.

JR: In that instance, it was kind of a chillyish night. I walked myself down there with my small jacket on.

CK: He had, you know, the banjo kinda slung, you know, over his shoulder or whatever.

JR: So I made myself a little, little baby fire. And—

CK: And he just would play.

JR: I can conjure up my own memories of playing with Joe. That's who I learned those songs from. That's sort of my most—my deepest connection to this music is through him. It connects me to . . . it connects me back across the ocean to African ancestors. And I can appreciate it, its sound. It sounds good.

FIN

JH: *Uncivil* is produced by Chris Neary, Chiquita Paschal, and Saidu Tejan-Thomas. We had more help from M. R. Daniel. Our senior producer is Kimmie Regler. Editing by Caitlin Kenney, Alex Blumberg, and Pat Walters.

CK: Our show is mixed by Bobby Lord, Haley Shaw, and Emma Munger. The music for *Uncivil* was composed by Bobby Lord and Matthew Boll in collaboration with Ann Caldwell and the Magnolia Singers.

We'd like to thank everyone in the low country for a fantastic week of recording.

Additional music features J. C. Brooks, Son Little, Rocko Walker, Haley Shaw, and Saidu Tejan-Thomas.

JH: Our show was fact-checked by Julie Beer. Our secret weapon is Christopher Peak.

Special thanks to Randy Snowden—those were great talks. For more on the Snowden family and the song "Dixie," check out the book *Way Up North in Dixie* by Howard and Judith Sacks.

CK: *Uncivil* is a production of Gimlet Media. Our website is uncivil.show. We're on Twitter and Facebook at "Uncivil Show." And don't forget to join our Facebook group: "Uncivil Podcast."

JH: I'm Jack Hitt.

CK: And I'm Chenjerai Kumanyika.

NOTES

1 Bertram D. Ashe, "Theorizing the Post-Soul Aesthetic: An Introduction," *African American Review* 41, no. 4 (Winter 2007): 614.
2 Ashe, "Theorizing the Post-Soul Aesthetic," 615.
3 Ashe, "Theorizing the Post-Soul Aesthetic," 614.

CHAPTER SEVEN

PERFORMING SLAVERY AT THE TURN OF THE MILLENNIUM

Stereotypes, Affect, and Theatricality in Branden Jacobs-Jenkins's Neighbors *and Young Jean Lee's* The Shipment

ILKA SAAL

WHEN BRANDEN JACOBS-JENKINS'S PLAY *NEIGHBORS* PREMIERED AT THE Public Theater in New York in 2010, Charles Isherwood of the *New York Times* complained about its use of "incendiary images and hackle-raising ideas," its "flame-throwing dramaturgy."[1] His acerbic commentary pertained above all to the playwright's bounteous use of racializing stereotypes, including blackface minstrelsy performances by characters named Mammy, Zip Coon, Topsy, and Jim Crow. Isherwood's choice of language bespeaks his anxiety over the continuing affective potency of these negative stereotypes of blackness, an anxiety he shares with a great number of critics. Perceived by some as cathartic, by others as offensive, by yet others as humorous and ironic, performances of racial stereotypes—particularly those emerging in the historical context of New World slavery and its aftermath—in the public spaces of the contemporary stage or museum tend to stir up heated debates over the function and ethics of art with regard to past traumatic histories.

This essay aims to shed light on the affective force of contemporary performances of stereotypes of blackness. It is concerned with how contemporary performances address not so much the actual history of slavery but the history of its various articulations, its enduring representational legacies. It focuses in particular on how these performances, by deploying various forms of theatricality, mediate the psychological and emotional hold that these negative images continue to have over contemporary subjects. For case studies I will draw on Branden Jacobs-Jenkins's play *Neighbors* (2010) as well as on Young Jean Lee's play *The Shipment* (2009). For a better understanding of the complex work of theatricality in these plays, of the ways they simultaneously trigger and mediate the messy encounter with the stereotype, I will begin by briefly sketching out the historical background for this inquiry, followed by some theoretical considerations on how the lens of theatricality can bring into focus the various layers of the affective exchange between performer, stereotype, and audience.

TWENTIETH-CENTURY REALISM
AND THE RETURN OF THE REPRESSED

For much of the twentieth century the dominant tradition for negotiating questions of racial identity on the American stage has been the well-made realist play. It allowed playwrights access to mainstream theaters and the dominant critical apparatus and provided a vehicle to make the everyday experience of subaltern ethnic groups palatable to mainstream—that is, predominantly white—audiences. With its focus on what Arthur Miller calls "the tragedy of the common man"[2]—on ordinary families and their struggles for upward mobility, and on attendant conflicts over one's personal sense of dignity, thwarted dreams, and betrayals—the well-made play in the United States is generally considered to speak to universal concerns. These "universal" concerns, however, as Richard Dyer and others have stressed, tend to articulate the privileged position of whiteness, a position of power that rests "on the equation of being white with being human."[3] Appropriating these representational forms of whiteness hence allowed playwrights of color to render racial Otherness in terms of universal, humanist concerns. Furthermore, in its claim to naturalize representation as a "slice of life,"[4] realism tends to give dramatic characters' struggles the ring of "truthfulness." Recall in this context, for instance, Lorraine Hansberry's ground-breaking Broadway success *Raisin in the Sun* in 1959; consider also the ways in which August Wilson built on this tradition in the 1980s and 90s by charting and documenting what is repeatedly referred to in summaries of his work as *the* African American experience.[5] Historically speaking, realism has clearly been instrumental for African Americans in combatting demeaning stereotypes of blackness and in replacing these negative images with positive ones.

While the emphasis on "uplifting the race" was foremost in African American cultural politics for much of the twentieth century (though never uncontested),[6] starting in the late 1980s and early 1990s playwrights and other artists increasingly began to turn toward precisely the negative images of blackness that the well-made realist play sought to leave behind. Truthful representations of *"the* black experience" and racial uplift no longer seemed imperative to a generation of playwrights that grew up in a post–civil rights era. Instead they aimed to trouble established definitions of blackness and to shed what Kobena Mercer calls the "burden of representation"—that is, "the impossible task of speaking as 'representatives'" of one's racial/ethnic community.[7] Undaunted by communal injunctions, this new generation of artists claimed the artistic freedom to explore the psychic and affective hold that racializing tropes, narratives, and images from the past continued to exert for contemporary subjects. Theatricality as a mode of direct and highly self-reflective communication with the audience proved to be an effective means for examining such fraught representational histories, including the traditions of blackface and minstrelsy. George Wolfe's *Colored Museum* (1986), Suzan-Lori Parks's *The Death of the Last Black Man in the Whole Entire World* (1990), and Robert Alexander's *I Ain't Yo' Uncle: The New Jack Revisionist "Uncle Tom's Cabin"* (1996) are cases in point—all of them setting out to gauge to what extent crude, racist stereotypes of blackness continue to matter today.

To be sure, much of this work is highly provocative. "The art of the stereotype," Shawn-Marie Garrett writes, "is offensive, or, at best, strange and uncomfortable; it raids history and brings some of its deliberately forgotten scenes to light. It is painful and appalling. It is sometimes hilarious."[8] Identifying a parallel trend in the visual arts of the 1990s, such as in the paintings of Michael Ray Charles and the silhouette installations of Kara Walker, Garrett diagnoses in this context a larger cultural trend at the close of the twentieth century: "the return of the repressed tropes of minstrelsy."[9] This trend has continued well into the 2000s and 2010s, as evident in Spike Lee's provocative millennial movie *Bamboozled* (2000) as well as in more recent dramatic productions by playwrights like Branden Jacobs-Jenkins and Young Jean Lee.

Some of this theatrical and visual work on stereotypes is straightforwardly satirical, exposing to ridicule past and contemporary attitudes toward race, attempting to exorcise them through the satirical laughter of recognition. Some other work, however, is less purposeful, somewhat messy, and therefore, perhaps also more disquieting in its approach. As Garrett writes,

> The most difficult and troubling of this 'art of the stereotype' . . .
> does not have a clear point of view. . . . This kind of work does
> not say black is beautiful, stereotypes are cruel and shameful, and
> whites are to blame. Instead, it asks, what is black? what is white?
> what is between them? what could one be without the other? . . .
> The most challenging new art in blackface is simultaneously

scatological and elegant, ugly and sexy, horrific and funny. Often the artists behind the work . . . are not only repelled but also titillated by the sadomasochistic aspects of racial mythologies and racist histories.[10]

Put differently, a good part of this work seeks not simply to debunk the racist stereotype but to investigate its affective relation to the beholder—a relation that is rather ambivalent, marked by repulsion and anxiety as well as desire and titillation. It examines the stereotype within a complex relational force field among object, performer, and audience.

This chapter focuses on these messy and disconcerting performances of the representational legacies of American racial history that articulate a rather ambivalent and decidedly affective relationship between the stereotype and its beholder. It aims to show in what ways theatricality, as a representational mode, enables an engagement with this relationship, how it can be deployed to tap the stereotype's complex epistemological as well as psychic and emotional hold over contemporary subjects and to what effect.

STEREOTYPE, AFFECT, AND THEATRICALITY

The work with racial stereotypes, minstrelsy, or blackface tends to trigger fervent debates, often dividing its audiences into fans and detractors. When Suzan-Lori Parks premiered *Venus* (1996)—a provocative restaging of the historic figure of Saartjie Baartman, a Khoikhoi woman notoriously put on public display in London and Paris in the 1810s as the "Hottentot Venus"— some critics saw in Parks's unconventional take on Baartman's history a "devilishly playful" archaeological dig at the various mythologies that underline historical and contemporary perceptions of the black female body;[11] others objected that the deployment of these crude stereotypes of the past simply reiterated "the travesty of objectification of 'Otherness,'" victimizing the historical Baartman for a second time.[12] At about the same time, Kara Walker's satirical silhouette renditions of plantation slavery caused similar consternation, as Derek Conrad Murray discusses in his article to this volume. Walker came under vehement attack from African American artists and critics for catering to the perverse tastes of a predominantly white art world—the verdict articulated by an older generation of artists: "Kara is selling us down the river."[13]

In the late 1990s, such heated responses to individual artworks by Parks, Walker, Charles, and others accumulated and were amplified by numerous public controversies over the function of racializing stereotypes in contemporary art.[14] While agreeing on the enduring legacy of racist iconographies, opinions largely split over whether these images should be suppressed and countered with affirmative images of blackness or whether they needed to be acknowledged and engaged and, if so, in what ways. Some critics avow that the violent nature of these negative images cannot simply be undercut by irony and playfulness but that it persists beyond the best of intentions. They also believe that in reiterating stereotypes, young artists are disrespectful to previous generations of African Americans who dedicated their lives to battling racist images of blackness. Other scholars, however, point out that the insistence on the creation of affirmative images not only "strengthens the negative stereotypes in both the white and black imagination,"[15] but is itself caught up in the reification of blackness, establishing another regime of (counter-) representation. For Manthia Diawara, for instance, the only way of depriving these negative images of their power is by "embracing" them, by revealing them as objects of desire.[16] Stuart Hall similarly insists on the affective purchase of stereotypes on what he calls the "inner landscape[s]" of both white and black viewers.[17] "If you want to begin to change the relationship of the viewer to the image," Hall writes, "you have to intervene in exactly that powerful exchange between the image and its psychic meaning, the depths of the fantasy, the collective and social fantasies with which we invest images."[18]

Diawara's and Hall's astute observations on the affective dimension of stereotypes are important here. They underline the extent to which a stereotype functions not only as an epistemological tool, as a way of producing and freezing knowledge, but also as a complex interplay of anxiety and desire, fear and fetish of and for the imagined Other. It engages the beholder, as Homi Bhabha also stresses, in an ongoing process of identification and disidentification, projection and displacement, pleasure and apprehension.[19] This complex intersubjective dimension of the stereotype also explains the heightened emotive register frequently used by critics in reaction to contemporary artworks—for the language of stereotypes is also the language of affect.

In Gregory Seigworth and Melissa Gregg's definition of the term, *affect* is the name we give "to generally *other* than conscious knowing, vital forces" that occur and circulate "in the intensities that pass body to body"—real and imagined ones.[20] These visceral forces can be minute and barely noticeable. They can also be quite powerful, leaving us stunned and paralyzed but possibly also driving us "toward thought and extension."[21] As Seigworth and Gregg insist, there is no "pure" state for affect; affect is always messy and complex since it "arises in the midst of in-between-ness: in the capacities to act and be acted upon."[22] In this regard, they also consider affect as very much synonymous "with *force* or *forces of encounter*."[23] To be affected, so the critics explain, drawing on Bruno Latour, means to be "'effectuated,' moved, put into motion."[24]

On this score, then, "going inside [the stereotypical] image,"[25] as Hall demands, entails the willful discharge of the affective encounter between subject and object—an encounter whose outcome is far from predictable. Ideally, it might expose the epistemological and psychic power of the stereotype, undermine its seeming "fixity" of representation, and open up again the play of difference, which alone can generate new forms of knowledges and new subjectivities, as Hall insists.[26] But the affective charge of the encounter with the phantasmagorical body of the stereotype might also exhaust itself in a myriad of other reactions: indifference, discomfort, embarrassment, silliness, and, yes, also impudence and vulgarity. This is the risk the artist takes in tapping the affective hold of the stereotype. In fact, as we shall see, it is often precisely the broad range of audience reactions that these theatrical engagements with racializing stereotypes aim to put on display.

Theatricality provides a useful theoretical lens with which to bring into focus the various affective layers and intricacies of the encounter between spectator and stereotype. A slippery term, theatricality has been used to describe a great variety of instances of performance, both onstage and offstage.[27] Three interrelated uses of the term, however, prove useful here: a) theatricality as the foregrounding of a communicative situation between performer and spectator; b) theatricality as referring to the self-reflective, meta-quality of a particular performance that foregrounds its own presentational qualities; and c) theatricality as the resistance of the performing object.

Regarding my first use of theatricality: Various scholars have emphasized the stage-audience relationship as the constitutive dimension of theater and performance. Willmar Sauter, for instance, defines theatricality as "the communicative process between the performer's exhibitory, encoded, and embodied actions and the emotional and intellectual reactions of the spectator."[28] Ironically, it is one of theatricality's most fervent critics who elaborates on the affective dimension of this communicative process. In his influential essay "Art and Objecthood" (1967), art critic Michael Fried complains about modern art's penchant for foregrounding its very materiality as an object. According to him, such "literalist espousal of objecthood amounts to nothing other than a plea for a new genre of theater," for the object sets up "a *situation*—one that, virtually by definition, *includes the beholder*."[29] It exerts "a kind of *stage* presence."[30] Fried notoriously adds that he considers such theatrical maneuvers "the negation of art."[31] His vehement antitheater bias aside, Fried's critique of objecthood nonetheless proves useful for thinking about the relationship between the artwork and the beholder that undergirds contemporary artists' powerful performances of race. For Fried understands theatricality as "a function not just of the obtrusiveness and, often, even of the aggressiveness of literalist work, but of the *special complicity* that that work extorts from its beholder. . . . [T]he beholder knows himself to stand in an indeterminate, open-ended—and unexacting—relation as *subject* to the impassive object on the wall or floor."[32] In other words, the complicity of the beholder/spectator and the attendant awareness of a fundamental, intrinsic relation between spectator and performance, beholding subject and performing object, is here conceptualized as a crucial part—if not the very focus—of the artwork/performance itself. As we shall see shortly in the case studies, this relation is anything but unexacting.

The "special complicity" of the spectator with the performance is at once of a profoundly affective as well as cerebral nature. It entails both the visceral experience of the force of an encounter between bodies (real and imagined) as well as the awareness that one is purposefully hailed by the performance into such an encounter. As Fried emphasizes, the spectator "knows himself to stand in an indeterminate, open-ended . . . relation" as subject to the object. Here a second definition of theatricality and, in a way, the most widespread one, comes into play: theatricality as a self-reflective mode of re/presentation that draws the spectator's attention to the very mediality of theater by highlighting the various mechanisms at work in the staging, performing, and often also reception of the theatrical event. Particularly when it comes to performances of race, theatricality tends to highlight the embodied performance of racial scripts as well as underscore the attendant scopic dynamics that interpellate the performing body into a visual regime that makes these scripts legible. In short, this kind of theatricality ensures that the spectator is conscious of his or her complicity, while at the same time also exposed to the full force of the encounter with the performing object.

Finally, I want to draw on a third notion of theatricality that I consider crucial in analyzing embodied performances of racializing stereotypes: Fred Moten's notion of the "essential theatricality of blackness," which is "able to mess up or mess with the beholder."[33] In a remarkable refiguration of Fried's notion of theatricality, Moten contemplates the "quite specific objecthood that joins blackness and black performance."[34] He here refers to the commodification of blackness that has historically conjoined "object" and "person," while also requiring the ongoing performance of objecthood. In this case, the object is the performer is the performance. The crucial question that Moten posits on this score is in what ways the object-performer might qua performance articulate objection to her ongoing objectification. How can racial performance be deployed to critique racializing categories?[35] Moten's elaboration of theatricality hence points us to possibilities of reading performances of race against the grain, of gauging the resistance of the performing object. It suggests that there are ways in which stereotypes can also be deployed to disrupt the economy of desire between object and beholder. In what follows, I will illustrate the work of these various layers of theatricality (complicity of the spectator, self-reflective mediality, resistance of the object) with the examples of Young Jean Lee's *The Shipment* and Branden Jacobs-Jenkins's *Neighbors*.

STAGING THE AUDIENCE

The Shipment by thirty-two-year-old Korean American playwright Young Jean Lee opened at The Kitchen in downtown Manhattan in January 2009. A year later, in February 2010, *Neighbors* by twenty-three-year-old African American Branden Jacobs-Jenkins premiered at The Public Theater in New York City. Both plays quickly drew critical attention for their provocative investigations of contemporary notions of blackness, which relied on the confrontational deployment of tropes of minstrelsy and blackface. Notably, both plays brought these tropes into conversation with forms of traditional dramatic realism.

This device points us to the first layer of theatricality at work in both plays: the self-reflective foregrounding of the mediality of theater that seeks to provoke reflection on representational techniques of blackness. *The Shipment* consists of two parts. Lee describes part one as a "modern-day minstrel show,"[36] composed of song and dance, stand-up comedy, and a series of comedic sketches on ghetto life and rap-star aspirations—all offering up reified tropes, narratives, and images of blackness, replete with racializing stereotypes. Part two follows up with what the playwright calls "a relatively straight naturalistic comedy,"[37] where the same cast of actors now enacts a realist drawing-room drama, addressing the pitfalls of friendship, collegiality, and love lives—issues seemingly devoid of racial specificity. Lee has commented on how she worked out this show together with her actors both to address the persisting stereotypes that performers of color repeatedly have to contend with in their profession and to provide them with roles "they'd always wanted to play,"[38] that is, roles not determined by skin color. In this regard, then, *The Shipment* might be read as an allegory of representational uplift—nimbly moving from a demeaning racial farce to lighthearted postracial tragicomedy.

But then again, Lee's dramaturgical choices also trouble precisely this reading. The play's two parts are played without interruption, in a continuous movement that blurs the distinctiveness of each part. The cast in both parts is identical, with the actors moreover wearing pretty much the same costumes (evening dress) and assuming some of the same character names. Furthermore, as the drawing room drama unfolds, we occasionally witness visual and sonic echoes from the earlier minstrelsy performance: a gesture, a shift in intonation—all slight, but distinctive enough to briefly jar us out of the habitual mode of perception we bring to realist acting and character development: the assumption of verisimilitude. Such continuities and irritations indicate that Lee's dramaturgy might, in fact, not signify an allegory of postracial triumph but rather underline how representational legacies are shipped across time as well as modes of representation.

Jacobs-Jenkins's *Neighbors* tells the story of two neighboring families: The Pattersons (Richard, Jean, and Melody), a young, urban professional interracial family striving for success and financial stability, and The Crows—named Mammy, Zip Coon, Sambo, Jim, and Topsy—a family of professional minstrelsy performers, who wear blackface around the house and tend to break out into song, dance, and slapstick routines during ordinary housekeeping chores. In the encounter of The Pattersons with The Crows, the playwright literally stages what Garrett calls the "return of the repressed."[39] The Crows, in Hilton Als's words, as "tokens of minstrelsy are loud and disruptive, caricatures of the kind of blackness that Richard Patterson has sought to escape."[40] Moreover, in staging The Pattersons and The Crows, the dramaturgy constantly switches between straightforward realism and vaudeville, minstrelsy performance. It soon becomes clear that neither characters nor performers nor the audience will be allowed a break from the racist stereotypes of the past. What's more, there is a virtuosity to The Crows' performance of minstrelsy, which despite its vulgarity and offensiveness is also oddly enticing. Richard Patterson, and by extension the audience, cannot help watching the neighbors' performances through his kitchen window, as much as he is appalled and angered by them. Notably, just like Lee, Jacobs-Jenkins does not resolve this conflict of representations of racial identity; in the end minstrelsy and the realist tragedy of the common man might collide, but they certainly continue to coexist. While Richard is preoccupied upstage with an intensely violent physical battle with his nemesis Zip Coon, downstage the rest of the Crow family stares out at the audience as minstrelsy music plays.

In interlinking nineteenth-century minstrelsy with twentieth-century realism, *Shipment* and *Neighbors* purposefully situate their investigations of contemporary meanings of race within the context of the long history of blackness in the American theater—a history that, in fact, begins in minstrelsy and supposedly culminates in the arrival of realism.[41] Such metatheatrical framing underscores two points regarding the history and legacies of representations of blackness. First, both Lee and Jacobs-Jenkins insist that minstrelsy and realism do not necessarily constitute polar opposites in this long history of racial representations, with realism at long last "coming to repair the damage of minstrelsy."[42] Rather, as Ryan Hatch suggests, the two dramatic modes represent "two points on an aesthetic Möbius strip,"[43] with realism partaking just as much in the discursive, visual, and ultimately ideological construction of blackness as the crude racist antebellum vaudeville show.[44] On this score, then, Lee's and Jacobs-Jenkins's skillful interweaving of minstrelsy and realism troubles naive and celebratory narratives of representational progress and racial uplift.

Secondly, by sketching out the *longue durée* of theatrical representations of blackness, the two playwrights also remind us that theater has long been instrumental in shaping ideas about blackness. Both the stages of actual theaters as well as the stages of everyday life constitute sites where notions of race are constructed and solidified in the collaboration and intersection of performative and visual regimes. Recall, for instance, how antebellum blackface performances by nonblacks for nonblacks served to negotiate boundaries of whiteness.[45] But also consider how race continues to be constructed every day in less spectacular settings, such as in the simple encounter between passengers on a train on a white winter's day somewhere in the middle of France, as poignantly recalled by Frantz Fanon. The moment a little white boy hailed him with "Look, a Negro," the student of medicine was "battered down by tom-toms, cannibalism, intellectual deficiency, fetishism, racial defects, slave ships, and above all, above all else, 'Sho' good eatin.'"[46] In the black subject's encounter with the white spectating gaze, a whole host of histories, mythologies, fantasies, and desires is instantaneously and indelibly inscribed onto skin. He becomes an object allowed to exist in the white looking space—the *theatron*—only by performing this objecthood. In sum, then, by alerting us to the long history of representations of blackness, *Shipment* and *Neighbors* also provide us with what Hatch calls a "meta-theater-history, a compendium of the ways [predominantly white] American audiences have fantasized the spectacle of blackness."[47]

This brings us to the second layer of theatricality at work in these plays: a direct, confrontational approach that seeks to engage the spectator in a conscious relation with the performance as well as to stake out an affective force field of encounter that taps the psychic hold of the stereotype. Both playwrights understand their work as provocations, as attempts to unsettle their audiences, to get under their skin. Branden Jacobs-Jenkins explains that he is interested in gauging people's anxieties about racial stereotypes, their "gut reaction to minstrelsy today."[48] Young Jean Lee describes her primary concern as jolting her audiences out of a sense of complacency, to destroy habitual perceptions and undercut attitudes of consumerism by putting "a little bit of gravel into their brains that irritates them."[49]

Lee's gravel work is somewhat devious. She does not provoke her audiences outright, but first lures them with a song and dance and well-worn assumptions about black expressive culture into a sense of familiarity and comfort with what is being presented. *The Shipment* starts off with a lively dance routine, followed by an explosive stand-up comedy performance that sends up stereotypes of whiteness and blackness alike, and, finally, a series of short comic sketches about ghetto life, replete with hip-hop tropes and postures—all of them stock narratives, images, and tropes of American popular culture. The actors' performance, however, undercuts the possibility of complacent consumption. The "bordering-on-goofy choreographed moves . . . are unidentifiable as a genre" and include occasional flashes of "possible minstrel reference."[50] The stand-up comedian takes the familiar *gestus* of the angry black comedian to such extremes in form and content (including fantasies about killing babies) that his jokes simply fall flat, triggering bewilderment and consternation. The cartoon-like Hip Hop saga is enacted in an utterly perfunctory manner, with a flat intonation of lines and minimal, automatized gestures (some of them borrowed from *Grand Theft Auto* video games). Lee comments, "The performers wore stereotypes like ill-fitting paper-doll outfits held on by two tabs, which denied audiences easy responses (illicit pleasure or self-righteous indignation) to racial clichés and created a kind of uncomfortable paranoid watchfulness in everyone."[51] The term "paranoid watchfulness" aptly captures the essence of the second layer of theatricality I see at work in Lee's play: in defamiliarizing stock forms of black entertainment through the interjection of some "unidentifiable weirdness,"[52] the performance undercuts the possibility of habitual responses to racial representations. It makes the audience unsure about what they are seeing and how they ought to respond. Watchful and anxious, they are compelled into a heightened sense of self-awareness—perhaps even self-consciousness—of their own subject position vis-à-vis the performance of race on stage.

Neighbors is similarly complex in its attempt to trap the audience into some kind of situation with the performance. While the shifting back and forth between dramatic realism and minstrelsy creates "a kind of weird destabilization, an alertness of some sort,"[53] the high degree of virtuosity at play in song, dance, and slapstick routines also aims to lure the audience into the sheer indulgence of entertainment. Take, for instance, the opening of the "Zip Coon Interlude" in *Neighbors*:

> Music plays. Zip is there, arms filled with musical instruments— a tuba, a violin, a viola, a trumpet, a bugle, a tambourine, a banjo— just a ton of instruments. He has so many that for every step he takes, he drops one and has to bend over to grab it, and every time he bends over to pick up an instrument and takes another step, his pants—which are ill-fitting and held up by a rope—fall down, lower and lower, so he has to continually stop and hike up his pants in between picking up the instruments that keep falling.[54]

What starts out as a humorous slapstick routine in the tradition of the Marx Brothers soon deteriorates into ever more bewildering action. At some point Zip picks up the bugle with his naked buttocks, "rolling his eyes in an odd mixture of pleasure and pain."[55] Interludes by other Crow performers likewise build up from innocuous beginnings to the most extreme racial grotesque. Mammy's attempt to extinguish a cigarette butt that has fallen into her décolleté ends up with her twirling two white babies clamped to her exposed nipples in a "Mata Hari-esque belly dance,"[56] while Sambo's struggle with a broken lawn mower leads to his unravelling of an "enormous fire-hose-esque phallus . . . from his groin into the offstage," with which Sambo eventually ropes in a watermelon.[57] These hyperbolic performances of the most flagrant racist clichés and mythologies of the black body are, moreover, painfully prolonged. They take up several minutes of play time and, hence, cannot be dismissed by a brief glancing off in mild embarrassment. The racializing stereotype demands attention, and as a spectator, one is inescapably drawn into an extended encounter with its most blatant phantasmagoric dimensions.

Similar to Lee's unidentifiable weirdness, such extended encounters with the hyperbolic racial grotesque trigger, in the words of one observer, a hyperawareness of oneself and the audience around one.[58] Reviews attest that this hyperawareness manifests itself in a broad range of reactions, including amusement, tension, silence, and indifference, but also arguments between spectators as well as walk-outs.[59] Notably, it is particularly laughter that is again and again mentioned as the measure of affect. "The laughs one hears at a Lee play can sound explosive, then shocked, then apologetic and perhaps timid—as if the audience is wondering whether they should be laughing at all," Eliza Bent comments.[60] Branden Jacobs-Jenkins adds that he is very much interested in audiences responding with laughter to the jokes of minstrelsy[61]—including what he calls "the wrong laughter," that is, laughter that is just a little too long, a little too loud, a little too indulgent.[62] It is through laughter that the playwright hopes to implicate the audience in the history of minstrelsy performances, for the laughter indicates that today, just as in the antebellum period, an audience continues to exist for these kinds of crude, racializing jokes: "We can't actually separate ourselves from those people safely," the playwright comments. "That's why we clam up and get angry and want everything shut down."[63] The articulation of laughter, particularly the wrong kind of laughter, begs the question of what exactly is the joke and "who is the butt of it."[64] In many regards, then, it is the audience and the broad range of its affective reactions that is brought into focus in these provocative theatrical performances. On this score, plays like Lee's and Jacobs-Jenkins's are not so much about race as they are about our contemporary relationship to it.

Related to such staging of the audience's complicity with the stereotype is a third layer of theatricality: the resistance of the object. In addition to provoking their spectators with "ill-fitting," respectively hyperbolic performances of stereotypes, both Lee and Jacobs-Jenkins incorporate moments into their plays where the actors halt their performance and turn downstage to stare at the audience for an extended period. In Lee's play this confrontation happens twice: briefly during the opening dance routine and then, more intensely, at the end of part one, when the entire cast assembles downstage, "looking at the audience in silence."[65] The stage directions specify, "They look at the audience for an uncomfortably long time. As they sing an a cappella rendition of the indie-rock song 'Dark Center of the Universe' by Modest Mouse, they continue to look around at the audience. They don't move or change expression, but they sing with feeling."[66] *Neighbors* similarly concludes with the powerful image of the members of the Crow family taking "their place on 'stage,' standing in a straight line," supposedly for the grand minstrelsy performance that they have been rehearsing throughout the play.[67] Yet, as the music begins to play, "they don't move. Instead, they simply look into every face in the room. . . . [T]he entire family looks the entire audience over. The minstrel music finishes, and there is silence before the entire theater, stage and all, is ever so slowly and completely washed in amber light. It is awkward and goes on forever. We watch them. They watch us. Occasionally, they point to people in the audience and whisper to each other, sometimes mockingly, sometimes out of concern. Occasionally, they giggle."[68]

With Fred Moten I want to read this "staring at the audience" as a highly theatrical moment that articulates resistance to the reification of blackness. There are at least two interrelated ways in which such resistance is made manifest. First, these moments effectively turn the tables: the former observer becomes the observed, and the prescriptive gaze of surveillance and desire that up to this moment had coproduced the performance of racial stereotypes is refracted back to the audience. Suddenly, it is the audience that is under scrutiny. In *Neighbors* it quite literally becomes "the butt of the joke," as The Crows watch and giggle about the spectators. In *The Shipment* the persistent stare-out at the audience during the rendition of a Modest Mouse song similarly troubles and reverses existing power relations. The song includes the lines: "I might disintegrate into the thin air if you'd like / I'm not the dark center of the universe like you thought. // Well, it took a lot of work to be the ass I am / And I'm real damn sure that anyone can, equally easily fuck you over. // . . . If you can't see the thin air then what the hell's in your way?"[69] The repeated apostrophe "you" in this moving yet confrontational rendition of the lyrics begs the question of who is being addressed here. If "you" means us in the audience, then is "I" a reference to the performer? And if so, what kind of epistemological, affective, and power relations do the lyrics articulate? Moreover, what is it we in the audience allegedly aren't seeing? The ambivalence of the lyrics in combination with the particular dynamics of the presentation thus serve to augment the "paranoid watchfulness" already induced in the audience by the preceding, perfunctory rehearsal of racializing clichés. Somehow one cannot help feeling that as an onlooker one has just been moved from the sidelines to center stage.

Second, in addition to refracting the gaze of the beholder, these moments also confront and challenge the audience with the concrete bodily presence of the performer. Since in performances of reified notions of racial identity, performer and object effectively merge, I suggest that we can also read these stare-backs as confronting the beholder with the very objecthood of the performer. Take, for instance, *Neighbors*, where the performers stare out at us in blackface, thereby underscoring their reification into stereotypes. Moten argues that it is precisely through such performative foregrounding of objecthood that the articulation of resistance becomes possible. He here elaborates on Fried's earlier-mentioned critique of the theatricality of modern art objects. According to Fried, the moment the modern art object accentuates its materiality as an object, it resists absorption into the aesthetic experience of the beholder, for the fullness of the artwork can then no longer be grasped instantaneously, at a mere glance. Rather the art object now demands the prolonged attention of the beholder; it no longer simply exists in the same space with the beholder, but puts itself in the way of the beholder.[70] Aesthetic experience as the experience of self-absorption, which for Fried is the sine qua non of "true art," is here effectively stalled.

Where Fried decries the end of art (and the start of theater), Moten sees a catalyst for fundamental change in the object-beholder relationship in the *theatron* of race. He here works from the example of Adrian Piper's provocative performances of the 1970s, in which "object, person, commodity, artist, and artwork" converge.[71] Piper reports that the moment she presented her black body in performances to white art connoisseurs as "silent, secret, passive, seemingly ready to be absorbed into their consciousness as an art object,"[72] she was no longer fully absorbable. Her "objectlike passivity" implied "aggressive activity and choice, an independent presence confronting the Art-Conscious environment with its autonomy."[73] Somewhat paradoxically then, it is in deliberately posing her objecthood that Piper attains subjecthood. Such manifest posing of objecthood, moreover, compels the beholder into a different attitude toward the object-performer. The "disruptive . . . pressure of an *other*," Moten writes, forces the beholder to move out of herself or himself, to encounter and acknowledge the interiority of the object.[74] And Moten significantly adds that "to be for the beholder is to be able to mess up or mess with the beholder. It is the potential of being catalytic. Beholding is *always* the entrance into a scene, into the context of the other, of the object."[75] The outcome of this encounter between self and other, beholder and object-performer, is entirely open, comprising all the possibilities of the affective encounter mentioned earlier in this essay.

Moten's refiguration of the disinterested Friedian beholding as an active beholding brings us full circle to our earlier consideration of the affective force of racializing stereotypes. It indicates how performance, in this case the performance of stereotypes, can be deployed to interrogate the visual and affective dynamics of racial formations. Theatricality, in the three uses that I have attempted to sketch out here (self-reflective mediality, complicity of the spectator, resistance of the object), proves to be an extremely useful representational mode for mediating the encounter with the stereotype: it can lay bare the stereotype's enduring epistemological and psychic powers and tease out the spectators' complicity with them; it can also articulate resistance to the ways it objectifies and freezes identities and reopen, as Hall puts it, "the practice of representation itself."[76] Above all, it can compel the spectator into a new subject-object relation. In all these instances, theatricality not only brings into focus the troubled relationship contemporary spectators continue to have with the history and legacies of representations of blackness, but it also affects/moves us—with all the risks and possibilities that movement entails.

The complex and self-aware use of multiple layers of theatricality for the purpose of exposing and interrogating the various performative dynamics and scopic mechanisms at work in reiterative enactments of racial identities is not unique to the work of Branden Jacobs-Jenkins and Young Jean Lee. In this article, I used their plays as exemplary case studies—exemplary because we can find similar dynamics at play in a great number of contemporary stage performances as well as in performances by visual artists. As I have shown elsewhere, Suzan-Lori Parks's play *Venus*, particularly in its 1996 production by Richard Foreman at the Yale Repertory Theatre, similarly deconstructs the discourses, performances, and scopic mechanisms at work in turning a person named Saartjie Baartman into the mythological construction we have come to know as "the Hottentot Venus."[77] This latter figure, as Parks makes clear, is a figure of the spectatorial imagination, a "visual signpost"[78] that makes manifest our various latent and not so latent fantasies, fears, and desires of and for "the Other." Kara Walker likewise dissects and refracts the spectatorial imagination with her 2014 installation *A Subtlety, or the Marvelous Sugar Baby*. This installation, located in the abandoned and soon-to-be-demolished Domino factory in Williamsburg, Brooklyn, featured a massive sculpture of refined sugar in the shape of a sphinx with prominent African facial features crowned by a handkerchief, a substantial female bosom, a massive behind, and exposed vulva. Similar to *Venus*, *Neighbors*, *The Shipment*, and Walker's own silhouette installations of plantation slavery, the installation triggered vehement debates over the ethics of form and the communal responsibilities of the artist, or more specifically, the artist of color. These performances not only draw their audiences into an extended situation of complicity with representations of race, they also "trouble blackness"—they playfully and iconoclastically dismantle canonical and sacrosanct narratives of what blackness has meant and what it should mean. In this regard, theatricality holds a prominent place in the repertoire of post-black poetic strategies that assert the fluidity of concepts of identity.

NOTES

1 Christopher Isherwood, "Caricatured Commentary: Minstrel Meets Modern," *New York Times*, March 9, 2010.

2 Arthur Miller, "Tragedy and the Common Man," in *The Theater Essays of Arthur Miller*, ed. Robert Martin and Steven Centola (New York: DaCapo Press, 1996), 3–7. Miller's essay was first published in the *New York Times* on February 27,

1949, shortly after the opening of Miller's landmark play *Death of a Salesman* at the Morosco Theater on February 10, 1949.

3   Richard Dyer, "The Matter of Whiteness," in *White Privilege: Essential Readings on the Other Side of Racism*, ed. Paula Rothenberg (New York: Worth Publishers, 2004), 12.

4   This influential term was coined by Émile Zola in his groundbreaking 1881 essay "Le naturalisme au théâtre." See Zola, "Naturalism in the Theatre," in *Theory of the Modern Stage*, ed. Eric Bentley (New York: Applause, 1977), 351–72.

5   See Bonnie Lyons and George Plimpton, "August Wilson, The Art of Theatre No. 14," *Paris Review* 153 (1999).

6   Consider, for instance, the fervent debates carried out within the Harlem Renaissance over what a 1926 symposium in *The Crisis* titled "The Negro in Art: How Shall He Be Portrayed? A Symposium."

7   Kobena Mercer, "Black Art and the Burden of Representation," in *Welcome to the Jungle: New Positions in Black Cultural Studies* (New York: Routledge, 1994), 233–58.

8   Shawn-Marie Garrett, "Return of the Repressed," *Theater* 32, no. 2 (Summer 2002): 32.

9   Garrett, "Return of the Repressed," 33.

10 Garrett, "Return of the Repressed," 40.

11 Michelle Wallace, "The Hottentot Venus," *Village Voice*, May 21, 1996, 31.

12 Jean Young, "The Re-objectification and Re-commodification of Saartjie Baartman in Suzan-Lori Parks's Venus," *African American Review* 31, no. 4 (Winter 1997): 700.

13 Betye Saar quoted in Juliette Bowles, "Extreme Times Call for Extreme Heroes," *IRAAA: International Review of African American Art* 14, no. 3 (1997): 4.

14 See, for instance, the special issue of *IRAAA: International Review of African American Art* 14, no. 3 (1997). Following the Saar-Walker controversy, Harvard University hosted the symposium "Change the Joke and Slip Yoke" in the spring of 1998.

15 Manthia Diawara, "The Blackface Stereotype," in *Blackface*, ed. David Levinthal and Manthia Diawara (Santa Fe: Arena Editions, 1999), 7.

16 Diawara, "The Blackface Stereotype," 15.

17 Stuart Hall, "The After-life of Frantz Fanon: Why Fanon? Why Now? Why *Black Skin, White Masks?*," in *The Fact of Blackness: Frantz Fanon and Visual Representation*, ed. Alan Read (London: Institute of Contemporary Art, 1996), 17.

18 Stuart Hall, *Representation and the Media*, produced and directed by Sut Jhally (Media Education Foundation, 1997), film. Transcript available at https://www.mediaed.org/assets/products/409/transcript_409.pdf, quote on p. 21.

19 Homi K. Bhabha, "The Other Question: Stereotype, Discrimination and the Discourse of Colonialism," in *The Location of Culture* (New York: Routledge, 1994), 66–84.

20 Gregory J. Seigworth and Melissa Gregg, "An Inventory of Shimmers," in *The Affect Theory Reader*, ed. Gregory J. Seigworth and Melissa Gregg (Durham: Duke University Press, 2010), 1, emphasis in original.

21 Seigworth and Gregg, "An Inventory of Shimmers," 1.

22 Seigworth and Gregg, "An Inventory of Shimmers," 1.

23 Seigworth and Gregg, "An Inventory of Shimmers," 2, emphasis in original.

24 Latour quoted in Seigworth and Gregg, "An Inventory of Shimmers," 11.

25 Hall, *Representation and the Media*, 21.

26 Hall, *Representation and the Media*, 21.

27 For discussion of the varied and complex history of concepts of theatricality, see Tracy Davis and Thomas Postlewait, eds., *Theatricality* (Cambridge: Cambridge University Press, 2003).

28 Willmar Sauter, *The Theatrical Event: Dynamics of Performance and Perception* (Iowa City: University of Iowa Press, 2000), 69. See also Erika Fischer-Lichte, *Ästhetik des Performativen* (Frankfurt am Main: Suhrkamp, 2004).

29 Michael Fried, "Art and Objecthood," in *Art and Objecthood: Essays and Reviews* (Chicago: University of Chicago, 1998), 153, emphasis in original.

30 Fried, "Art and Objecthood," 155, emphasis in original.

31 Fried, "Art and Objecthood," 153.

32 Fried, "Art and Objecthood," 155, emphasis in original.

33 Fred Moten, *In the Break: The Aesthetics of the Black Radical Tradition* (Minneapolis: University of Minnesota, 2003), 234–35.

34 Moten, *In the Break*, 234.

35 Moten, *In the Break*, 234.

36 Young Jean Lee, "Author's Note," in *The Shipment/ Lear* (New York: Theatre Communications Group, 2010), 5.

37 Lee, "Author's Note," 5.

38 Lee, "Author's Note," 5.

39 Garrett, "Return of the Repressed."

40 Hilton Als, "Branden Jacobs-Jenkins: From the Heart," *New Yorker*, March 6, 2017.

41 Cf. Jacobs-Jenkins's comment: "I wanted a play that dealt with the entire history of blackness in the theatre." Dan Piepenbring, "Branden Jacobs-Jenkins on His Play *Neighbors*," *Paris Review*, May 28, 2015.

42 Ryan Anthony Hatch, "First as Minstrelsy, Then as Farce: On the Spectacle of Race in the Theater of Young Jean Lee," *CR: The New Centennial Review* 13, no. 3 (Winter 2013): 94.

43 Hatch, "First as Minstrelsy, Then as Farce," 94.

44 For Jacobs-Jenkins the difference is their "very different relationships to the audience." See Rebecca Rugg, "Interview with Branden Jacobs-Jenkins," in *Reimagining* A Raisin in the Sun, ed. Rebecca Rugg and Harvey Young (Evanston, IL: Northwestern University Press, 2012), 408.

45 Eric Lott, *Love and Theft: Blackface, Minstrelsy and the American Working Class* (Oxford: Oxford University Press, 1993).

46 Frantz Fanon, *Black Skin/White Masks*, trans. Charles Lam Markmann (London: Pluto Press, 1986), 84–85.

47 Hatch, "First as Minstrelsy, Then as Farce," 104.

48 Patrick Healy, "New Play Puts an Old Face on Race," *New York Times*, February 2, 2010. See also Piepenbring, "Branden Jacobs-Jenkins on His Play *Neighbors*."

49 Eliza Bent, "Destroying the Audience: Young Jean Lee Talks about the Traps She Lays for Her Public," *American Theatre* 31, no. 9 (November 2014): 34.

50 Lee, *The Shipment / Lear*, 7.

51 Lee, *The Shipment / Lear*, 5.

52 Lee, *The Shipment / Lear*, 5.

53 Branden Jacobs-Jenkins quoted in Rugg, "Interview with Branden Jacobs-Jenkins," 409.

54 Branden Jacobs-Jenkins, "Neighbors," in Rugg and Young, *Reimagining A Raisin in the Sun*, 334.

55 Jacobs-Jenkins, "Neighbors," 334.

56 Jacobs-Jenkins, "Neighbors," 387.

57 Jacobs-Jenkins, "Neighbors," 358.

58 Playwright Teddy Nicholas in reaction to the use of blackface and racializing stereotypes in Jacobs-Jenkins's play *The Octoroon* (2014) in Chris Myers, "Teddy Nicholas talks with Chris Myers about his Obie-Award Winning Performance in *An Octoroon*," *New York Theater Review*, June 6, 2014.

59 See, e.g., comments by Branden Jacobs-Jenkins in Piepenbring, "Branden Jacobs-Jenkins on his Play *Neighbors*," and by Teddy Nicholas in Chris Myers, "Teddy Nicholas talks with Chris Myers." Charles Isherwood's review attests to the fact that the quick dismissal continues to be part of the repertoire of audience reactions. See Isherwood, "Caricatured Commentary."

60 Bent, "Destroying the Audience," 30.

61 See Chris Myers's comment in Myers, "Teddy Nicholas talks with Chris Myers," as well as Branden Jacobs-Jenkins in Tom Sellar, "Pay No Attention to the Man in the Bunny Suit," *Village Voice*, May 21, 2014.

62 Rugg, "Interview with Branden Jacobs-Jenkins," 409.

63 Sellar, "Pay No Attention."

64 Jacobs-Jenkins in Piepenbring, "Branden Jacobs-Jenkins on his Play *Neighbors*."

65 Lee, *The Shipment / Lear*, 29.

66 Lee, *The Shipment / Lear*, 29.

67 Jacobs-Jenkins, "Neighbors," 402.

68 Jacobs-Jenkins, "Neighbors," 402.

69 Modest Mouse, "Dark Center of the Universe," on *The Moon and Antarctica* (Epic Records, 2000), songwriters Eric Judy, Isaac Brock, Jeremiah Green.

70 Fried, "Art and Objecthood," 154.

71 Moten, *In the Break*, 239.

72 Quoted in Moten, *In the Break*, 239–40. Piper here reflects on "Untitled Performance at Max's Kansas City, NYC, 1970."

73 Moten, *In the Break*, 239–40.

74 Moten, *In the Break*, 239–40.

75 Moten, *In the Break*, 235.

76 Hall, *Representation and the Media*, 21.

77 See Ilka Saal, "Theatricality in Contemporary Visual and Performance Art on New World Slavery," *Oxford Handbooks Online: Literature*, June 2016.

78 This is a term used by Kianga Ford in her discussion of reenactments/ performances of Venus. See Kianga K. Ford, "Playing with Venus: Black Women Artists and the Venus Trope in Contemporary Visual Art," *Black Venus 2010: They Called Her 'Hottentot'*, ed. Deborah Willis (Philadelphia: Temple University Press, 2010), 100.

CHAPTER EIGHT

THYLIAS MOSS'S *SLAVE MOTH*

Liberatory Verse Narrative and Performance Art

MALIN PEREIRA

CRITIC JAY WINSTON ENDS HIS ESSAY ON THYLIAS MOSS'S "TRICKSTER metaphysics" with a key observation about Moss and her poetics: "She finds a kind of empowerment, if limited, in irony, in paradox, in humor, in recognizing the grave seriousness of situations yet choosing, for the moment, not to take them too seriously, to see what other possibilities there are and what can be done with them. In this regard, she might be said to take [bell] hooks's 'decolonization' a step further, to the point that even oppression and atrocity, the points that most political movements rally against, might be played upon, reimagined."[1]

Such a stance suggests a post-black artistic sensibility that insists upon the possibilities of play and imagination, even in depictions of deep oppression such as American slavery. In her 2004 narrative in verse, *Slave Moth*, Moss presents a reimagined enslavement through the words of Varl, a precocious fourteen-year-old girl enslaved on a plantation in antebellum Tennessee. As with other post-black reconceptualizations of blackness, *Slave Moth* revisits and revises familiar tropes, in this case those of freedom, literacy, and identity in the traditional slave narrative.[2] And in so doing, Moss reconceptualizes poetry and her artistic identity, producing a metanarrative commentary on post-black artistic freedom.

First, a quick overview of the narrative's characters, plot, and themes. *Slave Moth* follows Varl's daily life on a plantation owned by Peter Perry. Her mother, Mamalee, lives with her. The sixteen free-verse poem-chapters composing the narrative are written from the first-person point of view of Varl, so we see the plantation events and people through her eyes. She has been taught to read and write (her mother also is highly literate, often reading to the master and discussing books with him) and is very smart. Varl secretly embroiders her thoughts and feelings onto her underdress, making a cocoon of words from which she expects to emerge one day transformed and free. The problem of her circumstance is multiple: how to develop her identity as a person; how to achieve her freedom; and how to escape the developing sexual interest of her white master, who is disinterested in his illiterate white wife, is excessively close to Varl's mother, and wants to add Varl to his collection of rare things, especially as she enters womanhood. As the narrative progresses, Varl's circumstances become even more pressing. The mistress, Ralls Janet, and her daughter, Lusa, cause significant trouble for Varl, and the master's sexual interest in her grows. At the same time, Varl's feelings for a young man also enslaved on the plantation, Dob, become stronger, and he wants to escape. She wonders why she stays: "I should be in the north, Pennsylvania, Michigan, / New York, where I would not be an oddity, other / escaped slaves writing books. I want to run, but / haven't yet. Dob would, taking / one of the master's guns with him."[3] *Slave Moth* presents the matrix of slavery, literacy, identity, and freedom so common to the slave narrative tradition, yet does not pursue a physical escape to freedom for the main character.

The few reviews and the scholarship on *Slave Moth* position it within these frames. Reviewer Peter Campion justifies Moss's choice to write in verse, tying it to the issue of enslaved freedom: he writes that *Slave Moth* "is about acquisition of language in a state of opposition; heavily textured free verse offers Moss a way to create Varl's private echo chamber, that space where her body itself seems at turns to exult and keen."[4] Milton L. Welch's review underlines the importance of the word *narrative* in the book's subtitle, "A Narrative in Verse," a word choice which he argues "connects it to the prose tradition of slave narratives," revising and extending "familiar motifs of narratives written by men such as Frederick Douglass and Olaudah Equiano and women such as Harriet Jacobs and Mary Prince."[5] Alison Hawthorne Deming's review focuses on the theme of transformation embodied in the central metaphor of the luna moth, a theme noted by all reviewers and scholars.[6] Evie Shockley's essay on *Slave Moth* and Edward P. Jones's *The Known World* (2003) positions the texts' "representation of enslaved characters as, among other things, visual artists" against the backdrop of the "artistry as agency" exhibited in Harriet Jacobs's slave narrative.[7] Shockley employs Arlene Keizer's term "contemporary narratives of slavery" in her analysis rather than critical terms such as "neo-slave narrative" for multiple reasons having to do with a better fit for the two texts she interprets, especially in its focus on black subjectivity and agency. Through careful close reading of Varl's creation of her artistic identity by embroidering her cocoon-like dress—placing it in the tradition of the *künstlerroman* and as a revision of Sethe's bridal dress in *Beloved*, a key work in the contemporary period's reimagining of slavery and the slave narrative—Shockley shows how for Moss "imagination is a powerful form of agency, whereby the enslaved subject can, in a sense, alter her world by perceiving it differently."[8] Shockley identifies a core theme—creativity—that is central to Moss's redefinition of slavery in *Slave Moth*.

While Keizer's term "contemporary narrative of slavery" certainly has merit and yields insightful analyses such as Shockley's, I want to consider how Moss offers in *Slave Moth* a "liberatory narrative," which, while centered on literacy and identity, redefines the very idea of freedom. This builds upon Shockley's focus on imagination as a means of agency by tying it specifically to a redefined notion of freedom. According to Angelyn Mitchell, liberatory narratives provide "new models of liberation by problematizing the concept of freedom"; instead of the familiar trope of physical escape to freedom, they focus on "the protagonist's conception and articulation of herself as a free, autonomous, and self-authorized self" as a black female.[9] Employing this frame to read *Slave Moth* enables us to see how Varl demonstrates how to be black and female in a racist, sexist society, thereby offering a model of how to free oneself within confining parameters. Characteristic of liberatory narrative protagonists, Varl ultimately "wills herself to freedom"[10] regardless of external constraints imposed by remaining physically enslaved on the plantation. Mitchell's liberatory narrative framework focuses most closely on a paradoxical freedom within constraints and transformative black female subjectivity. As such, it allows us to address two elements unexplored in the current criticism on *Slave Moth*: its didactic enactment of a liberatory model for a readership imagined to be composed to some degree of black girls and women; and its empowering performance of Moss's post-black, postprint poetics for herself as a black female artist and American citizen. This essay will pursue each of these mutually constitutive readings in turn.

Robert Baker, in a long footnote to his essay on Moss's trajectory across several collections of poetry concluding with *Tokyo Butter* (2006), makes the case that Moss intends *Slave Moth*, unlike her other work, to reach a larger audience.[11] Citing a 2004 interview with Daniel Shapiro in which Moss describes *Slave Moth* as "a narrative in verse written to cause the likelihood of access by a wider, including younger, audience," Baker differentiates this accessibility, rightly so, from the precision and difficulty of (and thus narrow readership for) her other work, especially *Tokyo Butter*, which he characterizes as her elegy for the printed page, a point I shall return to later.[12] The text as a model for readers, especially young black girls, is one function of the liberatory narrative, according to Mitchell: "The protagonists of the liberatory narrative demonstrate how agency and the will to be free facilitate the liberation of the soul and the psyche. . . . How they prevail may offer paradigms of liberation for their readers."[13]

As *Slave Moth* comes to a close, Varl's reflection on the events in the narrative confirms her as a model of agency through which Moss offers a paradigm of liberation for readers. She remarks to herself:

> So much to think about
> And thinking is its own important thing.
> How to handle your situation. How to attack. Defend.
> How to become free.[14]

Scene after scene in *Slave Moth* shows Varl doing just these things: thinking, handling situations, attacking, defending, becoming free inside herself. These moments, akin to the "everyday practices" in slavery that Saidiya Hartman examines in *Scenes of Subjection: Terror, Slavery, and Self-Making in Nineteenth-Century America*, "illuminate inchoate and utopian expressions of freedom," Hartman theorizes.[15] Varl's behavior in *Slave Moth* thus not only resembles but also models for readers the "tactics of resistance, modes of self-fashioning, and figurations of freedom"[16] Hartman teases out from Works Progress Administration interviews with former slaves, thereby enacting what she calls, borrowing from Paul Gilroy, a "politics of transfiguration" as opposed to the more popular "politics of fulfillment" through physical escape.[17]

Varl's everyday practices always involve critical thinking. Throughout the text, her thinking involves curiosity and repeated questioning. For example, in the opening chapter, Varl, looking at a book her master has left open on his desk, the *Great Book of Insectean Marvels*, wonders, "What can I do / with insectean information? What can I do / with it; how can it take on value / for a slave? How can it matter? / What circumstances can it change?"[18] Moss emphasizes Varl's willingness to engage a subject and find its useful application for her life by ending the lines with—and thereby placing weight upon—the words *do, do, value, matter*, and *change*. Thinking thus can lead to transformation. Varl also remains reflective about her thinking, constantly checking herself and her assumptions. Considering her friendship and behavior with another slave, Jessper, Varl wonders, "Is it wrong to put this writing first? Myself? / How to think straight when everything's so twisted?"[19] Inquisitiveness, ascertaining value and meaning, applying knowledge to create change, reflection and checking assumptions—these all demonstrate important strategies for liberation.

Importantly, Varl's thinking allows her to name truths about slavery, its deformations of humanity (for both the slaver and the slave), and its atrocities. In "Sweet Enough Ocean, Cotton," Varl turns her attention to the agricultural product that fuels the economic engine of slavery in the southern United States, cotton:

> I've been thinking about this.
> While I'm working, I think
> about this. My mind is the part of me
> that gets the least rest.
>
> It's never quiet;
> there's always the hum
> inside me, the hive free inside me
> makes me think about honey, dipping
> all my thoughts into honey
>
> and even the thoughts honey won't
> stick to have been in the honey,
> have been next to honey so the knowledge
> of honey is on them and the knowledge
> all by itself can be sweet enough.
>
> I think about that, think about how thinking
> Can be sweet enough
>
> for now. Thinking about, thinking about
> so much that is buried in the cotton.
>
> Few months after we planted it,
> I called the pink blooms of cotton before it ripened
> An assault of endless sunset on the ocean.[20]

In a continuous metaphoric parallel between the Middle Passage ocean and the ocean of cotton, this poem-chapter subverts the collective "assault" of slavery by tracing the powerful workings of an individual mind. Varl's thinking, enabled by the cocoon-like underdress embroidered with her writings, dominates the second half of the poem, achieving a sweet knowledge that names plantation slavery an "endless sunset." That knowledge, "for now," identifies an important truth "buried" in the pretty pink blooms of the cotton, one that Varl is then able to name. Moss thereby emphasizes the importance of analyzing and naming the systems of oppression that constrain the individual.

In addition to modeling through Varl the power of thinking within constraints, Moss crafts scenes in which Varl handles difficult situations by shifting power. As Moss comments in her online work, "Project Genealogy," "The fact that power shifts makes it difficult for any one person to wield it well or consistently."[21] Varl makes use of this. In extended chapters with both Lusa, the young daughter of her master, and Janet Ralls, the master's wife, Varl demonstrates how to reverse others' attempts at disempowerment. In one exchange, Lusa insists that Varl call her Miss Lusa, so Varl replies: "It would be better if you were gone / so that I could *miss* Lusa. You're always / around; I don't get a chance to miss Lusa."[22] Wordplay, humor, deflecting attention—Varl uses these effectively to shift power and refuse disempowerment. In an extended scene in "Lusa and the Mud Man," Lusa insists that Varl coat her with mud so she can have black skin. When Lusa makes it an order, Varl can no longer put her off. However, Varl employs several strategies to maintain a degree of agency and control, first walking away to think, then considering that "it might be good / for Lusa to wear a mud skin. She's not seeking / that good, but it might be good anyway" and ultimately deciding, "That's all right. I'm glad."[23] Never does Varl give up her agency or control in the situation. In a Pygmalion-like moment, Varl decides she is an artist, and Lusa, her sculpture brought to life. Varl then decides "to talk to my artwork," taking advantage of Lusa not being able to speak without getting mud in her mouth (which effectively silences her). Varl's storytelling aims to educate Lusa about slave conditions, telling her about the "muddy slave graves / over in Landry" where "the slave bodies weren't buried / deep enough."[24] When the "river flooded and the bodies started rising," justice was served, as "the darkest day in Landry" destroyed the town.[25] In this scene, Moss presents Varl as a model of how to claim an empowering role for oneself, speak up, and take advantage of teachable moments with the oppressor.

Aware that shifts in power can be unsafe, Moss includes attacking and defending in the list of "how to" strategies Varl models for readers. While Varl herself survives her situation, the story she tells of Clarie Lukton illustrates how one must sometimes attack in order to defend oneself. Clarie killed her master after years of sexual abuse and was found guilty and executed.[26] Clarie—whose name suggests clarity and light—models for Varl (and thus for readers) a tougher choice with harsher consequences. Moss depicts Varl's thoughts about Clarie as affirming agency, new perspective, and identity, all of which are represented as freeing Clarie despite her ultimate death. Varl thinks, "She did not die / Lukton's [her master's] way, the body alive / but nothing else," and repeats, "She did not die his way." Instead, she chose to refuse his assault and to kill him, asserting her agency over the situation. Varl wonders what "something allowed for her to refuse" continued sexual assault, deciding "the something must be how she saw things. / The day must have given her new eyes to see the new sun." The gift of a new perspective is imagined as "ropes of light," a "cocoon of light" that allows her to say no, and in that act she "found herself in emancipation." When "she saw a self in herself, she refused" sexual assault. Varl takes Clarie's story as an inspiring model of black female liberation, thinking, "I would do that, too, / I hope."[27]

Varl's self-emancipation in *Slave Moth* ultimately is achieved through many of the tactics she has employed throughout the narrative, including thinking and questioning, engaging in wordplay, shifting power, claiming agency, naming truths, and gaining new perspective, all of which provide instruction for readers. At the key turning point in the narrative, Varl realizes that she is free even while enslaved on the plantation, thinking, "Your freedom doesn't come to you / because of your location; you have to feel it inside / or you'd just be a slave in a free place. Lost."[28] In the scenes that follow, a series of power reversals occur that create a momentary space of freedom for everyone. After her mistress insists she wear a too-small dress of Lusa's, Varl discovers that "it won't succeed / in belittling me as Ralls Janet hoped. / The dress is small, / not me. In it, I seem even bigger."[29] Even better, Varl realizes that the stars embroidered on the shoulders by her mother are likely to make Lusa envious and want the dress back. Another reversal occurs with the master. Named at birth after the master's favorite horse (instead of Free, as her mother had planned), Varl has worked on her mental cocoon "extending Varl's definition to include *Free*"[30] to the point that, when at the end of the narrative the master decides to rename their town from Perrysburg (after his surname) to Varlton, it is clear that Varl has effected a major power reversal through the power of naming. While she still carries the name he gave her, it now includes Free as both a name and a condition, and is no longer connected in her mind or the public's with the horse. The town is now named after the slave, not the master.

The final poem-chapter, "A Day in Varlton," offers a fleeting and perhaps emergent space of freedom closely resembling the "expressions of freedom" Hartman focuses on in nineteenth-century slavery. She points out that sometimes the "utopian" acts are labeled as "fanciful" but are important because they gesture toward "unrealized freedom."[31] The scene does indeed seem utopian.[32] Varl watches "something becoming free / in Varlton," something "becoming free / however briefly." Small, freeing acts in everyday practices occur: "Sully stopped feeding the horses"; "Pearl ignored the chickens"; even the mistress "moved out of the way." Varl feels "most of everything was freed for a moment." Varlton is affirmed as her "home" and a "particularly welcoming" one. And the prospect of physical freedom—whether through the rebellion Varl learns Dob has been planning and collecting guns for or imaged through the luna moths who escape in their "flight out of Varlton"—is possible and imminent, although not yet realized. Such a "fanciful" resolution to the narrative thus celebrates with its readers achievable freedoms within constraints.

Slave Moth's liberatory model for contemporary readers, showing how to practice freedom within racism and sexism, implicitly draws running parallels between the historical period and the present—what Hartman calls "the tragic continuities in antebellum and postbellum constitutions of blackness"[33]—and foregrounds a common problem-to-be-solved of black female agency within restrictions shared among the protagonist, the author, and the readers. Mitchell's discussion of the liberatory narrative names Harriet Jacobs's *Incidents in the Life of a Slave Girl, Written by Herself* as the ur-narrative of black womanhood in US literature; the claim is particularly apt because of Jacobs's repeated scenes of constrained agency and problematized freedom. Choosing her own lover rather than submitting to her master, hiding in an attic for seven years, achieving legal freedom only through being bought by a white friend—in all of these circumstances, Jacobs provides a model of not-free freedom and thus a model of black female agency in the racist and sexist United States that over time has proven to transcend eras.

For Moss, in her creation of *Slave Moth*, being owned and thus legally not-free is the central and, indeed, only constraint she puts on Varl, her protagonist. In our interview, she explained: "The vileness of slavery wasn't the forfeiture of humanity by the enslaved; I contend that no humanity was lost. The vileness existed within the concept of ownership, the human treated as property. . . . Therefore, in *Slave Moth*, to demonstrate the insidiousness of the system of slavery did not require a setting of physical brutality; that Varl was owned was sufficient. I removed as many popular constructs of slavery as I could."[34] Such an artistic decision places the focus entirely on the idea of being not-free due to ownership. It works deliberately to undo popular and established understandings of slavery and freedom in the United States. As the blurb on the back of *Slave Moth* explains, "*Slave Moth* is a fresh look at slavery and freedom."

By removing as many "popular constructs of slavery" as possible and instead focusing on a highly paradoxical not-free freedom, Moss as a contemporary black female artist participates in the post-black project of replacing familiar tropes and civic myths with complex truths. This suggests that we consider *Slave Moth* as more than simply a model for readers. Salamishah Tillet argues in her *Sites of Slavery: Citizenship and Racial Democracy in the Post–Civil Rights Imagination* that many contemporary black artists and writers have returned to what she terms "sites of slavery" in the antebellum period to make claims "about how best to remember American democracy and to construct national identity." As she explains, "Following [Toni] Morrison's sites of memory, I argue that post–civil rights African American writers and artists claim and reconstruct pivotal figures, events, memories, locations, and experiences from American slavery in order to provide interiority and agency for enslaved African Americans and write them into the national narrative."[35]

Through this lens, it becomes apparent that Moss's depiction of Varl as an agentive citizen of Varlton despite remaining enslaved on the plantation signals *Slave Moth* as an intervention in the national narrative of slavery. Moss enacts what Tillet would term a "critical patriotism," a stance that allows her to appropriate founding narratives as a model citizen engaging "the metadiscourse of American democracy." Importantly, Tillet contends that contemporary artists and writers refuse to separate slavery from the story of American democracy, representing instead the founding coupling of freedom and slavery as "ironic and constitutive" and the "mnemonic property of the entire nation, . . . not the exclusive property of blacks."[36] In particular, Tillet seeks to theorize how post–civil rights artists "reimagine black women as a source of critical patriotism and model citizenship." Their "peculiar citizenships" move "between slavery and subversion," Tillet claims, stretching "the black radical tradition into the present, while modelling challenges to ongoing forms of racial retrenchment and imagining an unfinished revolution."[37]

To fully understand Moss's critical patriotism and model citizenship, her needs as an artist, her black radicalism, and her full contribution as a contemporary artist and writer, we need to move beyond the boundaries of her written text, *Slave Moth*. *Slave Moth* was produced at a key time of artistic transition for Moss. As I mentioned earlier, Baker both begins and ends his essay on Moss by suggesting that her 2006 book "*Tokyo Butter* may turn out to be . . . [Moss's] farewell to the traditional printed page or book."[38] I would argue that this process of moving beyond the book—becoming postbook—already was significantly underway for Moss during the time she was creating *Slave Moth*, 2002–4. In our interview, Moss revealed that her work had become unmarketable due to her "artistic growth in multiple directions

MALIN PEREIRA

and on multiple scales." She identified plans "to do further work on poetry as sculpture . . . [through] *Bubbling* poams [which] will also exist as a huge quilt."[39] Moss's emerging theory, Limited Fork Poetics, including her redefinition of the poem as a "poam"—her acronym for "product of the act of making"—and her artistic identity as "forkergirl," expresses her move beyond the printed page to a boundaryless artistry.

Moss, long known for dramatic performance of her poetry with music, at this time began to produce performance artifacts in multiple media. The relevant "products of the act of making" that Moss produced before, during, and after her composition of the book *Slave Moth* take a variety of representational forms, including public dissent; written, oral, and musical performance of a "movie poam"; an author interview; and repurposing of a collectible object through sewing and photography. While these may seem an odd array of material to claim as art, as Uri McMillan points out in *Embodied Avatars: Genealogies of Black Feminist Art and Performance*, "performances are indeed captured and stored, albeit in unusual ways."[40] It is important to treat these artifacts not as accessories to the printed book or incidental contextual material, I contend, but rather as fully artistic products that demand to be understood as forming, together with the text of *Slave Moth*, an entire work of performance art.[41]

In this larger work of performance art, Moss reimagines blackness, poetry, and herself as an artist. In our interview, she explicitly ties her need to expand beyond boundaries as an artist to "definitions of *Blackness* that deprived me of the complex structure of identity." She explains, "If I am capable of an endeavor, then that endeavor evidently falls within what is possible within a definition of Blackness, or I couldn't execute that endeavor. So I redefine Blackness, redefine it, reconfigure it, as it must be able to embrace anything I do, anything I think, anything I imagine."[42] Just as Moss felt the need to reconfigure blackness, so too did she feel the need to reconfigure artistry. Her faculty appointment as professor of art and design in addition to her appointment in English at the University of Michigan recognized her branching out beyond print poems to create in other media. The artifacts produced in conjunction with the text of *Slave Moth* recommend recasting Moss as not just a poet who has written a contemporary liberatory narrative but also a black female performance artist producing multiple layers of performance to consider with her "text" as part of the "work of art." Consideration of these artifacts and Moss's artistry beyond the printed page have not been discussed in scholarship on Moss's work.

One difficulty for scholars interested in apprehending and experiencing these artifacts in order to study the larger work of performance art created by Moss is indeed the unusual ways the work has been captured and stored, such that almost none of the artifacts are represented in the book *Slave Moth*. Moss complains in our interview about publishers' unwillingness to work beyond the traditional print text; their limits created a very narrow version of her intended work. Only the dress Moss sewed (at night, by candlelight)[43] to represent the one created by Varl in the text is reproduced on the book's cover. All the other artifacts I have identified are stored apart from the text: in other print sources, online on her website, in her personal possession, or in photographs she has shared via personal email. That they have not been collected together as a total work demonstrates the difficulties of capturing a polytemporal, polymedia, multiartifact work of performance art.

I have two goals for the remainder of this essay. First, I intend to identify, describe, and document the larger body of material that constitutes this work of performance art so that other scholars can consider these when discussing Moss and her work. To distinguish this reconceptualized work of performance art from the bound print text of *Slave Moth*, I will call it *Slave Moth, Unbound*. Second, I want to show how the performance artifacts constituting *Slave Moth, Unbound* allow us to see the full enactment of Moss's critical patriotism performing multiple interventions in the national narrative of slavery. This performance art positions Moss in the company of other black feminist performance artists whose work Uri McMillan discusses. As McMillan explains, female performance art is a time-based medium in which the artist typically uses the body as an object to subvert norms and explore social issues.[44] Most strikingly, McMillan finds that these artists employ both embodied and disembodied avatars of black female subjectivity. In other words, in their performance art they use their own bodies, others' bodies, and object bodies as avatars to explore the range of black female subjectivity. Moss's *Slave Moth, Unbound* enacts several features McMillan finds common to black feminist performance art, including a challenge to foundational and fetishized notions of truth about slavery, disruption of presumptive knowledge of black subjectivity, and a reimagining of black female objecthood as a strategy toward agency.[45] *Slave Moth, Unbound* thus subverts normative understandings of slavery and freedom from an agentive black female perspective as part of an ongoing intervention in contemporary discourse about slavery. It also frees Moss from poetry.

An important place to begin looking at this work of performance art is the event that prompted Moss to write *Slave Moth*, the dissent she voiced at her son's school in response to African American parent complaints about a class genealogy assignment. Two artifacts have been produced to reperform this moment by Moss, one in a movie poam, "Project Genealogy," available online, and another in her interview with me. Moss's written text online framing "Project Genealogy" sums up the situation: During a meeting at her son's school, "some parents wanted to ban a required ninth-grade ancestry assignment that [they felt] was embarrassing, humiliating, and demeaning for disclosing that their sons could trace their ancestry no further than slavery." Moss writes that she "realized the need for other models of slavery" and wrote *Slave Moth*.[46] This description confirms that, indeed, Moss conceived *Slave Moth* to provide another model of slavery. "Project Genealogy," however, allows yet another frame for slavery, one probably not possible in the print text, *Slave Moth*, due to its focus on reimagining the slave narrative. "Project Genealogy" instead takes the broad view that we are all descended from stardust. Moss describes how the scene at the school ended: "I commented that [my son] Ansted had traced his ancestry all the way back to the big bang, and considered himself a descendant of stardust." This universe frame forms the main theme of the approximately seven-minute soundtrack of "Project Genealogy," enacted through echoing space music and vocals moving from the spoken words "slavery" and "heavy genealogy" to "stardust" and "breathe." Moss incorporates elements of a poem her son, Ansted Moss, wrote, called "Ancestry Poem": "We all came from a single cell a vast time ago specks coming to life in the oceans of the planets and in space everyone of us evolved from star dust into the form we take on now looking at space through telescopes at the next generation of star dust that will breathe." Ansted also composed the soundtrack, making "Project Genealogy" a collaborative performance. A trace of the universe theme from "Project Genealogy" is discernible in the text of *Slave Moth* in the stars embroidered on the shoulders of the too-tight dress Varl is made to wear near the end of the narrative.[47] Placed with the text *Slave Moth* as part of a larger work, "Project Genealogy" broadens the frame Moss intends for her revision of the "heavy genealogy" of slavery to the universe.

The second artifact performing the scene of Moss's dissent is our interview, in which Moss describes in much greater detail the position of the parents and her response.[48] She adds information, such as the fact that student population at the school was 98 percent white, as was the head of school, and elaborates on her pride in being the descendent of survivors, her awareness of its "powerful legacy." Echoing her big bang theory in "Project Genealogy," Moss argues in the interview that her heritage, like anyone's, has been here "from the beginning of humanity." Insisting on the humanity in enslavement is thus a key element of her critical patriot project. Moss reveals that she was embarrassed by the parents' "vision of humanity that was way too narrow, way too constricting for the mind to inflate, unfold, blossom, expand." She was embarrassed by "the embarrassment of these parents." The "failure to imagine history beyond certain popular constructs" concerned Moss. While she agrees there is "accuracy to prevailing notions of slavery in the general black community," she was disappointed to see that "the model of inarticulate uneducated slaves brutalized and physically victimized by affluent white owners was so fixed [in the parents' minds] as the only possible fact of slave experience that no imagination could assist them in visualizing a range of human experience within the slave experience. They accepted the inhuman status of the slave." Moss seeks to disrupt this presumptive knowledge of black subjectivity in national narratives of the slave experience.

The interview version of Moss's dissent from the parents' popular construct of slavery presents a more staged performance than that in "Project Genealogy," one more focused on Moss as an avatar. Moss's "I spoke" moment enlarges:

> So I spoke, and informed the parents, teachers, and administrators present that my son, new to the school as a sixth-grader, had been given an ancestry assignment that he had no trouble completing. He was not embarrassed by history, I told them. If my son is put in a box, I said, he would enjoy discovering ways to get out of the box or to transform the box; he would invent windows, doors; he would raise the ceiling, explode the roof. My slave ancestors survived long enough to produce the generation that ultimately produced my generation, my son's generation. I then added, before I left the room, that my son had no problem with slavery being in his past; he traced his ancestry *all* the way back, I said, *to the big bang!*[49]

Moss underscores the declarative, performative element by repeating phrases that mark this as a spoken act to an audience: "I spoke," "I told them," "I said," "I added," "I said." This is more emphatic and performative than her "I commented" in "Project Genealogy." Note, too, the italics for emphasis, to give a sense of rising inflection, and the use of an exclamation point for dramatic effect. In this performance, Moss's avatar moves to take advantage of a teachable moment to head off what Moss calls the "pathological resolution" of banning the assignment.

Whether or not this is how it happened at the meeting is not the point; what matters is that, in the four or five years since the event and its initial depiction in "Project Genealogy," Moss has reimagined and reproduced this moment as a staged intervention in the national discourse of slavery, disrupting foundational notions of truth about slavery. High school genealogy assignments are ubiquitous across the United States (I remember completing one myself), and certainly schools are one of the key sites in which civic myths get reproduced for consumption by another generation of citizens. As depicted in our interview, Moss's staged dissent from civic myths of slavery enacts her critical patriotism and presents an avatar of herself as a model citizen declaiming at a majority-white school that African American students, too, can complete an ancestry assignment despite tracing their roots back to and through slavery. Moss's performance thus insists upon black citizenship both in the United States and in the universe.

Another important artifact in the performance artwork *Slave Moth, Unbound* is the dress Moss sewed by hand and modeled on an American Girl doll she had custom made.[50] The three photographs taken by Moss—one of the dress alone and two of the dress on the doll—are shown in figures 8.1, 8.2, and 8.3. Moss's creation of a doll-size version of the dress the character Varl embroiders to wear as part of her protective chrysalis not only reenacts Varl's identity-formation process and self-shielding, but also suggests that Moss as an artist is undergoing a similar identity metamorphosis. Moth and Moss are homophones, after all. From this perspective, *Slave Moth, Unbound* functions on one level as Moss's own chrysalis, which she stitches with words, sewing, and performance, through which she transforms herself into a flying moth—her "forkergirl"—a black female performance artist postprint.

Moss speaks of the importance of the everyday practice of sewing in our interview, connecting it to poetry as sculpture, with an emphasis on the slow process and the realization of self:

> Varl's courage comes from the reinforcement of that identity that penetrates cloth, that is locked into cloth with her stitches. This is a slow and deliberate form of making text; there is much effort required beyond the mechanics of knowing how to write. Stitched words are thread sculptures. The words are raised on the cloth just as healed scars are raised on the skin. There is ceremony implied here, transition from childhood to adulthood, which is also the accepting of the responsibility of an identity. With that proof, although she is still legally owned, she is not mentally or emotionally owned.[51]

Moss's focus here on the ceremony of the stitching underscores her own stitching and modeling of the Varl dress as performance art. Moss felt it so important to replicate the stitching act exactly as Varl would have done it that she sewed the dress at night, in the dark, by candlelight, as Varl would

all of my name Varl
fits into larva,

into what undergoes
complete metamorphosis.

Lots of small things enlarge
in opportunity to. Actias luna
moths fly like green angels
of the insects. I want
to blossom to prove the wide
world inside.

My master is a collector.
Rare things delight him;
Deformity piques in him
an unwholesome joy.

8.1   Photo of Varl dress, hand-sewn by Thylias Moss. Photograph
by Thylias Moss. Courtesy of Thylias Moss.

have had to do.[52] Moss sought to make the text of *Slave Moth* as close as
possible to enacting the performance of stitching, insisting on a font for the
poem-chapters that would replicate embroidery, but the publisher refused.[53]
The only representation, then, of the stitching act in the print text *Slave Moth*
is Moss's photograph of the handmade dress (figure 8.1), also represented on
the cover of the book, representing an everyday practice that gestures toward
an (as yet) unrealized freedom.

Beyond her photograph of the dress on the cover, Moss's modeling of the
dress on the American Girl doll and photographing of the doll produces
another performance, one that repurposes an iconic collectible object—an
American Girl doll—into another avatar of black female subjectivity. This

move aligns with McMillan's understanding of how black feminist performance artists reimagine black female objecthood as a strategy toward agency. It also enacts a critical patriotism that subverts the American Girl narrative for African Americans, and thereby dominant American narratives of slavery. McMillan argues that in black female performance art "objecthood provides a means for black subjects to become art objects"; for this, the artists employ "simulated beings" as avatars. This process McMillan terms "performing objecthood," rescripting "how black female bodies move and are perceived by others."[54]

Crucial to Moss's project in *Slave Moth, Unbound*, then, is not only her creation of the embroidered Varl dress but its modeling on a black doll body, a performance that enables a rescripting of black female enslavement. The dress is white, suggesting unsullied innocence and sexual purity; while pretty, it also appears to be sturdily made, not flimsy. Leaves and flowers embroidered next to the cursive words imply growth. Once the dress is on the body of a black female doll, these symbolic features adhere to the black female body and the avatar. In one of her photographs of the doll, Moss places in her hand a piece of cloth in an embroidery hoop, thereby having the avatar perform the act of stitching so important to the identity formation process. In both photographs (figures 8.2 and 8.3) I have seen of the dressed doll, Moss places the embroidered dress—conceived of as a hidden undergarment in the text *Slave Moth*—over a long-sleeved country print dress. She also situates the dressed doll in a rustic farmlike setting of rough-hewn fencing and, in one photograph, grass. The Little House on the Prairie look of both the underdress and the setting place this avatar firmly within American visual discourse, thus making Moss's rescripting part of the national narrative. Moss's photographs draw upon what Hartman identifies as the "dominance of the pastoral in representing slavery," appropriating it, as Tillet would argue, to launch her critique.[55] Just as Varl in the text *Slave Moth* stays on the plantation because it is her home, so too does this Varl avatar look entirely at home and in possession of both herself and her place. Moving the undergarment to be a top layer is obviously necessary for it to be seen in the photographs, but it also symbolizes the unearthing of a previously silenced narrative of agency and black female subjectivity constructed in the face of oppression.

With an increasing number of black dolls available on the market, and thus a range of choices possible, Moss's artistic selection of a custom-made American Girl doll merits further scrutiny. Scholarship on American Girl dolls focuses on how girls use the dolls to create identity, and those identities are constructed in relation to what scholars have termed a romanticized version of American history and nationalism that is centered on whiteness

8.2. Photo of Varl doll in dress hand-sewn by Thylias Moss, seated and sewing. American Girl doll custom-made to specifications by Thylias Moss. Photograph by Thylias Moss. Courtesy of Thylias Moss.

as the norm.[56] Each of the dolls has a story—both of herself and of her time—and the only African American doll from the antebellum period in the collection, Addy Walker, is no exception. Addy's story is, predictably, one of slavery and freedom: she escapes to the North.[57] Tillet's theory of sites of slavery helps us think about the American Girl doll Addy as a site of slavery that repeats dominant tropes about slavery. Moss's swerve around the readily available Addy doll by instead ordering a custom-made doll for the dress and the photographs reimagines these tropes through an avatar of Varl, who, rather than physically escaping, remains enslaved and stitches her thoughts on her clothes to create an interior identity that is free. Important to Moss, too, was that the doll be multiracial in appearance and origins, like Moss herself, "as mixed as many slaves were."[58] This artistic choice of a customized American Girl doll replaces the dominant, single story of blackness and slavery represented in the American Girl Addy Walker narrative with more complex truths about slavery, thus providing an alternative model that intervenes in national narratives about slavery, girlhood, and blackness.

MALIN PEREIRA

all of my name Varl
fits into larva ,

into what undergoes
complete metamophosis.

Lots of small things enlarge
in opportunity to. Actias luna
mothe fly like green angels
of the insects. I want
to blossom to prove the wide
world inside.

My master is a collector
Rare things delight him ;
Deformity piques in him
an unwholesome joy.

8.3   Photo of Varl doll in dress hand-sewn by Thylias Moss, standing
in grass by fence. American Girl doll custom-made to specifications by
Thylias Moss. Photograph by Thylias Moss. Courtesy of Thylias Moss.

How is such an alternative model of slavery received? Can one effectively disrupt popular constructs of slavery? Can *Slave Moth* or the performance work I have identified here as *Slave Moth, Unbound* change anyone's conception of slavery? The answers should matter for post-black artists. Reception of Moss's *Slave Moth* (the text, the dress, and the doll) and scholars' representation of it at a public conversation illustrate the difficulties of and limits on Moss's intervention in the national narrative of slavery and democracy as a model citizen enacting a critical patriotism. In 2012, my colleague in the English and Africana Studies departments at University of North Carolina Charlotte, Janaka Lewis, and I gave a presentation on representations of slavery in African American literature at the Harvey B. Gantt African American Cultural Center in Charlotte, for Black History Month. The audience was mostly African American and either middle-aged or retired, with just a smattering of younger people; Janaka is African American, and I am white. Janaka presented on the nineteenth-century writer Elizabeth Keckley, who worked as a seamstress for a time for First Lady Mary Todd Lincoln, and I presented on *Slave Moth*, explaining how in it Moss revises dominant tropes in the slave narrative tradition. I also showed a picture of the dress and the Varl doll. What followed in the discussion afterward confirms McMillian's emphasis in his book on "critical moments where black performance art, objecthood, and avatars meet challenges from foundational (and often fetishized) notions of 'truth' and accuracy that are thought to reside in more typical forms of evidence."[59] In an interesting redux of the point of origin of *Slave Moth*, I came right up against the same inability "to imagine history beyond certain constructs, constructs that might indeed be valid," as Moss describes the parents at her son's school.[60]

During the Q&A following our presentations, one older gentleman waited patiently while some of the younger audience members asked us questions about Keckley and Moss and seemed excited to learn about them and their work. When he finally spoke, he was very measured and respectful but also clearly unhappy about Moss's depiction of slavery. He was concerned, he said, to hear that a contemporary writer would be so unthinking as to make slavery seem survivable or even a situation in which one could form an identity. He very carefully schooled me in the history of slavery and its horrors. He wanted to make sure that I knew, that I was not swayed by Moss's depiction of Varl, and he wanted to make sure the younger people in the audience also knew their history. He asked me what, really, was the value of Moss's depiction of Varl staying in slavery? What was the good in that? I tried to give him a good answer—that Moss definitely understood the horrors of slavery but wanted to open up additional possibilities, not to erase the history but to enlarge it. I assured him she was not an apologist for slavery or a sellout. He remained unconvinced. A couple of the other older members of the audience at that point began nodding their heads in agreement with him. It seemed that Moss's alternative model of slavery was not going down well with this audience.

I have thought many times about that moment and the concerns he raised. I have thought about the comforts and the dangers of a single story of slavery. I have thought about a better answer for him and that audience. This essay is in part an effort to give that gentleman a better answer, or at least a more convincing answer. Post-black artists need advocates for their interventions and reimaginings in order to be heard and considered and for dominant narratives about race to change. Moss aims to present a broader, more complex view of the possibilities for blackness not only in slavery but also in the continuing systems of oppression blacks experience today. *Slave Moth* and *Slave Moth, Unbound* are thus didactic works in the best of the African American literary tradition, works that teach us all to recognize black humanity and black citizenship, an ongoing pair of themes Phillis Wheatley brought into American public discourse so many years ago. Teach it forward.[61]

NOTES

1 Jay Winston, "The Trickster Metaphysics of Thylias Moss," in *Trickster Lives: Culture and Myth in American Fiction*, ed. Jeanne Campbell Reesman (Athens: University of Georgia Press, 2001), 145.

2 Thylias Moss, *Slave Moth: A Narrative in Verse* (New York: Persea Books, 2004).

3 Moss, *Slave Moth*, 99.

4 Peter Campion, "Review of *Slave Moth* by Thylias Moss," *Poetry*, November 2004, 137.

5 Milton L. Welch, "Review of *Slave Moth* by Thylias Moss," *Modern Language Studies* 35, no. 1 (Spring 2005): 106.

6 Alison Hawthorne Deming, "Walking on Rough Water: Review of *Slave Moth* by Thylias Moss," *Women's Review of Books* 21, nos. 10–11 (July 2004).

7 Evie Shockley, "Portrait of the Artist as a Young Slave: Visual Artistry as Agency in the Contemporary Narrative of Slavery," in *Contemporary African American Literature: The Living Canon*, ed. Lovalerie King and Shirley Moody-Turner (Bloomington: Indiana University Press, 2013), 139.

8 Shockley, "Portrait of the Artist as a Young Slave," 146.

9 Angelyn Mitchell, *The Freedom to Remember: Narrative, Slavery and Gender in Contemporary Black Women's Fiction* (New Brunswick, NJ: Rutgers University Press, 2002), 4–5.

10 Mitchell, *The Freedom to Remember*, 16.

11 Robert Baker, "The Sprawling Genius of Thylias Moss," *Religion and Literature* 47, no. 3 (Autumn 2015): 99–118.

12 Baker, "Sprawling Genius," 116.

13 Mitchell, *The Freedom to Remember*, 16.

14 Moss, *Slave Moth*, 149.

15 Saidiya V. Hartman, *Scenes of Subjection: Terror, Slavery, and Self-Making in Nineteenth-Century America* (New York: Oxford University Press, 1997), 13.

16 Hartman, *Scenes of Subjection*, 11.

17 Hartman, *Scenes of Subjection*, 13.

18 Moss, *Slave Moth*, 5.

19 Moss, *Slave Moth*, 14.

20 Moss, *Slave Moth*, 41.

21 Thylias Moss, "Project Genealogy: Why I Wrote *Slave Moth*," accessed May 9, 2018, https://player.fm/series/limited-fork/project-genealogy-why-i-wrote -slave-moth.

22 Moss, *Slave Moth*, 43.

23 Moss, *Slave Moth*, 47–48.

24 Moss, *Slave Moth*, 50.

25 Moss, *Slave Moth*, 51.

26 Moss, *Slave Moth*, 69–75.

27 Moss, *Slave Moth*, 74–75.

28 Moss, *Slave Moth*, 119.

29 Moss, *Slave Moth*, 148.

30 Moss, *Slave Moth*, 119.

31 Hartman, *Scenes of Subjection*, 13–14.

32 Moss, *Slave Moth*, 150–52.

33 Hartman, *Scenes of Subjection*, 7.

34 Malin Pereira, "Thylias Moss" (interview), in *Into a Light Both Brilliant and Unseen: Conversations with Contemporary Black Poets* (Athens: University of Georgia Press, 2010), 143.

35 Salamishah Tillet, *Sites of Slavery: Citizenship and Racial Democracy in the Post–Civil Rights Imagination* (Durham: Duke University Press, 2012), 5.

36 Tillet, *Sites of Slavery*, 11.

37 Tillet, *Sites of Slavery*, 15–17.

38 Baker, "Sprawling Genius," 101.

39 Malin Pereira, "Thylias Moss," 144–45.

40 Uri McMillan, *Embodied Avatars: Genealogies of Black Feminist Art and Performance* (New York: New York University Press, 2015), 15.

41 In an email exchange with me about this essay after it was written, Moss's response to my statement that the artifacts and *Slave Moth* together constitute performance art was "thank you so very much; it was always performance art, indeed Malin." Thylias Moss, email to the author, June 30, 2018.

42 Malin Pereira, "Thylias Moss," 137.

43 Moss, email to the author, July 26, 2018.

44 McMillan, *Embodied Avatars*, 5–6.

45 McMillan, *Embodied Avatars*, 7–9.

46 Moss, "Project Genealogy."

47 Moss, *Slave Moth*, 148.

48 Malin Pereira, "Thylias Moss," 140–44.

49 Malin Pereira, "Thylias Moss," 142. Italics in the original.

50 Moss, emails to the author, July 27 and July 30, 2018.

51 Malin Pereira, "Thylias Moss," 144.

52 Moss, email to the author, July 26, 2018.

53 Moss, email to the author, July 29, 2018.

54 McMillan, *Embodied Avatars*, 7.

55 Hartman, *Scenes of Subjection*, 11.

56 Carolina Acosta-Alzuru and Peggy J. Kreshel, "'I'm an American Girl . . . Whatever That Means': Girls Consuming Pleasant Company's American Girl Identity," *Journal of Communication* 52, no. 1 (2002): 147; Elizabeth Marshall, "Consuming Girlhood: Young Women, Femininities, and American Girl," *Girlhood Studies* 2, no. 1 (Summer 2009): 95–96.

57 Ian Elliot, "Connie Porter: Telling It the Way It Was," *Teaching Pre K–8* 25, no. 2 (October 1994): 42.

58 Moss, emails to the author, July 27 and July 30, 2018.

59 McMillan, *Embodied Avatars*, 14.

60 Malin Pereira, "Thylias Moss," 142.

61 I wish to express my appreciation to two colleagues in English and Africana Studies at University of North Carolina at Charlotte, Jeffrey Leak and Janaka Bowman Lewis, whose support for this project moved it forward and whose suggestions made it better, and to Thylias Moss, self-styled "Maker," recipient of both MacArthur and Guggenheim fellowships and winner of five Pushcart Prizes. She has recently completed "Shawsheen Memorial Broom Society," a collection of poetry, with several collaborators.

CHAPTER NINE

PLANTATION MEMORIES

Cheryl Dunye's Representation of a Representation
of American Slavery in The Watermelon Woman

BERTRAM D. ASHE

EXACTLY THREE MINUTES AND FORTY-FOUR SECONDS INTO CHERYL Dunye's 1996 film *The Watermelon Woman*, the camera slowly pans left to gradually display a cluttered apartment-cum-studio. A coffee-table book titled *Philadelphia* lies on its side, and above, below, and beside it are stacks of newspaper, books, videotapes, manuscripts, markers—even a Gumby-like yellow toy. Eventually the camera dips slightly to reveal a VHS box lying in front of a tape dispenser. The VHS film is labeled *Plantation Memories*, but the camera doesn't linger; its persistent pan continues before stopping to focus on an empty chair. Since it's so early in the film, there's no clear indication that the *Plantation Memories* film box has any more importance to *The Watermelon Woman* than the tape, the coffee-table book—or Gumby. What viewers will soon discover, however, is that *Plantation Memories* will, indeed, mark a length-of-the-film running critique on the portrayal of American slavery in American film.

The setup for Dunye's commentary begins when, moments after the camera settles on that empty chair, a young black woman wearing an extremely short afro and smallish hoop earrings pops into the frame, sits in the chair, picks up a lavalier mic, and clips it to the collar of her long-sleeved white T-shirt. Her head and torso are perfectly framed as she briefly smiles pleasantly into the camera and then earnestly says, "Hi. I'm Cheryl, and I'm a filmmaker. . . . Nah, I'm not really a filmmaker, but I have a videotaping business with my friend Tamara and I work at a video store, so I'm *working* on being a filmmaker. The problem is that I don't know what I want to make a film *on*. I know it has to be about black women because our stories have never been told."[1]

On first viewing, of course, *The Watermelon Woman* unspools in dynamic real time, and I watched, as I would watch any other film, to see what would happen next. After multiple viewings, though, I couldn't help but recognize the precision and clearly rehearsed fluidity of that early scene. Cheryl's motions appear to occur spontaneously but upon closer scrutiny are obviously carefully imagined and blocked beforehand. There is an obviousness, an intentionality to the action. In much the same way, a generation earlier, Shirley Clarke films like *The Connection* (1961) and *Portrait of Jason* (1967) pointedly incorporated camera movement and focusing-while-filming to signal that the camera was an active part of the filming process rather than a passive recorder of events. Dunye, in character as Cheryl, literally moves the camera on-screen, sits down in front of it, jumps up and out of the picture frame moments later to stand behind it and pan to a monitor, pushes in to focus on the monitor, and so on. Perhaps most noteworthy is the way she allows the black cord of her lavalier mic to dangle, left of center, in front of her white tee as a constant reminder, for those who notice, of the fluid artifice she is insisting on portraying as the film rolls. And so this introductory scene does two things at once: first, perhaps without realizing it, viewers are presented with something that seems fluid and real but is actually a carefully constructed reality, one that persists, in one way or another, throughout the film. Secondly, and importantly, given the film's extended examination of mediated slavery, viewers are introduced to Dunye's relationship to history. Cheryl's key contention, which she shares in that early scene, is that "black women['s] . . . stories have never been told." That assertion animates the plot, archival intent, and faux-documentary style of *The Watermelon Woman*. So much so that, very late in the film, during the closing credits, shortly after "Written and Directed by Cheryl Dunye" appears, the following words emerge, alone and centered on-screen:

> Sometimes you have to create your own history.
> The Watermelon Woman is fiction.
>   Cheryl Dunye, 1996

Dunye's *The Watermelon Woman* recalls Trey Ellis's 1989 comments about what is now referred to as post-blackness.[2] The school "is not an apolitical, art-for-art's-sake fantasy," Ellis asserts. "What most all the New Black Artists have in common is what Columbia University philosopher Arthur Danto calls 'Disturbatory Art'—art that shakes you up." Ellis insists that with post-black art, "you won't find many Spartan tales of suburban ennui or technicolor portraits of Fred and Barney."[3] Indeed, each of the three points on the post-black matrix I devised for my own "Theorizing the Post-Soul Aesthetic: An Introduction"—the cultural mulatto archetype, "blaxploration," and the use of what I call allusion-disruption gestures (moments in texts where figures, concepts or tropes are specifically alluded to and then disrupted)—figure prominently, in various ways, in *The Watermelon Woman*.[4] The sense of formal play, the construction of a queer black world—and within that world the wide, sometimes warring, variety of black personae and perspectives that Dunye displays—all, in total, suggest a post-black sensibility. This testy exchange, for example, features a traditional black perspective versus that of a cultural mulatto, as two lead characters converse on a back porch:

TAMARA: All I see is that—once again—you're going out with a white girl acting like she wanna be black, and you being a black girl acting like she wanna be white! I mean, what's up with you, Cheryl? You don't like the color of your skin nowadays?

CHERYL: Tamara, I'm black. I mean, who's to say that dating somebody white doesn't make me black? I mean, who's to say anything about who I fuck in the goddamn first place, okay?

Dunye's insistence on building such intrablack tensions into her film—a film, mind, comprised almost totally of lesbians—executes blaxploration on multiple levels: gendered expectations, traditional racialized dating patterns, black cultural expectations, and black "freedom" of sexual expression, all wrapped up in the ongoing struggle for identity between these two characters, a struggle echoed with other characters throughout the film: *The Watermelon Woman* clearly rests firmly within the school of post-blackness. The most prevalent nod to post-blackness, however, is Dunye's use of a series of key allusion-disruption gestures that collapse time and pointedly link the late twentieth century with American slavery—perhaps the most important level of historical engagement in *The Watermelon Woman*.

During the above introductory scene, the clip in which Cheryl excitedly leaps out of her seat to play for the camera is a scene from *Plantation Memories* that features Elsie, an enslaved woman, and her brief conversation with her mistress, Missy Barbara. The post-black gestures that inform *The Watermelon Woman* begin as early as Cheryl's sit-down in front of her camera, when Cheryl utters a sentence that I have been unable to match anywhere else in recorded American culture—it's entirely possible this is the first and thus far only time this sentence has ever been captured on film, in literature, or in American popular culture: "I saw the most beautiful black mammy." Cheryl made the observation about the character Elsie, played by actress Fae Richards, otherwise known as the Watermelon Woman, in a fictive 1937 film called *Plantation Memories*. Using the words "most beautiful" in front of "black mammy" destabilizes, by itself, common American historical expectation. It's one of several ways Cheryl Dunye undermines common beliefs about antebellum black womanhood. As Matt Richardson suggests in "Our Stories Have Never Been Told: Preliminary Thoughts on Black Lesbian Cultural Production as Historiography in *The Watermelon Woman*," "Dunye challenges the historical renderings of the 'mammy' figure as asexual, calling attention to the underlying sexual tensions between the white mistress and black female slaves. In *Plantation Memories* the sexual tensions between the mistress and the female slave are masked and mediated through the heterosexual romance plot."[5]

Dunye, in *The Watermelon Woman*, has deftly managed to use that core fictive clip from *Plantation Memories* to explore and examine the tension between "mistress" and "female slave" at various stages in the film. In a key moment, sometime after establishing the importance of the clip, Cheryl impersonates Elsie, the mammy in *Plantation Memories*. In addition, a tense scene that occurs late in the film mirrors the power dynamics from the *Plantation Memories* exchange. As a result, what appears to be merely an early, momentary clip in Dunye's film actually becomes three interrelated allusion-disruption gestures, each having to do with the relationship between a white female authority figure and a black female subordinate. Importantly, these vaguely similar, somewhat-connected scenes occur whether the power relationship takes place in a fictional film clip, or in Cheryl's imagination, or in a Rittenhouse Square living room; the scenes take place during slavery and after slavery, during both the mid-nineteenth and late-twentieth centuries.

There is, of course, no documentary footage of whites and enslaved blacks; motion pictures, as we know them today, did not exist during the antebellum era. That reality means, though, that whatever we see on-screen—and whatever imagery we hold in our heads as "authentic" or "legitimate" scenes of enslavement—stems either from our imaginations or from previously viewed recreations of American slavery. Part of why the carefully careless staging of Cheryl's introductory face time three-plus minutes into the film is so important is because it establishes and reinforces the representational aspect of images of American slavery: Cheryl literally holds up that VHS tape box of

Plantation Memories for her viewers to see. The film doesn't exist in our reality, but it is very real inside the reality of Dunye's faux documentary. Cheryl projects authority as she plays specific on-screen roles during the scene—we're watching her direct herself, right there on-screen. And the direction is tight; the picture is crisply framed, the camera movement is seamless and smooth: it pans, pushes in, pulls back, focuses, all while we intently watch. Most films don't want you to notice camera movement; they just want you to sense the effects of it. Not Dunye—we're inside the direction, here, in some fundamental ways.

And when we view that highlighted scene from *Plantation Memories*, we're actually and actively looking at the clip *through Cheryl's point of view*. It's actually not a clip, really, so much as an on-screen moment that features the *presentation* of a clip—and we're meant to see it that way. There are visual cues suggesting that if viewers weren't meant to notice the clip *as* a "presented" clip, then Dunye would have seamlessly spliced the clip into the film the same way she did the many, many other scenes of archival footage—and fake archival footage—placed on-screen throughout the rest of the film. Countless films have done that: wiped or faded into the scene from another film in ways that conform to established film grammar, and hence don't attract attention to themselves *as clips*. In fact, *The Watermelon Woman* itself frames Cheryl's introduction at 3:44 with a cinematic gesture that has the film expertly fold in on itself as it fades to black. Similarly, at 6:28, when the introduction ends, Dunye's skillful edit freezes Cheryl's image and toggles it left, into black, and then, as the music swells, the brief, watermelon-colored pink-slash-green opening title sequence fills the screen.

In addition, the sound—the dialogue viewers hear while watching a screen during which the clip is being played—clearly emerges from the speakers on the monitor through the lavalier mic Cheryl wears clipped to her collar. Room sound is noticeable; the air in between the monitor's speakers and the lavalier is obvious. No competent sound designer would ever tolerate such grungy sound unless we were specifically meant to experience diegetic monitor sound rather than the clean, nondiegetic soundtrack we would otherwise hear. Indeed, the *frame* of the monitor stays around the edge of the film after Cheryl gets behind the camera and pushes into the monitor's screen, as if to remind us that we're not really watching a scene from *Plantation Memories*— we're watching a monitor that has a scene from *Plantation Memories* playing on it. This key introductory clip, then, is designed not only to present a scene of American slavery, but to do so while pointing to the fact that *Plantation Memories* was not a presentation of slavery but rather a 1937 *representation* of slavery.

Our viewing position, relative to both the screen and the screen-on-the-screen, implicates us, the viewers, and insists that we view, or attempt to view, this clip through, if not Cheryl's eyes, Cheryl's *reality*. On that screen is "the most beautiful black mammy": the character's name is Elsie, the film is *Plantation Memories*, the actress's professional name is the Watermelon Woman, the Watermelon Woman's actual name is Fae Richards, and Fae Richards's birth name is Faith Richardson. The layered identities attendant to this clip ripple out in concentric circles, over time and history: *Plantation Memories* features a white female slave owner and a black mammy. *Plantation Memories* was directed by Martha Page, a white woman who was in a relationship with Fae Richards at the time of filming. As on-screen filmmaker/historian Cheryl is discovering and uncovering this cinematic on-screen-and-behind-the-camera history, *she* is similarly involved with a white woman named Diana. The pairings of Martha Page and Fae Richards and Cheryl and Diana are obvious, and they are directly commented upon during the film. ("Diana just threw me for a loop," Cheryl says after the first time they had sex. "I mean, she's not my type, but I liked it. I don't know what to say next—maybe it all has to do with this film project which is, finally, coming together: Hollywood, The Watermelon Woman, Fae Richards and . . . Diana?") Less obvious but still significant was Dunye's expansive comment on the power dynamics of American slavery—and the representation of American slavery through Elsie's relationship with her mistress.

And yet one of the ways the film complicates Dunye's assertion is by the reactions of other black female characters in the film and, indeed, Fae Richards's own feelings about representing slavery. When yet another collection of 1930s films arrives at the video store where Cheryl and Tamara work, Tamara scoffs, vocalizing exactly the feelings of many African Americans about excavating the past: "I can't believe you're wasting the tape scam to order *them*. I can barely stand the stuff that Hollywood puts out now, let alone that nigga-mammy shit from the Thirties." And there's also this, from a letter to Cheryl from the woman who took care of Fae Richards in her last years: "I think it troubled her soul for the world to see her in those 'mammy' pictures." It seems clear, then, that Dunye is not just concerned with telling black women's stories; she's also concerned with the task of complicating those stories (and complicating the way those stories are filmically rendered—and apprehended).

The clip itself is remarkable for how utterly unremarkable it is. Missy Barbara, mistress of the plantation, is distraught, worried about whether her husband, Master Charles, will return, presumably from the Civil War. Her faithful enslaved woman reassures her that he will, indeed, return. End of clip. What's interesting about the clip and its placement in *The Watermelon Woman* is that undoubtedly, if *Plantation Memories* had actually existed, the film would have focused intently on the travails of Missy Barbara, the same way plantation-era films like *Gone with the Wind* focus on characters like Scarlett O'Hara. Dunye, however, alludes to traditional American representations of American slavery, and then—by focusing our attention completely on Elsie—disrupts the representation, undermining and critiquing traditional filmic racial hierarchy.

Dunye could have left it there, but she signifies on that clip nearly a half-hour into the film as she actively imagines—directly to viewers, in front of the camera—what it must have been like to play Elsie in *Plantation Memories*. Cheryl's lip-synching of the dialogue that Elsie speaks to Missy Barbara is by far the most fascinating twenty-eight-plus seconds of a film that is fairly stuffed with fascinating moments. Cheryl plants her body in the now-familiar studio chair, next to the now-familiar monitor. We can't see all of the screen as the scene plays out on the monitor, but we can see enough of the screen to know that what we're hearing and seeing is happening in real time. Cheryl is wearing her usual street clothing, a blouse, complete with a chain and matching earrings and her closely cropped hair—all stylistic and sartorial signs of late twentieth-century black lesbianism—but she tops off her nod to the scene from *Plantation Memories* by wearing a blue bandanna tied up in a bow much like Elsie's character in the film itself.

There are a dizzying number of identity-laden layers to the lip-sync scene and what it projects. There is, of course, Cheryl Dunye, director of *The Watermelon Woman*, playing Cheryl Dunye's character—also named Cheryl. And while it's true that Cheryl is representing the character Elsie, it is the fictive actress Fae Richards / Faith Richardson who brought Elsie to life—there is no Elsie without Richards / Richardson / the Watermelon Woman; and yet while Dunye is miming the movement and voice of a character named Elsie, she is also technically imitating Lisa Marie Bronson, the present-day actress who played the Watermelon Woman in the film *The Watermelon Woman*. This key scene, then, is an embodiment of—and critique of—both American slavery and filmic representations of American slavery. Dunye previously decentered a culturally familiar American antebellum scene of a white mistress and black mammy in order to place our attention on the black mammy—and in addition, Dunye made her beautiful. In this scene Dunye goes one farther by executing some nifty time travel—wrenching the antebellum scene out of the fictive nineteenth century and into the late twentieth century, while never fully leaving the antebellum era behind as she maintains fidelity to the dialogue in the original scene:

ELSIE: Oh, don't cry Missy! Master Charles is comin' back, for sure! I know he is!

MISSY BARBARA: Do you really think so, Elsie?

ELSIE: Oh yes, Missy Barbara, I know he is. I prayed to God all night long, and this morning this little angel told me he's comin' back—back to ye.

The invitation, for the viewer, is to pay attention not only to the acting body within the character on-screen but to the critique/exploration of slavery embedded within the multiple representations of black bodies in this one key scene of mimicry. This allusion-disruption scene, perhaps more than any other single scene in the film, troubles and disturbs viewer expectations. It is in some ways a difficult scene to watch, a scene that tugs at a deeply black, tragicomic sensibility. The viewer might see it as purely comic, or as wildly inappropriate, or as an uncomfortable combination of the two. Viewers are left on their own to figure out how to feel and how to respond. In the same way black characters on-screen like Tamara are uncomfortable with Cheryl's historical exploration—as well as her relationship with Diana—the discomfort and what-do-we-do-with-this?-ness of the scene presents that discomfort to the viewer and invites, if not forces, them to contemplate the scene's difficulty.

This brief lip-synching scene has, perhaps not surprisingly, garnered significant critical attention. For example, Laura L. Sullivan suggests in "Chasing Fae: *The Watermelon Woman* and Black Lesbian Possibility" that this scene "invites the reader to connect the history of the black lesbian actress who rose to fame through a series of denigrating roles as servant and slave, with the present black lesbian filmmaker before us, Cheryl Dunye, who is playing a version of herself."[6] In another analysis of the film, "Body and Soul: Identifying (with) the Black Lesbian Body in Cheryl Dunye's *Watermelon Woman*," Mark Winokur argues that this scene should be read as one in which "Dunye creates a representation of the negative oedipal stage of both identification with and desire for the body of the black lesbian mother."[7] Perhaps Sydney Fonteyn Lewis, in "Looking Forward to the Past: Black Women's Sexual Agency in 'Neo' Cultural Productions," provides the most convincing reading of the scene when she argues that "the scene must be read both socially and psychically." "In fact," continues Lewis,

in her unearthing of The Watermelon Woman's history, Dunye discovers that her real name is Faith Richardson, her stage name

Fae Richards, and, of course her Hollywood nickname, The Water-melon Woman. The title of Cheryl's final documentary refers to Fae as all three of these names. These multiple layers of naming are suggestive of the complexity of Fae Richard's identity—the many figures she inhabits in one body—and none of these figure(s) trump the other. This reading, like the film's style and structure, further destabilizes the concept of real/essential versus stereo-type/fragment and any attempt to uncover the 'truth' behind the stereotype. In other words, in *The Watermelon Woman* the mammy figure is re-presented in the film as more than just a (negative) stereotype that Fae is performing; it is more than a "haunting image" which limits and fragments Fae. Instead through the collapsing of boundaries between the character and the actor, the stereotypical character is re-visioned to be, in itself, as complex as the actor performing it.[8]

Well. Paul Beatty's novel *The White Boy Shuffle* has an extended early section in which a central character's ancestor runs away *into* slavery. Dunye uses a similarly playful tone to inhabit an institution that would not at all seem the place or site for play. Indeed, Cheryl's face and manner are difficult to read conclusively as she imitates Elsie. On the one hand, there's clearly an element of affection for a character whom Cheryl refers to as "the most beautiful black mammy" and about whom she also said, nearly in the next breath, "Girl-friend's got it going *on*."

But on the other hand, Cheryl's facial expressions make it equally clear that she's also making fun of Elsie. Take, for instance, the five-plus seconds that Cheryl is on-screen as Elsie with Missy Barbara speaking. Cheryl takes a break from exaggeratedly emoting while presenting Elsie's dialogue and begins to make petting motions, as if she's calming, say, a puppy. This gesture surely serves to heighten the mollifying and pacifying of Miss Barbara, but it also speaks to the role Elsie was forced to play as an enslaved woman, a role that may or may not have been sincere, no matter how convincing it might seem.

The difficulty in telling exactly which parts of this lip-synching, play-act-ing scene are allusion and which are disruption goes, I contend, to the core of "squishy, hazy"[9] post-blackness: post-black artists "trouble blackness, they worry blackness; they stir it up, touch it, feel it out, and hold it up for exami-nation in ways that depart significantly from previous—and necessary—preoccupations with struggling for political freedom, or with an attempt to establish and sustain a coherent black identity."[10] Not only would it be unlikely

BERTRAM D. ASHE

that an artist from before and during the civil rights movement would leave her imitation of an enslaved woman ambiguous, but treating slavery with the irreverence Dunye does here seems to trouble blackness, gesturally, no matter what.

Deeply embedded in this disruptive moment—and the biggest difference between the original clip and Cheryl's imitation—is Cheryl's snatching the bandanna off of her head twenty-one seconds into the lip-synching scene, calling attention to both the bandanna and her use of it as a prop heavy with symbolism. It was effective while on her head; once it gets to her hand, the bandanna is heightened as a sign of not just enslavement but a particularly female form of enslavement. In addition, her removal of the bandanna prompts our visual reengagement with—just in case certain viewers needed to get used to it—her extremely short haircut. But Cheryl doesn't just remove the bandanna and dramatically clutch it to her chest (think a present-day clutch-the-pearls gesture) in order to heighten the emotionality of the scene. She *then* executes the one-two punch of (a) an exaggerated, honking clown-sneeze *into* the bandanna and (b) intentional comic mugging as the scene fades. As is often the case in *The Watermelon Woman*, it is sometimes difficult to tell when something is done for mere humor or if there's also an ulterior motive. Obviously those two modes are not mutually exclusive, and this scene appears to be one of those overlapping instances. If the original clip from *Plantation Memories* Cheryl screened at the beginning of the film was what an imagined clip from an actual 1937 film set in the antebellum era might have looked like, this twenty-eight-second send-up of the now-familiar clip both alludes to familiar narratives of the mammy figure and at the same time pries them apart.

If Dunye's film exists as an exploration of the filmic representation of American slavery, the comic gestures at the end of this key scene also seem instructive. As Karin D. Wembley suggests, "Dunye manipulates the mammy stereotype as a means to create Fae, recuperating agency from the mammy stereotype. However, Dunye the parodist takes this ironic, comic scene one step further by commenting on the intellectual absurdity that recuperative readings of mammy could entail, thus collapsing the very recuperative model she posits."[11] Are they funny, these fake-sneezing, mugging, scene-ending gestures? Sure. They are also, though, a way to manage historical pain, a way to take late twentieth-century ownership, if you will, over even a fictive filmic representation of racially hegemonic American enslavement. Indeed, since it's difficult to tell where affection ends and mockery begins in this scene, my sense is that they are both layered upon each other; they're both there at the same time. There's an impish delight to Dunye's performance here, one that isn't quite matched in any other sequence in the film. It's a moment of willing simultaneity that actually becomes, if you will, *trimultaneity*: It's not just Cheryl, on-screen, in 1995, imitating the actress the Watermelon Woman, in 1937—the actress of *Plantation Memories* is also acting as an antebellum enslaved woman of a particular location (the South) a particular time (likely Civil War era) and a particular place (the plantation). *The Watermelon Woman* wouldn't have suffered much from an exclusion of this imitation scene—if, say, the scene had ended up on the cutting-room floor, viewers would not have missed it, since we would have had no idea it would ever have existed. But, such as it is, its inclusion is telling blaxploration: asking questions about blackness, about enslavement, about acting that speak to historical representations of American slavery in early—and late—twentieth-century film.

Beyond the initial presentation of the clip, and the subsequent lip-synching to the clip, *The Watermelon Woman* includes a late-in-the-film mirror scene of that clip from *Plantation Memories*. The mirror scene is set up, however, by the power dynamic that sustains itself from the antebellum mistress / enslaved woman relationship to the postbellum ma'am/maid relationship. The difference, of course, is that the black maid is not enslaved and has drastically increased agency. But that agency is limited at best. Dunye shifts the slavery context to the limited-agency context by constantly referring to the fact that being a maid is one of the few areas of employment open to black women in the pre–civil rights movement era. For instance, when Cheryl begins to narrate the biography of the Watermelon Woman late in the film, she says,

> The first record of Fae that I could find was this photo, "Faith Richardson, winner of the Beechie Beacham Bicarbonate Jingle Contest, Philadelphia, 1922." I know that she worked as a maid for several years, and I know that she danced in the chorus on South Street. But I'm not sure how she got into her first film. She must have met Martha Paige at some club or something. This one is stamped, "Newark Studios," and on the back it says, "The Watermelon Woman and Sandra Vincent in *Jersey Girl*, 1931."

Over the nearly thirty seconds it takes for Cheryl to narrate the above voice-over, exactly four maid photographs are displayed on-screen: two of them feature an unhappy Watermelon Woman in full maid uniform, attending to white women; in the remaining two she is dutifully dusting while the white woman in the photo happily chats on the telephone. It is instructive that, according to Cheryl's biographical information, Richardson worked in real life as maid for an undisclosed number of years.[12] This blurring of Richardson's real life and her on-screen life spoke to the diminished agency she had. The lack of a grinning, happy maid visual helps to express this tension, although another photo of the Watermelon Woman is displayed throughout the film, where she is expressing surprise next to a vase of flowers—that photo is closer to the happy maid stereotype, but even then the photograph stops well short of a stereotypical darky attribution. Since Cheryl makes it clear that Richards's early years included work as an actual maid, the photographs of the Watermelon Woman playing an on-screen maid once again collapse the distinctions between reality and film, here regarding labor and, perhaps more importantly, servitude. There are multiple moments, throughout the film, where Cheryl holds up photos of iconic black female actors (Butterfly McQueen, Hattie McDaniel, etc.) in maid/servant poses and uniforms.

The scene that echoes the Elsie–Missy Barbara clip occurs two-thirds of the way through the film, when Diana and Cheryl visit Mrs. Page-Fletcher, the younger sister of Martha Page, the white director/partner of Fae Richards. When, after a haughty, self-important, middle-aged Page-Fletcher refers to "all those coloreds" her sister employed, Cheryl objects strongly, and a confrontation ensues. The way the scene is composed and constructed, Diana and Page-Fletcher sit on a cream-colored couch as Cheryl sits facing them on an adjacent flowered chair. The couch and chair are on a side of the room that has a mantle and a bookcase behind them, but when Page-Fletcher rises in outrage as Cheryl insists that Martha Page and Fae Richards were lovers, Page-Fletcher essentially cuts the room in two: to the left of her is the lit portion containing Cheryl and Diana, and to the right of her is darkness; she fronts what appears to be a dark wooden panel of some sort. As the tension escalates and Page-Fletcher asks Cheryl and Diana to leave, a door opens behind and to the right of Page-Fletcher, a door that appeared moments earlier to be a wall. So, quite literally out of nowhere, at the moment of greatest opposition between Cheryl and Page-Fletcher, a pliant, obsequious, heavy-set, middle-aged, light-skinned black maid, wearing a white apron and a baggy teal blouse, emerges from the kitchen. She slowly walks a step or two and then, fairly oozing with schmaltzy, unctuous concern, asks Page-Fletcher, "Is there some problem, ma'am?" Page-Fletcher completely ignores Her Maid (the character is listed as Her Maid in the credits), and they both stand, one indignant and the other blandly puzzled, while Diana apologizes and Cheryl crisply unclips the lavalier mic from Page-Fletcher and walks out, but not before announcing, seemingly in response to both Page-Fletcher *and* her maid, "This is a mess."

Obviously, the scene is not a beat-by-beat mirror scene of the Elsie–Missy Barbara clip; indeed, there's no explicit indication that this scene should be read as a mirror scene. What prompts me to do so is the presence of the black maid—and her excessively supportive and seemingly selfless relationship to her employer, and the way it brings to mind Elsie from *Plantation Memories*. Page-Fletcher could easily have invited Cheryl and Diana to leave without the maid appearing—viewers didn't even know she existed until she appeared. Instead, Dunye's placing a black maid into the scene conforms with the white-slaveowner-combined-with-twentieth-century-madam / enslaved-mammy-combined-with-twentieth-century-maid dynamic that floats through the narrative from beginning to end, and again seems to collapse historical time and make a veiled reference to American slavery. The differences between the antebellum film clip and the Page-Fletcher interview are many, but in the end the power dynamic between white mistress and black mammy is so similar to that between white female employer and black maid—as is the performance of white female power and black female subservience—that it seems as if the latter scene is, indeed, signifyin(g) on the first. But if Gatesian signifyin(g) is "repetition and revision, or repetition with a signal difference,"[13] the "signal difference" here is the insistent, disruptive presence of Cheryl at the very site that alludes to the white female / black servant power dynamic. Indeed, Dunye does several things with this Page-Fletcher scene: She blurs the difference between mammy and maid. She points to the distinction between *being* a maid and *portraying* a maid. And in *this* scene Dunye inserts *Cheryl*, herself, directly into that dynamic. Here the disruption emerges from inside the action.

In a way that recalls her signification on Elsie as she imitates her earlier in the film, Cheryl is *present* here. Cheryl, in voice-over, introduces the scene this way: "What you're watching now is footage from an interview Diana arranged with Mrs. Page-Fletcher, Martha's younger sister. The whole thing was quite disturbing. First she started by describing Fae all wrong. She started talking shit about Fae and all those 'coloreds' her sister employed? Humph!" From the very beginning of the scene, in which Cheryl is narrating over footage we can see in progress, Cheryl very much wrests narrational control over the interview. She frames it for the viewer as "disturbing," and in a key moment in the scene, Cheryl bluntly tells Page-Fletcher that Fae Richards "was lovers with your sister."

Page-Fletcher jumps to her feet, insisting, "My sister was *not* that kind of woman!" Cheryl says, in voice-over, still dominating viewer perception of the scene, "Diana kept quiet most of the time, but I wasn't going to be quiet, *no way*. I went off on that *old woman*." And she did, although in Cheryl's familiarly soft-spoken, fairly unobtrusive way. No screaming, no shouting, no raised voices; no fists—or epithets—were thrown, no profanity was uttered, no insults were hurled. But what Cheryl did do, in her own way, while staying very much in character, was to clearly advocate for her own position, her own historical knowledge. She held her own. She pushed back at Page-Fletcher's attempt to alter her older sister's history, and then once her point was made, she left, appropriately and definitively declaring the situation "a mess."

This echo scene extends, complicates, and informs that key, original clip from *Plantation Memories*. For good measure, as a way, perhaps, to solidify the extended, film-length commentary on slavery, Dunye replays parts of these key scenes during the "documentary," the nearly five-minute-long biography of Fae Richards that Cheryl narrates at the end of the film, interspersed with the closing credits. She includes stills from *Plantation Memories*, in particular one called "Elsie Calls on the Lord," with Elsie near a building outside, in her bandana, on her knees, hands clasped, praying to God. Cheryl narrates, "I wrote to the studio and got these glamour photos of Fae taken in 1938. It looks like she was trying to bust out of mammy roles, but of course in 1938 that couldn't really work." What *The Watermelon Woman* does, in the end, is rehabilitate Fae Richards, as an actor and a person, and present viewers with badly needed context—from scenes of enslavement through scenes that recall enslavement—by constantly collapsing time and inviting viewers to grapple with the present-day echoes of an enslaved past.

Post-blackness, as an artistic school, is steeped in a critique-filled, non-traditional, critical and explorative black stance, and when it comes to addressing slavery, Cheryl Dunye's *The Watermelon Woman* provides viewers a way to think about, think through, and deeply consider black enslavement by presenting a representation of a representation of American slavery. By including an example of imagined slavery along with imitation and repetition and alignment with postbellum domestic work, the film offers a pathway to apprehending and pondering the full, expansive realities of enslavement itself. Visual images have the power to form and shape narratives of enslavement, and films like *The Watermelon Woman*, particularly since it blurs the fictive and the real, the documentary and the faux-documentary, provide a site for viewers to recognize and critique these narratives of slavery. As Robert Reid-Pharr—who himself makes a brief, memorable appearance in the film—argues in "Makes Me Feel Mighty Real: *The Watermelon Woman* and the Critique of Black Visuality," "The process of stitching together the history of a community necessarily involves a somewhat idiosyncratic interpretation and representation of the cultural artifacts that one encounters." "I think," continues Reid-Pharr, "that *The Watermelon Woman* takes us a step further down this particular path, however, by not attaching differential values to the various levels of evidence, the many remnants, on display. Dunye tells us that film, photographs, documents, gossip, storytelling, and her own narration are all suspect, open to interpretation."[14] Indeed, when Cheryl stares into the camera near the end of *The Watermelon Woman*, she is speaking as expansively to a critique of representing slavery as she is speaking to what exploring the life of Fae Richards / Faith Richardson / the Watermelon Woman has meant to her. She concludes, "It means hope, it means inspiration, it means possibility . . . [I]t means *history*."

NOTES

1 *The Watermelon Woman*, directed by Cheryl Dunye (1996; First Run Features, 2000), DVD.

2 Names for this post–civil rights movement artistic school were various from the start: *the New Black Aesthetic* and *post-soul* were the most widely used terms. Trey Ellis, "New Black Aesthetic," *Callaloo* 38 (Winter 1989): 233–43; Nelson George, *Buppies, B-Boys, Baps, and Bohos: Notes on Post-Soul Black Culture* (New York: Harper Collins, 1993). *Post-blackness* is currently most widely used, and I have adopted it here for that reason. The reason I can so easily move from *post-soul* to *post-black* is because I see no distinction between the various names; they all describe what I once referred to as a "fundamental break" with the Black Arts Movement of the 1960s beginning with some young black artists of the 1980s. Bertram Ashe, "Foreword," in Trey Ellis, *Platitudes* (Boston: Northeastern University Press, 2003), iv.

3 Ellis, "New Black Aesthetic," 239.

4 Bertram D. Ashe, "Theorizing the Post-Soul Aesthetic: An Introduction," *African American Review* 41, no. 4 (Winter 2007): 609–23.

5 Matt Richardson, "Our Stories Have Never Been Told: Preliminary Thoughts on Black Lesbian Cultural Production as Historiography in *The Watermelon Woman*," *Black Camera: An International Film Journal (The New Series)* 2, no. 2 (Spring 2011): 105.

6 Laura L. Sullivan, "Chasing Fae: 'The Watermelon Woman' and Black Lesbian Possibility," *Callaloo* 23, no. 1 (Winter 2000): 459.

7 Mark Winokur, "Body and Soul: Identifying (with) the Black Lesbian Body in Cheryl Dunye's *Watermelon Woman*," in *Recovering the Black Female Body: Self-Representations by African American Women*, ed. Michael Bennett and Vanessa Dickerson (New Brunswick, NJ: Rutgers University Press, 2001), 244.

8 Sydney F. Lewis, "Looking Forward to the Past: Black Women and Sexual Agency in 'Neo' Cultural Productions," PhD diss., University of Washington, 2012, 132.

9 Ashe, "Theorizing the Post-Soul Aesthetic," 619.

10 Ashe, "Theorizing the Post-Soul Aesthetic," 614.

11 Karin D. Wembley, "Framing the 'Art of Stereotype': The Politics of Race and Representation in African American Literary, Visual, and Performance Culture, 1985–2005," PhD diss., University of Chicago, 2012, 119.

12 I'm put in mind of the rejoinder Hattie McDaniel (one of seven people, including Butterfly McQueen, to whom Cheryl Dunye dedicates her film) offered when some blacks of her era complained she was playing a maid on screen too often: "Why should I complain about making $700 a week playing a maid? If I didn't, I'd be making $7 a week being one." Maria Bukhonina, *Inspired! True Stories behind Famous Art, Literature, Music, and Film* (New York: Museyon, 2016), 125.

13 Henry Louis Gates Jr., *The Signifying Monkey: A Theory of African American Literary Criticism* (New York: Oxford University Press, 1988), xxiv.

14 Robert F. Reid-Pharr, "Makes Me Feel Mighty Real: *The Watermelon Woman* and the Critique of Black Visuality," in *F Is for Phony: Fake Documentary and Truth's Undoing*, ed. Alexandra Juhasz and Jesse Lerner (Minneapolis: University of Minnesota Press, 2006), 139.

CHAPTER TEN

"AN AUDIENCE IS A MOB ON ITS BUTT"

An Interview with Branden Jacobs-Jenkins

BERTRAM D. ASHE AND ILKA SAAL

BRANDEN JACOBS-JENKINS IS AN OBIE-AWARD-WINNING MACARTHUR Fellow who, at the age of thirty-three, has already published six plays. Three of those plays in particular—*Neighbors* (2010), *An Octoroon* (2014), and *Appropriate* (2014)—are, among many other things, searing commentaries on race in America, and all three grapple, either directly or indirectly, with blackness and the legacies of slavery in the United States. We had the opportunity to talk with him on September 21, 2018, at the historic Park Avenue Armory on the Upper East Side in Manhattan, where Jacobs-Jenkins is an artist in residence. After the three of us settled in the gorgeous, elegant room where Jenkins plies his trade, Ashe opened the interview by asking him to talk about his stance on the term *post-black*.

BRANDEN JACOBS-JENKINS: Well, the term, as I understand it, originated with Thelma Golden, and it's one of those phrases that I'm like, "I don't really know what it means," so I hesitate to attach myself to it in any sort of significant way. But I would say that the post-black artists that Thelma was sort of highlighting at that time, like Glenn Ligon, Lorna Simpson, and Kara Walker, those people were very, very significant in terms of the work I started making at the time. I studied Kara Walker's writing; I studied everything that she did. And for some reason, I just felt that there was something happening in that pocket of artists. All these visual artists are very significant models for me in making my work, more so even than theater artists. It just felt like they had stumbled upon a patch of the forest that was speaking to my needs at the time.

198

BERTRAM ASHE: And by "forest" you mean . . . ?

BJJ: Meaning, in some fantasy of why people make art. It's like uncovering new territories of being and explaining the present and explaining the world around you. Do you know what I mean? I felt like no one in the theater was really thinking through representation in that way. I mean, there was George Wolfe during his time at The Public [Theater], but they weren't quite visible at the time that I began working and writing. Kara Walker had just won a MacArthur at the time, and Glenn—I love Glenn Ligon's work so much—I think he might have just been doing the neon signs. I was just really struck by the way he was thinking about materiality. And he was my way into David Hammons. I suddenly was like, "Oh, I feel like I found a network of people that I needed to know!" There was no equivalent of them in the theater. Of course, Suzan-Lori Parks, but she wasn't quite where she is now. But her work also was helpful. It felt like she, and maybe Robert O'Hara, were the only ones sort of thinking through these ideas and these concepts in some way.

BA: You used the term *representation*, and I'm curious about what's sometimes called the burden of representation of African American cultural production. Do you feel as if it's something that you have to pay attention to, something that you don't pay attention to, something that you willfully ignore?

BJJ: "Burden of representation." Can you talk about that concept a little more?

BA: Sure. It probably takes us back, in some ways, to Du Boisian double consciousness, and the idea that "they" are watching us, and therefore, black artists must create art that represents all blacks, and that art must represent blacks in a way that is respectable. Some black artists consider it a burden and wish they could just be free to create art in any way they desire.

BJJ: Yeah, right. It's funny; in a very positive review of mine, early on, that really kinda haunts me, the critic said that I was writing about "self-consciousness," which really struck me. I didn't feel [I was doing that then]; I still don't feel that, but I do wrestle with that idea in interesting ways . . . To be honest, the impulses for me were just coming from a very personal place, a place of confusion and questioning. So it wasn't that I felt an obligation to do *anything*, and in fact, a lot of that work was questioning the obligation I was *feeling* to do something, and why I was "supposed" to do that. Why? I didn't know. No one's answering the question of *why*. And if there was anything called provocative about that work, it was me trying to provoke an answer to that why—which wasn't happening.

My parents are both collectors of black memorabilia. They actually met at an auction for black memorabilia. So I grew up around these images in my house that are just, like, things in my house. They were just dolls to me because I haven't been racialized fully. To me, they were just frightening objects, full stop. The way that children are frightened of dolls and things like that. And so, it was interesting to have normalized these things, these images in my life that have been around me and then to kind of be socialized and understand that those things contained very specific coded information for other people. So, with *Neighbors*, which was the first play, when I look back I can feel that was me trying to understand why people were afraid of these images. Whereas for me, they were like matter, they were like the weather. They didn't contain any affect that wasn't extremely personal, extremely rooted in childhood. [*Chuckles*] You know what I mean?

BA: Got it. Got it. Yes, absolutely.

ILKA SAAL: I've read somewhere that you said you wrote *Neighbors* to be done with race. It was supposed to be your first and last play about race. And then you mentioned that in a way it also became a door opener, and you followed up with several other plays thinking about representations of blackness. I was wondering about what it is about the *theater* that allows you to explore these questions of race and blackness there?

BJJ: Well, you know, no one really gets to hide in the theater. In order for theater to happen, a bunch of strangers have to agree to be in a room together and have a shared experience. In television and film, people get to hide behind their laptops; they get to be at home; they can start and pause, stop and restart it. There's the kind of privilege of privacy that prevents you from having to be responsible for your emotional response in some way. We know those things all cater to a kind of sense of the private, the personal. Whereas the question of race and of blackness— those have always been social questions for me. You can't answer a social question without society, without the social element. The theater has always been essentially a social form. You can't really do it unless there's an encounter with public faces.

IS: This would be a good opening to talk about the audience. I liked what you said about how we can't talk about these social issues unless it's in a public forum. And you can't hide, right? And what struck us in watching your plays, and also reading them, is that you really confront the audience in various ways. In *Neighbors*, there's the scene at the end where they all step to the front of the stage and stare at the audience for a very, very long time. And in *An Octoroon* you have Br'er Rabbit walking across the stage, and at one point—I think that role was played by you, right?

BJJ: Mm-hmm.

IS: You literally do this onstage: [*gestures with index and middle fingers extended, pointing first at her own eyes, then points fingers out at imaginary audience*] I'm watching you watching us—

BJJ: Yeah. Yeah [*chuckles*].

IS: So what about such confrontations with the audience? How do they matter to your thinking about theater?

BJJ: I guess I wouldn't think of those moments as "confrontations" with the audience. For me, there's a lot of power, or there's assumed to be a lot of power in the role of the watcher. Again, it's that feeling of no one is safe from judgment in this space, so your judgment is not supreme. Part of what makes the theater the theater is, like, "the actors are still here, guys." This is actually a space of exchange, not a space of ownership. You don't control what's happening here. We're all kind of taking a leap of faith together to underscore the value of this encounter. I think there's something important about that. I'm always thinking about the audience as a democratic space. I'm less obsessed with that now, [but] that was such a strong MO for a long time, trying to understand what is American theater. What is it supposed to be if our idea of Americanness is about pluralistic voices? We all make a choice to coexist together in our diversity. That's the dream. But an audience is a mob on its butt.

So, first, the theater has this idea that a success of the theater is the audience all feeling the same thing, but I knew that wasn't true. And I was having lots of experiences going to the theater and being the only person of color in the theater and having moments of being with everyone and laughing, and then something kind of unsavory happens on stage—usually along racial lines—and suddenly I'm not laughing; I feel alone in that space. And I'm like, "Wow. This is such a vivid experience." And I wanted to see, is there a value in this feeling? Because, suddenly, the show is not just a show. The show is the people around me, too, you know? So the idea was how do I constantly destabilize, how do I constantly remind us that we're all participating in this? Like, we're equalizing everyone. So that's sort of the idea behind it. Again, I hate to call it confrontational because confrontation, to me, feels like there's aggression in it, and it feels more like a reminder to me.

BA: I completely understand why you would prefer *not* to use the word *confrontational*. I think, though, the reason why it *felt* confrontational is because it *almost never happens* that characters on stage say nothing and stare at the audience. And *then* go over and *whisper in the ear* of another character while gesturing to the audience . . . [*laughs*]. I have to say, that *felt* confrontational.

BJJ: It's funny because they are not talking about you, you know what I mean? So, really, when we're talking about the end of *Neighbors*, I'll tell you all the things I was thinking about going into that. One is that I wanted to create a situation where you had to look *through* something, to look through someone to see something else. So the play kind of does this at the end. The story of Richard and the kind of real world of the fight [the fight Richard has onstage with Zip Coon]—everyone is invested in that fight. But there's something in front of you that's preventing you from actually seeing, like, the black face. You have to *look through* the representation to actually see an existential struggle in some way. And then that thing is looking back at you. That's the thing. People aren't animals to be dissected, you know? That felt important.

But also, there's two events in that. One is that [the characters] start looking at you, which has roots in, like, the '70s Living Theater. But the real event is when they start whispering—it goes from a tableau of actors to conspirators. That's when people turn. That's when the audience will be like, "You *talking* about me?" No, they're still actors doing what they wanna do. It's still a play. But what *is* it about the fact that when those two actors started talking, suddenly, people felt attacked? That was the phenomenon we were kinda after. And then, the play does these crazy things; the play goes into the lobby, and then these actors are talking, but actually the play's still happening, you're hearing the play happen. I think I was, like, twenty-four when I wrote [the play], trying so hard to break a thing and figure out what made it work.

The thing is that there was no confrontation. I think there was maybe a little *provocation* in that, like, you're all gonna make a choice or take an action, but we're just being us. You know what I mean?

BA: Sure. Sure. Absolutely. I guess it's the difference between you doing something confrontational versus someone *feeling confronted*, even if you weren't intending to do so—

BJJ: That's kind of right. That's right. The other thing that drives people nuts about *Neighbors*, or drove people nuts, is that there's no curtain call—or there's half a curtain call. People were irate that they didn't get to applaud for these other three actors. But the play was just like, "I don't know if I really care what you think. Maybe this wasn't for *you*." And that's the thing. That's where people, I think, began to break down.

IS: Can I pick up on what you just said about feelings? At some point in one of your other interviews you mention that theater should be a safe place for feelings. And then you add, "But also for ugly feelings,—*especially* for ugly feelings." And I was intrigued by that. Could you say more about the relevance of ugly feelings in your plays?

BJJ: Well, I just think in some ways we're trying to document the truth of a present. And the present is full of negative feelings. I guess I always want to believe that the theater is supposed to be—not an instructive tool, but it's supposed to give you something to live with that makes living easier. Maybe that is a lesson . . . My teacher, Marsha Norman, always talked about how she felt story was based on survival information. The reason stories even began was because someone was like, "If you wanna eat food, there's this great lake down the street. I should tell you about how I first got to it." The whole point of story is that it's supposed to help—

IS: —nourish you?

BJJ: —nourish, but also, make us better at living. Anyway, so for me the theater has always been about rehearsing feelings. I mean, I certainly believe that there are people who make theater that harms people, and that's not what I'm trying to ever do. But the idea is . . . For example, this past election, I was in the MacDowell Colony in New Hampshire. And I got there maybe four or five days before the actual election. I was in eastern New Hampshire; I was driving around, and I just saw tons of Trump and Pence signs. I have all these friends I was working with who were like, "He's never gonna win. He's never gonna win. He's never gonna win." And then I was like, "Are you *sure*?" Every day I would drive—I had a rental car—and I would just drive as far as I could, until I felt like I saw a Hillary sign, and I didn't see any! And every day I would go farther and farther and farther and farther. And then, when that night happened and everyone was being traumatized, I actually felt very calm. Because I felt like I'd seen the writing on the wall. And that, to me, is what theater is supposed to *give you* in some way. I think it's tied to that idea of growing up with these images of mammies and sambos. I don't feel afraid of those images at all. And so, I feel like that allows me to move past the trigger of them to ask questions about how they're actually weaponized or used. Does that make sense?

BA: Yes, it does. Sure.

BJJ: Part of what I was figuring out with *Neighbors* was—well, everyone wants to blame the blackface; it's the blackface that shuts the thing down. And I'm like, "That feels so lazy because it makes the *paint* the enemy." As opposed to thinking about "Well, no. There's human actors involved." I just felt we're distracted by the surface of things, and the theater is supposed to be the space where we move that aside, and we actually get to the real issues. We get the real conversations about history in action, as opposed to how things *look*. I feel like theater, when it really works, it imbues the material with meaning. Or you feel like you go through the physical to get at the spiritual, when it's *amazing*. I don't know if you ever had that experience.

IS: Yes, this is very interesting what you say, and I can completely follow you. But at the same time, you know, the use of, for instance, stereotypes, racial and racist stereotypes, is also very controversial, right? A number of artists are using them today, and their works have triggered vehement controversies over the ethics and politics of using stereotypes. Some critics believe that *regardless* of the playwright's intention, they just revive the violence inherent in them. Other critics say, "No, you have to go inside the stereotype, you have to use, for instance, hyperbole and blow them up from the inside," et cetera. So I can see that you use stereotypes in a way to clear this discussion, right? To engage it and clear it, so you can get to the spiritual issues, or the other issues beyond it. But at the same time, I also think that some audience members might be blocked precisely because there's a stereotype.

BERTRAM D. ASHE AND ILKA SAAL

BJJ: Right. Yeah.

IS: Bert, you had an experience of this sort at a talkback in Washington, right?

BA: I did. I went to see *An Octoroon* at the Woolly Mammoth. At the talkback, that scene where Pete was on the auction block came up. Now, the production had him performing in a way that I, personally, found hilarious. It was supposed to be funny. It *was* funny. The actor who played Pete [Joseph Castillo-Midyett] was very good at projecting a kind of physical humor in a way that caused me to laugh. And yet, at the talkback it was very clear that there were African Americans in the audience who did not find that funny at all. For them, the idea, the visual, of a black body on an auction block precluded any sort of humor whatsoever. Obviously, I disagreed, but—

BJJ: —also, it wasn't a black body [*laughter*].

BA: Huh?

BJJ: Yeah. It was black paint on a body, a brown body.

BA: Yes, there is that. But the perception, from their point of view, is that it was, indeed, a black body on an auction block. And as a result, it was in this moment when the stereotype was preventing certain black theatergoers from reacting in ways that they *might* react—if they wanted to—it seemed to me. And I'm curious as to whether you enjoy and hope for those sorts of complicated moments?—find them fruitful, a place for exploration? Or if you're just writing a play, and they happen if they happen.

BJJ: I don't even *know*! [*Laughs*] Of course, I chose that; I chose for that moment to happen and with the body that it happens with, asking for those things. In that situation, that's exactly what I'm after, which is those people have to own their perception. In reality, I think that might have actually been a First Nations actor. You know, one of the things I was doing in that play was "Okay, a white guy in blackface is offensive. A black guy in whiteface is complicated." I was like, "So, what if it's just a different body in blackface, are we still upset?" That was one of the questions. And that was that moment. I get very intense, very interesting critiques from Native American actors and communities about that play because of the representation of Wahnotee. And I'm excited about that, because I'm like, "Oh my God, *please* speak up in the audience, because now we [blacks]'re not the only ones! Please, like, let's everybody talk about how widely offensive American history is."

I will talk about *Neighbors* too: what I wanted was something so crazy that an audience would turn to a stranger and go, "What just happened to us?" Maybe these "ugly feelings" are a space where we come together as well. That's the argument too. Not just when we're happy and joyful, but when we are feeling irate about something.

BA: Yeah, yeah.

BJJ: To get back to your question: I don't remember the DC production very well, but I had a similar issue in London recently, where that character [Pete] is written specifically to *interrupt* his minstrel act. For me, that moment *fails* if he gets applause. Which has happened, because he'll do like a [*singsong*] "Zippity do da, and we'll get to the end, and we'll feel"— and they're gonna clap for him. That happened in London, and I was like, "That is bad, that is bad." Because then you are *doing* a minstrel show. If the action completes itself, you have successfully recreated the minstrel show. The point is that this character has had the agency to be self-aware enough to be like, "Just kidding." That's sort of the Brecht of it, where it's constantly trying to get someone to feel a thing, and then be like, "Oh, you just felt something—did you feel it? did you feel it?" How do you get people to be *aware* of their sensory apparatus? And that is actually a political moment, you know.

BA: Well, now, I think that I have read that laughter, as an action, releases tension.

BJJ: That's what they think. Yeah.

BA: And so, if that's true, and it may not be, but if it is, then, doesn't it become difficult to actually have a moment that is willfully, intentionally humorous? Because under ordinary circumstances, the willfully, intentionally humorous moment leads to laughter if it's successful, but it sounds like you're saying that you want a moment onstage that is, indeed, willfully and intentionally humorous, that should produce laughter, but if it does, it fails? Am I getting that right or not?

BJJ: No, no, no, no. I think, for me, laughter is a bodily reaction—like breathing, you know? Sorry, let me be clear, it was *applause*; we get applause.

Applause is actually a conscious communication. But, for me, the idea is that I want people to feel an emotion *passively* and then realize they've just felt something passively, and that's, again, me trying to be a five-generation-removed Brechtian [*laughs*]. Because that is where we begin to legitimately have a discussion about the insidiousness of a racial construction.

BA: Got it. Sure. Good.

BJJ: One of the things I realized [with *Neighbors*] was that it's very difficult for an audience *now* to realize that it is as naive as an audience two hundred years ago. In some ways, we dismiss those audiences of original minstrel shows, but they were as aware of their world as we are. They did not know the future; they did not know the things they were looking at would be considered offensive. In the same way that we do not know in ten, fifteen years what's gonna happen, what will be right or wrong. And that, to me, feels like us getting close to a real conversation about existence and the human experience, moving through time. It's stuff that I wanna be talking about in the work. But then, when we get to fetishized stereotypes we *deflect* that thought process that might lead us to being like "how might we be implicated in the furthering of these ideas?" We instead get to say, "Oh no, it's the paint, it's this picture." You erase the human actor behind it, which means you erase the politics behind it. That's my feeling.

BA: And that's at least, in part, I'm assuming, the reason for why the dramatis personae listing in *An Octoroon* has so many options—for a person of color or someone who looks like one—so that it complicates the body behind the paint.

BJJ: Yeah, that's right. And it also forces theater makers to suddenly be, like, "Wait a minute, what is this? The system I'm using is a failure." Like, you know, what does it mean to cast someone, when it says "comma black"? What does that mean? Can anyone with dark melanin skin play this? *Why*? One of the experiences I had with *Neighbors* was that I had this character Melody, and I wanted actual biracial actors to play her. And all these women who played her would be like, "I've never played myself on stage before." *Why* is that? It's because most casting offices have a drawer that says "black" or "Native American." They open it up, and you just somehow wound up there. You know, it's illegal to actually ask an actor what their ethnicity is. And so you get a lot of people who wind up in a drawer because they look a certain way. Again, here we are, playing the theater game of race and being bad at it.

IS: Can I ask you about the role of humor in your plays? Because there's a lot of humor—even, as you said, in very disturbing moments, one feels prompted to laugh. Maybe you can comment on this? How important is humor to your explorations? And another question building on that: you also mentioned, at some point you became interested in the wrong kind of laughter—particularly after Dave Chappelle left his show.

BJJ: Mm-hmm. Mm-hmm. Yeah.

IS: Might there be a Dave Chappelle moment for you at some point? When there's too much wrong laughter?

BJJ: Oh my God—or have I already had it? Humor, for me . . . You know, during my brief jaunt in grad school, I was reading a lot of Freud and thinking about melancholia and humor and jokes and the subconscious. I guess when you work in the theater, all things that are attached to emotion are just fair game, in terms of tools that you have to manipulate and use. There's a lot of language in the theater, too, around laughter, how humor happens in threes—[*in response to IS's reaction*] yeah, exactly, you want jokes to be always in threes. You're taught that you wanna create a button, so like in the first eight minutes of a play, you have to have a big joke or something that lets the audience know that this is a show you can laugh at. Because audiences want to laugh, right?

BA: And they want permission to laugh?

BJJ: They *need* permission to laugh. Especially if you're an artist of color. Because everyone is showing up ready to feel a lot of guilt, and they don't wanna laugh, you know? So laughter becomes an important device in terms of opening up a group of people. Because I think when you laugh together, you feel connected. In the same way that if you sang together, there's something about the group sound that actually locks the mob in, you know? So, I do think of humor. I do think of it, oddly, almost like paint. I think of it as material. And I think of when jokes happen. Because laughter also creates periods of nonthinking. That's the other thing they teach you. If you make something that's too funny, no one's gonna hear the next line. So, don't plant information behind it. I think of humor in that way.

But the wrong laughter was very key for me because I loved Dave Chappelle's stuff so much. I was in that pocket of where that show hit, and we were all watching it—that and *The Boondocks* were the two things that I was kind of beginning to flirt with. And Dave Chappelle kinda gave up because he felt this wrong laughter, and that really haunts me as an idea. This is actually what I wound up writing about in grad school: What is right and wrong laughter? And that's what led me to Freud. He has this idea of tendentious laughter. He posits the joker, there's the object of the joke, and there's the audience. And the game is to always win the audience to the joker's side. And that's the point of the joke: the joke has to be at the expense of something or someone. Because again, you always believe that the audience wants to laugh. That means the audience doesn't know what's right and wrong, the audience is just an actor in a game that you've set up. So, if the audience feels wrong, it feels wrong to you because you have rules as to what right and wrong laughter is that you aren't communicating, if that makes any sense.

IS: Yes, it does.

BJJ: So what happened for me was—and this is really just talking about *Neighbors*—I was interested in those moments, almost like a social experience, where an audience began to judge itself laughing. One of the interesting phenomena in *Neighbors* is that if, for whatever reason, our audience had bought tickets in such a way that the room was fully integrated, they were joyful, wonderful shows. Everyone felt fine; everyone fell in line laughing with everyone else. But if ever there were more people of color on one side of the room than the other, this phenomenon began where people would hear laughter coming from one side, and they would turn against that side, and those would be the most tendentious and contentious shows. And that's when I was, like, "Oh, right, there's something those people are hearing, they are deciding that that laughter is wrong"—but when they're mixed in with everyone, everything is fine. There's no Other. There's no butt of a joke; you don't feel like the butt of a joke. That was just one of the many horrible things I learned about dramatic process.

So I think that, oddly, as I have written before, I have feared that idea of wrong laughter. I don't know if I [now] feel more in control of it, or I think I built a discourse around myself where my work is called "uncomfortable," so people go in ready to feel sort of uncomfortable; they already feel wrong in some way even being there. So that's allowed me to relax. I mean, again, my fear is making things that harm people, and I don't feel that I have actually done that.

BA: Interesting, yeah.

BJJ: I was just in London for two weeks, where they just sort of encountered *An Octoroon* for the first time, which was so surreal. And I had this young black woman, black British, who is actually a critic there, come up to me, not identifying herself as a critic, and she said some phrase like, "If you're a black person, you don't need to see that show twice." And I was like, "Oh, you've seen it again," and she's like, "Oh no, a black person? You don't need to see that [again] if you're black." And I was like, "That's so craz—. That's so interesting. Because I know many, many people of color who've seen the show *multiple* times. And so you're taking it upon yourself to be the arbiter of this?" And that's the thing, this delusion is what I'm actually attempting to peel back. The trap that racial constructions are always laying for us is this illusion that we are going to represent anyone, that we can essentialize anyone in ourselves. Again, that's a bit tied to my whole idea of you're not the only watcher in the room.

BA: In a certain way, that takes us to *Appropriate*, where there're no black bodies on stage—but black bodies *everywhere* on stage.

BJJ: Yeah, they're underground, they're outside, in a jar . . .

BA: . . . trapped within photographs in a book . . . I'm curious as to how you explore blackness in that play, at the same time that you kind of explore whiteness in that play?

BJJ: So, that play kind of came out of my experience with *Neighbors*, actually. As I tried to write this "last play about race," or whatever we're going to call it, one of the strategies I felt myself really evoking creatively was like, "Okay I'm just gonna put all the blackness you can think of on stage, and then you're gonna tell me which one is really black." So I am going to put someone who has a black body who sounds white on stage; I'm gonna put, like, a biracial girl on stage; I'm gonna put a person of color in black-face on stage—actually, I don't specify who the actor is—I'm gonna put blackface on stage, and I just want to talk about which of these is black in the context of the theater? What are we talking about when we talk about blackness in the theater? Because the reference for it in the theater is actually blackface. And that's what I want to do. And that really upset everyone [*chuckles*]; the play really upset people. And I was like, "Okay, now that I've kind of come to this notion of blackness as a material, as a dramatic material, and a narrative material that contains, as a signifier, its own kind of nexus of meaning and feeling and that's like a palimpsest, how little does it have to be, for it to charge the room?"

This was sort of around the time Tracy Lett's *August: Osage County* had become this gauntlet thrown. It won *everything*—it was, like, the Thing. And I had this very interesting obsession with Tracy Letts as a writer, 'cause I really loved his early plays, and I came to New York when the play *Bug* had happened. And then something kind of happened in his work, which all writers are allowed to do, but his work kind of transformed, and suddenly there were people of color on stage, and I felt like they were "magical." Do you know the phrase the "magical negro"?

BA: Oh, God. I do. Yes.

BJJ: Anyway, so, I was sort of astonished because all of these plays, no one was saying they were about race. In *August: Osage County* there is a Native American woman who lives in the attic, and the last scene of the play is, like, the matriarch, in her arms, having a song. And no one was seeing the race allegory in this, which I thought was wild. But they were reading it into Lydia Diamond's play *Stick Fly*, which I really loved. Which was her, honestly, I believe, writing a good old-fashioned melodrama. It's just that everyone just happens to be black; it's a family drama. But all the reviews were like, "She's not going nearly deep enough into social issues," and you're like, "Whoa, look at this crazy double standard." Because one of these plays won the Pulitzer and won the Tony, its melodrama was considered a positive element, and here's this other play where it was just, like, "Wow, so we're only allowed to write about certain things?" That's when I began to be like, "Oh, something's up," you know? And so I had this idea that I wanted to write a play where there were no black bodies on stage [*laughs*] and that, actually, they don't really talk about race. I mean, they talk about their grandfather in this kind of elliptical way, but really it's about this brother, who was troubled and an addict, and may or may not have had some kind of illicit goings-on with an underage girl.

Because an element to me in the active dynamics of (again, I hate using this word, but) "race"—for me, it's antiblackness, it's specifically about blackness—is how it is avoided, how deftly it is avoided. And that we have entire vocabularies built around coded speaking about it, which we see politicians employing literally every single day. That's actually, to me, the thing to document about the moment. So I wanted to just have people [*chuckles*] doing that: just avoiding, avoiding, avoiding, avoiding.

Also for me it was partly an experiment within the industry. It was well and good to attack a kind of generic white subscription-based audience. But I was like, "No, there are actually more people complicit in the system, which are the people who run these institutions." And I wanted to see how the discourse worked differently. Because it wasn't just the audience or critics coming down on Lydia Diamond. Something was wrong, you know? So I wrote this play. And first of all, this is the play that everyone wanted. I mean, there was a bidding war to do the premiere. And then I realized that my thing was like, "I want you to market this exactly like you marketed *August: Osage County*." That's what I wanted. And it was amazing to watch marketing department after marketing department have a total meltdown about this. And that's when I realized that part of the value was actually my own race. *That* was the selling point. That it wasn't actually the work I was doing; it was me as a black author because they believed that I would draw a black audience, de facto. Listen, I'm not mad at that, but I'm like, "How *interesting*!" Because I seem to possess a *special skill* that makes me valued.

We had this crazy fight with one of the theaters, where with their poster they were like, "Can it be you holding a plantation?" I'm like, "No! I'm not in the play! I only *wrote* the play!" It was wild. And they were like, "What about you *standing* on a plantation?" I'm like, "No! I'm not—Did you make Tracy Letts stand in the middle of a field for the poster?!" It was really profound. I was like, "W-wow." You know, "Wow." And then basically after that they confessed and were like, "We're just afraid that if we don't use you we're not gonna get black audiences." And I was like, "Okay, this is interesting. So, why do you care about black audiences for *this play* specifically? And what is that saying about what you crave for the other half of the audience that is not black?" So, now, as I said, we're actually teasing something out about the ways that we think about what a black presence means. What does it translate to you? Because I guarantee that once they're in this room, you're not gonna invite them back for your Christmas show. So why do they need to be in this room? And then you start —it's like *The Wire*—you follow the money. And you're like, "Oh my God, it's about *funding*." It's tied to these economics that are around guilt. These feelings are actually political because they're wrapped up in economics. That was sort of the space I came to. So part of the metaphor that's working in *Appropriate* is what these photos mean, right? These portraits of legitimate black annihilation, black suffering . . .

BA: And the commodification therein!

BJJ: Right, exactly! Because they don't care about them until they learn what they're worth. I ask my parents a lot about the community of collectors they came out of because this is the stuff they're collecting. And my dad was like, "I've literally only seen a lynching photograph twice in all my collecting. That stuff belongs to a very specific group of people who it's hard to get an entrée in." *Without Sanctuary* was *massive* because that form of collecting was basically behind closed doors in collecting. It's like snuff films or something, right? They were. That impulse is fascinating. What *is* that? What is that *thing*, you know? Does that answer your question?

IS: [*Laughing*] You answered *many* questions. Did your experience with the industry trying to use you to market the play to black audiences—did that repeat itself with *Gloria*? Or was that off the table then?

BJJ: Well, that's a good question. So let's think about *Appropriate*. So the Signature Theatre production of New York—their marketing brand of that year was the playwright's face on the playbill. And so what happened is people [watching] that show would look down and see a picture of me smiling at them from their lap. At the theater in Louisville, you would leave the theater, and there was a huge poster of my face! It was crazy. So then, I kinda took that into *An Octoroon*. I was like, "Oh, okay. I'm gonna put myself in this." And that really actually opened the play up in a crazy way. I think that weirded people out more because this avatar began to exist. It was not played by me; I was the bunny. They're like [*sounding desperate*], "I don't know who this person is! *Who is this person*?" And then for *Gloria*, I think there is a way in which I, having learned through these plays, I realized how to scramble the race machine a little bit. People walked into that play looking for the race category [*chuckles*], and they spend about an hour investing in . . . you know, because she's the Asian one, he's the black one. [*Laughs*] And then halfway through half of them are murdered [*laughs*]. They're like, "Oh, that wasn't the play." That's actually a weird thing I think I learned from *Game of Thrones* [*chuckles*] because I realized the trick of *Game of Thrones* is that it's all about genre.

The game of that show is that it understands that genre is like a template. And we love it because we know how to feel. We feel at ease because we're like, "Okay, I'm investing in this bad guy, I'm investing in this person. Oh, no. It's a twist. I kinda knew a twist was coming, but that was a good twist." You know you're playing that game. But then what happens in *Game of Thrones* is that the first season is a detective story—but then they kill the detective! There's a funny way in which affect in the theater is kind of like a system of banking. You're constantly storing up, um—you've heard the phrase, "likeability?" People would say about someone, "She's not likeable!" It's because you haven't given her enough things to make us like her. She doesn't crack enough jokes; she doesn't save enough cats from trees. You're constantly playing this game of making people invest in people. And then it's like taking a chess board and flipping it. And suddenly they're like, "But I just spent all that time!" You know, audiences feel like affect is labor. That's my experience of it. So once you've done all this work, you're like [*quickly, frantically*], "Well, this work has to mean something! This work has to mean something!" So, you try to redirect it into a different conversation. So, then, the second movement of *Gloria* is this kind of strange allegory of victims versus nonvictims but also minorities versus nonminorities. Suddenly you're following along and then the chessboard moves again, and that's actually the "Game of *Gloria*" for me in the composition of it. So it confused people so much that all that people really talk about is that I used to work at the *New Yorker*, which has so little to do— [*Laughs*] It has so little to do with a play that only takes place in a magazine for like forty minutes.

What I also learned from *Gloria* is the way that people invest differently. They invest in different bodies differently. I wanted, again, for people to see their own perceptions at work. Because that, to me, is the seed of racial antagonism: it's just the idea that people mean different things, based on things they have no control over.

BA: Well, here's the good news: I saw *Appropriate* in Richmond, Virginia. At the Virginia Rep. Full capacity. I think my wife and I were two of maybe five or six black folk there that night. And you know, watching a Southern space on the stage, in a Southern theater, added another layer of complexity to the play—well, another layer of complexity that *I* was aware of—

BJJ: [*Laughs*] No. It was there. It was there.

BA: And I don't know how much unself-conscious, middle-class Southerners who showed up for the play that night were aware of that layer of complexity. They may or they may not. But I don't recall seeing your face anywhere in the lobby! [*Laughs*]

BJJ: Oh. What a relief! Here's what's funny: So I followed *Appropriate* to several cities. And it premiered in Louisville, Kentucky. I learned a lot about whiteness, actually. Because Southern whiteness is different than Western whiteness and in the Northeast, and that was really affirming for me. And you know, when the kid comes down the stairs at the end—in the South—the audience went *nuts* because it felt like they all had that happen—and they needed that story! [*Laughs*] But then it's true. When it premiered, I had some people come to me like, "Oh yeah, when my grandpa died, we found all this crazy stuff in his house." You know, and it was just so lively. I think they were *fully there*. It was—

IS: They laughed at that scene?

BJJ: They *laughed*. It's always this amazing sound. It's my favorite sound at my plays, where you hear people go like [*the laughing sound he demonstrates here is a combination of surprise, horror, and then over-the-top hilarity*] "Oh, Go-o-o-o-o-o-od! Oh, Go-o-o-od! Oh, Go-o-o-od!" You feel them move; you see them move; you hear them move through the emotions of horror and absurdity. And just the sound of people, as the lights go down; the sounds of people in that depth, like darkness laughing. I still remember that one very vividly. But then what's funny is when I went to New York, it was deadly serious when that kid came down the stairs. And then in California, it was the totally other thing—actually, in California the person who got the most laughs was River, the kind of hippie girl. I felt I had done something right. It was like a litmus test. But in the South and in DC it was a very anxious audience. And I could never figure out why.

IS: I would like to ask you about the voice you use as a playwright in your plays because I love your stage directions.

BJJ: Oh, thank you.

IS: And there's so much going on in your stage directions. There's deliberate vagueness, nonchalance in some of your directions where you say, "Well, something whatever—you figure it out." Then there's this moment—I think it's in *An Octoroon*—where you wonder whether you're too Brechtian. And so it seems to me you are having a slightly different conversation with the reader of your play than you have with the spectator of your play. Could you comment on that?

BJJ: Yeah, I've noticed I've actually gotten quieter in my stage directions. Well, I am and I was very much obsessed with Tennessee Williams and Eugene O'Neill and with the idea that stage directions are just a very seductive place for a playwright because it's where you feel like you have power—and you don't really have power, as you learn. Two productions in, and you realize that everybody just crosses you out and ignores you . . . [*laughs*]. But it's the only place where you're actually allowed to reveal yourself and reveal your own needs. And then [in] *Neighbors*, I remember feeling this is the only place where the reader will find comfort, and so I have to stay there with them. Otherwise, they would stop reading. And otherwise, they would actually feel that this is a play that was attacking them. The thing that was also a concern was Sambo's olio of the lawnmower moment, where there is that line "Or that might be too much" [*laughter*].

BA: [*Laughs*] Yes. I remember that clearly.

BJJ: Exactly. But that, for a reader, I think allowed them to keep going. Because they're like, "Right, there *are* boundaries . . ." And then we keep moving. Because I didn't want to be accused—which I have been—of anything pornographic or licentious. It's a way of holding the hand of the person.
 So what happened with *Appropriate* was that—I was reading all this Faulkner, and I was reading all this Southern Gothic stuff—and I felt that I wanted something that felt novelistic. And so I think that that play has this. I was also living in Germany at the time, and so I was spending my days speaking just really basic bad German and feeling like a child. I'm sure you've had this experience when you're learning a language, and you're in a place where you don't know the language, you become very close to your own mind. Because you feel like you're always living right here [*places hand on forehead*], and the struggle is to get it out. I found a comfort in language suddenly with *Appropriate*, and that's why I think that play has this sort of strange upset-like language—the stage directions are very, like, gnarled and rococo in some way. And then, *An Octoroon* I

thought was a return in some ways of the voice of the *Neighbors* stage directions. In the game of that play is this notion of the author disappearing. So the action of that play, in a classical sense, is a playwright who wants to write a play. And that [voice in the stage directions] felt like I was keeping with the shape that I was building. But then it sort of disappears, and actually, that voice becomes Act 4 on-stage, that becomes them building the play. So again, I felt like I was alienating voices and material that I could rework in some ways. But then *Gloria* feels very stark in terms of the stage directions; I don't know why. I don't think I used first person in that at all.

So, anyway, for some reason the play announces its needs to me as I'm writing it. I'm very aware of it because I'm someone who reads more plays than I see—or I used to be—so I feel like I was always more interested in the reading, or I care about the reading experience in a way that a lot of [playwrights] take for granted because they get their plays done all the time. I feel like the life of a script was always fascinating to me, that you had to write a thing that convinces someone to want to see it in space.

BA: Yes. Actually, the last couple of pages of *Appropriate* describe something that there's no way someone sitting in the audience could see. And yet as a reading experience, it's profound. It really takes us somewhere.

BJJ: I think in Providence they tried to read [it aloud]; they had the young boy read [that last page]. I'm like, "Go for it, try it!" But you're right—I just think that you can't approximate the theater of the mind. And yet, the play wants to live in both your interior and on your exterior; that's a play, that's why a play is so magical to me.

BA: After reading Dion Boucicault's *The Octoroon*, I'm pretty sure I can see why you would want to play with it. And yet your revision of the play, intentionally or not, had some post-black elements to it. You know, the cultural mulatto aspect of Zoe and BJJ and what I call allusion-disruption gestures—where you allude to something that preexisted and you disrupt it in a certain way. And you explore blackness and race in a variety of ways. The Minnie and Dido characters were fascinating to me. It wasn't just their speaking in a contemporary black and idiomatic dialect—which was disruptive and fascinating and fun on its own. But when Minnie and Dido were openly lusting after Captain Ratts? A slave owner?

BJJ: [*Chuckles*] Unclear, yeah.

BA: I wonder what prompted that inclusion; at least in part because it felt like—and I'm using words that you may or may not sign on to—but it felt like an almost deliberate provocation. Now, look, in the original play, there was no black interiority at all. Black people were characters, but they were characters that only served the play and served the interest of whites. There was only one scene where black people talked to each other without white people around.

BJJ: They talk about selling themselves! It's like the Bechdel Test—they were talking about selling themselves.

BA: Yes! I was just thinking about the Bechdel Test. And here your intent, clearly, was to create a sort of black interiority on Terrebonne. But what you *do* with that interiority is to infuse it with "Woo, that dude over there he's kinda hot; I hope *he* buys us!" [*chuckles*]. So tell me what you were doing with those sorts of scenes and how those worked.

BJJ: As it relates to this idea of interiority? Or as it relates to the lusting after Ratts?

BA: Well, both—because that's part of what we *get* from a peek inside their interior world.

BJJ: I mean anyone with half a brain—any person of color with half a brain— who reads *The Octoroon* is immediately thinking, "They are never by themselves." You're like, "What are they actually talking about when not on-stage?" Boucicault in some ways wrote the play, insidiously or not, to kind of capitalize on or compete with the popularity of *Uncle Tom's Cabin*. And his whole argument was like, "No—no, that is dramatic; that is over-dramatic. This is how slavery *really* is; this is how black people *really* are." And I was like, "Yeah, you would know, white man in a room with them [*laughs*]. Why would you ever assume in this moment that you would ever see a black person be some private self?" I found places in the play where I was like, "Oh, actually you could sneak this in here." I remember the first thing, when the curtain comes up, it's when a white person walks on. No! Actually, what if we imagine the curtain came up like ten minutes *prior* to this entrance. What are they doing with these bananas? And so yes, there is this desire to see or to imagine what slaves might be talking about outside of a white gaze.

I felt what that space had to be was—The only thing I can identify with in my life was having a job that I didn't like but I had to have; there was no other option. And I thought about the ways of resistance or of claiming one's time. But you know, part of when you felt free on that job was when you *weren't* doing that job; no one was looking around, and you were just talking to your fellow, for lack of a better phrase, wage slave. Those conversations were not about politics, but they were about what we could pretentiously call the questions of being. We were talking about like, "Who are you dating? What are you doing later? Who do you know? What's your boyfriend like?" Because you were definitely—

BA: —shootin' the shit—

BJJ: —shooting the shit! You were desperate to know, what is this person's life outside this room with me? That felt important to me, and I just wanted to create female slaves who weren't living fully in fear of their exploitation because that exploitation is normalized. That was the tragedy. Part of the struggle with that play was trying to get people to see how they literally don't know anything about slavery, really. And that's actually the fucked-up thing about slavery. It is like all that we have of it is filtered through white ethnography . . . and *Gone with the Wind*. Like, your ideas of slavery that you think you have are actually probably from Hollywood. That is the *tragedy* of these lives that were erased from time in history.

Also, one of the funny things about the original is that they are actually [on] a good plantation [Terrebonne]. You know, we only hear about *bad* plantations. Why would they want to ever leave? It's so great here. And I was like, "Yeah, well, if it'll make you feel great; you aren't that afraid; you just figured it out; this is where you live; this is where your people are . . ." I just didn't think that they would have these noble discussions. I don't know why. That made me think a lot about people who are in hostage or captive situations. They don't know anything but their own lives.

It also felt important to me that these women [Minnie and Dido] were different in that one of them had been brought up on this plantation and the other actually had moved around, and they had different temperaments. It's obvious, but it's what a lot of people don't see because they hear *Real Housewives*, and are like, "Oh my God, this is crazy." No. There is a dynamic here. This is the sort of women who are actually trying to find equal footing, and once they find it, they are stronger for it.

In terms of Ratts, there was the joke that *I* play Ratts. And again, when I made the show I didn't think anyone would ever do it again, but I'm definitely a black man in a fat suit playing a white man. I thought the kind of layers of crazy, the amount of work an audience has to do to imagine me as a tanned white man who is beautiful—that was part of the game, visually at least. Actually it's only Minnie who says that he is fine; Dido does not lust. But they do manipulate their female wiles to get what they want, which is a new life; they want to be free of this place.

And I felt the language thing was about—I just remember feeling so anxious. I mean, you write after him [Boucicault]. Can you imagine how to stage these scenes? It would feel like a joke; it would feel like at a museum. I just knew that I had to create a tether between these women and the audience, and language felt like the quickest way.

BA: It also made it feel contemporary in a way that I appreciated. You know, the way that they talked with each other. Your—intentionally or not—your exploration of the difference between *nigger* and *nigga* was interesting [*laughs*].

BJJ: Yeah, you feel like it sort of lands everywhere. I know, I know.

BA: I mean, the word *nigger* in *The Octoroon* is, like, every third line. And completely unself-consciously, completely, you know . . .

BJJ: —like the weather

BA: Yeah, exactly. But then to use the term *nigga* colloquially and affectionately between two black characters, who are outside any sort of white presence, complicated those words a little bit, in ways that I appreciated.

BJJ: Right. And it was also about feeling ownership of the language; that's the point, you know.

BA: Including Pete and his code-switching that's evident in *An Octoroon* in ways that it completely isn't in *The Octoroon*.

BJJ: I know, because it's only white men.

BA: Right [*laughs*].

BJJ: One of my favorite moments in the play, still, is when Dido comes back in and she's like, "Here it be, Mas'r George." And you're like, "Oh wait, she is [code-switching] also!" She just says, "Girl don't you see, he does that every time," and she is doing it too. And Minnie's whole thing is like, "Aah, I'm I supposed to put on a weird voice—is that our job here? You will be Mas'r George."

IS: Regarding *An Octoroon*, I thought it was brilliant that you went back to this period in American theater history, melodrama—just as before you had gone to minstrelsy—to look at how different theater periods dealt with questions of race, how there's this strong connection between theater and race. And then you move on to realism. You sort of investigate the racial legacies of these forms of representation. But what struck me with regard to your use of melodrama is that you don't make fun of it. You play with it; you cite it, you include all these hyperbolic gestures and tableaux. To a certain extent it *is* making fun of melodrama, but to a certain extent some of these scenes are still played very emotionally. So I think you walk a fine line between completely debunking the genre and making it work for contemporary audiences.

BJJ: I know, yeah. Well, when I have these investigations of form—and I feel like I'm running out of forms—I do always feel really respectful of them. Because I always think that form is not something predetermined; it's like a cultural object that has evolved, that had an evolution to it. So I always feel invested in understanding how these things come together because like anything working in a market, the theater is evolving because of demand. It's shaping itself based on what it's seeing itself do in the society. Melodrama, in the history of theater, was a very successful formal evolution. I felt it would actually be hypocritical to set this up as an outdated form, because it's everywhere. It's television.

So I thought, I start from that place. And I felt also that working on that play was a lesson for me in what emotion is in the theater. That whole theory of the economy of affect, that's all coming out of my readings about what melodrama was, and I was just curious. It's like people trying to put together old cars or something. Once I saw the power of it, I felt to throw it away would be a mistake. I think when you say things like "melodrama," it's such a derogatory term; people are predisposed to dismiss it. I think when *An Octoroon* is working, people are like, "Holy shhhi—, this is working. [*Laughs*] This melodrama is still making me feel."

BA: Well, there are a couple of times—once in *An Octoroon* and the other at the very end of *Neighbors*—where you have characters who say to the audience, "Are you feeling something?" Or you have a couple of people who are conversing *about* how they can make the audience feel or not in ways that bring it out of the merely conceptual and thoughtful and right *into* the present and onto the stage itself. And I thought that was really interesting. It allows the audience to be aware that it's being asked to feel something instead of *just* you, by virtue of what you put down in the characters' mouth and stage directions.

BJJ: Taylor Mac has this line he keeps using: "Whatever you're feeling is appropriate." It's that thing about ugly feelings, or complicated feelings even. We encounter them so little that when we feel these things, people get insecure. I think that's why they get angry when they feel insulted or something, because they feel out of control. Because the only thing you bring into the theater is your own body—and your purse—but that's the only thing. So when your own body is feeling something and you don't necessarily want to be feeling that feeling, it creates an anxiety. And I think those moments in the play for me kind of are [*laughing*] "Yeah, you are right. You are doing great, everyone is doing great!" Another moment I can think— You saw *Neighbors* at The Public Theater: after this crazy scene where [Richard is] hitting his wife, and it's just like "Oh my God," and we have this pulsing soundtrack, Topsy comes on to do her extra act, her extra olio, and the first thing she says, which is scripted, is [*to the audience*] "How you guys? How is everyone doing? You enjoying the show? [*Loud laughter*] Oh, you're not? Yikes." But you always feel the audience is like, "Right!" [*Laughs*] And that moment, of course, is all about the overload, of like, "Let's be in this cerebral space and just—everyone relax!"

IS: So you are still Brechtian enough to not let the emotions *completely* carry everything.

BJJ: That's exactly right. It's just the theater, guys, it's just the theater, you're all gonna go home and watch something fun.

BA: When I alerted my sister that she should go see *Neighbors* in Los Angeles, she and her husband went, and just like at The Public Theater, some people walked out!

BJJ: I love it when people walk out, because they're taking ownership. When I'm writing, I think a lot about the rewards for people to stay. A lot of people would walk out of *An Octoroon* after the first act. So first of all, people walk out—amazing! Because that is you making a choice, you're performing that choice, you're telling the civic community, "I'm done. This is my line—I'm out of here." I walk out of stuff *all* the time. I do! I'm like, "I paid for this, I'm reclaiming my time." But what happens, though, is you always have to live with the fact that you missed how it ends. That regret has to be real, you know. So in *An Octoroon*, I do remember feeling that first prologue goes on for *way* longer than it should. And it's so gross. It's an empty black box; he's coming in with a plastic bag of stuff. I think people are so used to being told that they're going to see the Disneyland of everything that they are angry at the play twenty-five minutes in because they are like, "Is this it? Did I pay for this guy to just sit here on a stool and ramble?" And then people leave. In the New York production we had this huge set thing, which most people actually kind of mimic now. But then the show really starts, and people are like, "Oh." And they feel glad that they spent those twenty-five minutes listening to these guys ramble. But then the melodrama kind of keeps going, and you never hear this guy again. And everyone is like, "Is this just gonna be this weird melodrama?" And then our act break happens, and people leave. They are so doubly angry—they are like, "Why am I watching a reconstruction of an old, bad racist play?" But then actually the juice of *An Octoroon* in some ways is the second act because that's where the perceptions just go like this [*gestures as if on a roller-coaster*]. You're suddenly on a ride. So I always feel like, "Yeah, you walked out, you missed the ride." Theater rewards the people who *show up*—that's my feeling about the theater.

Another example is in act 4—I barely pull this off, by the way. The actor comes out, and he's like, "We don't have any money; we have no resources; we have no idea how we're gonna make this act work." And that is about lowering an audience's expectations. The audience is like, "Oh, my God, we're back in this black box? And now all they have are, like, chairs?" But then the theatrical game of pleasure in that act 4 comes out of the actors putting the show together; they build a solution in front of you. The velocity of it; the intensity of it! We experience—when it works—we experience *virtuosity*. And that's like, "Right! See!"

IS: Absolutely.

BJJ: A very formative moment for me, creatively— I have this whole thing about August Wilson. He was the only model when I started, and I had such a push-pull, love-hate thing with him. He would talk about how his moment of birthing as an artist was listening to a Bessie Smith record. And he was like, "I heard in this the story of black struggle blah-blah-blah like the jelly roll song"—I think it's called "Jelly Roll," that "nobody makes a sweet jelly roll like mine." I listened to that song on repeat, waiting for that moment to happen for me. I was like, "I'm not feeling it— [*Getting increasingly agitated*] What are you *talking* about, August Wilson? This doesn't make any sense! You're *lying*." But then I had a moment in that period of time—I had a moment with Nina Simone's "Mississippi Goddam." And I remember very vividly—and this is also what I was talking about with *Neighbors*—there's a moment in that song where she goes, "I bet you thought I was kidding, didn't you?" And you feel the audience stop laughing for the rest of the song. I was like, "*This moment* is what I want to make; this is the moment that's supposed to be the Thing." It sort of happens, I hope, in *An Octoroon* quite a bit. I'm always interested in that moment when the audience realizes that it was laughing. An artist has to be like, "Yeah. I know you're going to stop laughing."

BA: It's an absolutely fascinating example. Nina Simone didn't have to use the form of the show tune to sing that song! Even though the execution is brilliant, the selection of *that form* is what makes it the legendary song that it is.

BJJ: I know, because in that form we are predisposed to have black artists make us feel good. And everyone jumps on that train—they laugh at that joke! I just finished reviewing Imani Perry's new Lorraine Hansberry book [*Looking for Lorraine*], and there's a direct relation between Lorraine Hansberry and the fact that Nina Simone started using the vocabulary of theater in her catalog—isn't that amazing? "Pirate Jenny"? And Lorraine Hansberry's whole thing in the theater was appropriation. She appropriated this performance of social realism. I kind of got chills when I figured that out. And I was like, "Right! Lorraine Hansberry!" I'm sorry, I just went down a tangent . . .

IS: This is great; tangents are great! I want to ask you about your use of visual media. Earlier you mentioned that you actually started out feeling influenced by visual artists: Kara Walker, Glenn Ligon, David Hammons, and others, who were an eye-opener for you. There's a strong element of visuality in your work—and I don't just mean these moments where you thematize that the stage is looking at the audience looking at them and vice versa. That's only one of the elements. Another one is your use of these grotesque, hyperbolic stereotypes, which also have an element of visuality in them. And then you project a lynching photo, which is a very strong visual. Have you ever thought about your use of visual elements?

BJJ: Yeah, I think a lot of the kind of big, very formative plays for me starting out were Sam Shepard's one-acts and plays by Mariá Irene Fornés and Adrienne Kennedy, which were part of the Theater of Images. That was the tradition I had locked in, in my sort of early avoidance of what I interpreted as the sentimentality of August Wilson and these sorts of depictions of black life. I was looking for models elsewhere, and that's where I felt like, "Oh, it's here!" It felt to me race is a visual thing; it's a visual trick. We judge things based on sight, not on what we hear generally. So I knew that I had to play in the visual, and I was like, "That's where I'm gonna shore up the answers to whatever questions I'm asking: in the visual." It was the act of looking that was on trial for me. Another person of great importance was Adrian Piper. When I encountered *Cornered* in grad school I was like, "YASSS! This is it!" She just had a retrospective here [at the Museum of Modern Art, New York City], and I was shocked that it wasn't as big of a deal as I thought it should have been. I was like, "Right, there's something *happening* in this idea of black visual culture, black visual art." Because that place is just out-looking, that's what visual art is, and they sort of cottoned on, for lack of a better phrase, quicker to what's at stake in the visual and these conversations than the theater had. That's because, I think, the theater has been disseminated primarily through the scripts. I realize now that more people have read my play than seen it.

One of my major moments of understanding, when my view of Boucicault changed in the middle of working on his play, was when I started visualizing his scripts. Because he never wrote these scripts to be published and read as plays; they were blueprints for a visual event. That sounds like "Oh, he's a visual genius." Because that entire play is about white actors in brown face, and a white woman playing a brown one. It's like proto-Brecht. He knew that there was something about the tension between what you see and what you're being told about what you're seeing. That actually is where the gold is. So I felt kinship. Because I had been trying to do that in *Neighbors*. I've been trying to talk about, like, "Guys, everything on stage you have called black at some point. What *is black*?" But it was getting lost in the kind of sheer noise of the overload of what was happening for the audience.

BA: Part of what was so interesting about those interludes in *Neighbors*, aside from the fact that they were complicatedly hilarious, was the fact that there was one of the neighbors, the Crows' neighbors, *watching* at all times. It was either Richard or Melody, so it becomes part of your sense of the visual—even though it's not just the audience, it's other characters who are, like, silently waiting and watching.

BJJ: And it's creating a relationship between you and that person that you're like, "Uh, do I want this relationship here?" That kind of pocket was where I think *Appropriate* kinda came out of. Because I was interested in a play where you were just watching people watch something horrible or look at something that we would consider horrible and that that created the desire we need to see that thing as well.

I can point to the artists I obsess over for all those plays— Kara Walker was a huge part of *Neighbors* to me, especially building these olios. I remember reading about [her artistic] process. She's like, "I just start cutting," and I was like, "Okay, I'm supposed to start writing." And all those things are kind of one long jag of thought that kind of completed itself. I remember I was obsessed with Glenn Ligon's "Wanted" [*Runaways*] posters. I was really leaning into that and also what he did with the *Black Book*. That was all over *An Octoroon* for me. It was writing my own "Wanted" poster, you know. "I'm going to deface this *thing* and make it a new thing"—I felt that was part of it. *Appropriate* really came together when I saw Kerry James Marshall's *Heirlooms and Accessories* paintings, which are the ones where he takes a lynching photograph—have you seen these? they are *amazing*—but he paints over them with white, and he finds one face in the crowd, and he draws it. It really blew my mind, and I think *Appropriate* was born in some ways out of that encounter with that piece of writing.

IS: For me, your plays really clarify to what extent theater is a looking space.

BJJ: Oh, yeah, absolutely.

IS: —and, in a way, quite often a white looking space, right?

BJJ: Yeah. I don't know if you saw or heard about *Fairview* by Jackie Sibblies Drury, a play that just opened; her play is all about that. But there's a real conversation to be had, because I'm not ready to cede this space to whiteness. The tradition of theater to me is sort of white. [*Chuckles*] But I don't know if I can say that the action of sitting communally and kind of collectively hallucinating a story—I don't think I'm gonna give that to anyone right now.

BA: Thank you. It's just deeply, expansively human, with so many different cultures, over so many different, you know, hundreds, perhaps thousands of years.

BJJ: Exactly. I think the challenge and a trap a lot of artists are falling into—and I may have fallen, I don't know if I ever fell into it, to be honest, but maybe I have— I think it's a mistake to assume that your audience is white. Because the truth of an audience is that it can be *anyone*. Anyone can show up; anyone if they *want* to can pay that money. And that's different than what happened sixty, seventy years ago when these were segregated spaces. I think that's the kind of underexplored element of this sort of canon-revision thing that we're all kind of working through. There weren't black people in the audience in *The Octoroon*; they probably didn't care. In some ways that's like Minnie and Dido. They actually just don't care about this drama.

BA: I'm not seeing many productions of *Neighbors* currently. Are people producing that play?

BJJ: No . . . because I'm sort of not allowing it.

BA: Oh you're not *allowing* people to! Do you mind sharing why not?

BJJ: Well, I feel like . . . So, one issue is that there is not a publishable draft of *Neighbors* because it changed so much over the course of its life. I'm still trying to collate the best version of it. And ironically, there's this ten-year anniversary of *Neighbors* next year, in 2020 . . .

IS: Already?

BJJ: I know, I know, I know. And there's a theater [in New York] that's been kinda flirting with doing, like, *Neighbors Revisited*. So part of it is like, "What does it mean to finally publish it if we're just gonna redo it." So, it's oddly in flux. I also saw—I mean speaking of wrong laughter—I have seen productions of it where I was like, "Oh no-o-o-o!" And they weren't major productions. But I was like, "I don't know if I can trust just any old body to do this play." Now, when I wrote that play, I never thought anyone would do it. I legitimately thought it was just gonna be this play that gets read and not produced. So what does happen is that people apply to do readings of *Neighbors*, which I'll let them do. What's so funny is that I wrote that play in 2008, 2009? It kind of made the rounds, and no one would touch it with a ten-foot pole. I mean everyone would read it, and they would talk to me, and they'd give me little awards and stuff. But it wasn't until Obama was president that they actually were like, "We're gonna do it." And I was hesitant about it. I feel very protective of actors in that play, because we work in a theater now where marketing has an enormous amount of power, and theaters always want to take press photos. And I will say, "No, you can't do that without asking these actors' permission, because the actors are gonna have pictures of them in blackface floating around the internet, and it's forever. And they are not being paid enough to have to answer for this play for the rest of their lives. So, 'no!'" So, I have all these stipulations that people don't like. And that's part of why it became very difficult for me. I don't trust people to take care of these actors, who are really doing the hard work. That's why it has become more of a reading-only thing, but maybe one day it will [get produced again].

BA: Well, this has been a wonderful conversation. We have deeply appreciated your time and your insights. Thank you!

IS: Yes, thank you so much!

CONTRIBUTORS

BERTRAM D. ASHE is professor of English and American studies at the University of Richmond, Virginia and the author of *Twisted: My Dreadlock Chronicles* (2015), which was a finalist for a Library of Virginia Literary Award. His scholarly and teaching interests include jazz, basketball, post-blackness, and black hair. He has published widely in academic journals and essay collections, including coediting and writing "Theorizing the Post-Soul Aesthetic: An Introduction" for the special 2007 Post-Soul issue of *African American Review*. Other publications include "Paul Beatty's *White Boy Shuffle* Blues: Jazz Poetry, John Coltrane, and the Post-Soul Aesthetic" in *Thriving on a Riff: Jazz and Blues Influences in African American Literature and Film* (2009). He is currently working on a book on the varieties of black hair statements in the United States and beyond.

KIMBERLY NICHELE BROWN is associate professor in the Department of Gender, Sexuality, and Women's Studies at Virginia Commonwealth University in Richmond, Virginia. She specializes in contemporary African American women's literature and culture, black feminist theory, Africana film, and twentieth-century American and Africana literatures. She has published articles dealing with race and representation, black agency and self-actualization, black subjectivity, the black body, as well as questions of audience and spectatorship. Her publications include *Writing the Revolutionary Diva: Black Women's Subjectivity and the Decolonized Text* (2010). Her new book demonstrates how racial passers and other liminal figures use racial ambiguity as a strategy she calls "cross-racial espionage" to combat antiblackness.

MOLLIE GODFREY is associate professor of English at James Madison University, where she teaches African American literature. She coedited *Neo-Passing: Performing Identity after Jim Crow* (2018) and is currently working on a book project titled *Black Humanisms: Race, Gender, and the Fictions of Segregation*. Articles related to these topics have appeared in *MFS: Modern Fiction Studies, MELUS, CLA*

Journal, Arizona Quarterly, and *Contemporary Literature.* Mollie has also orga-nized several community-engaged projects dedicated to preserving and making accessible local African American archives. Her work on this topic has appeared in *Pedagogy: Critical Approaches to Teaching Literature, Language, Composition, and Culture,* and *Public: A Journal of Imagining America.*

JACK HITT contributes regularly to the *New York Times Magazine* and the public radio program *This American Life.* He is the cohost of the 2018 Peabody Award–winning program *Uncivil.* Jack also won a Peabody Award for his hour-long Guan-tánamo Bay special "Habeas Schmabeas" (2006) for *This American Life,* being the first to interview detainees who had been held there. He is the author of the book *Bunch of Amateurs* (2012) and a number of essays anthologized in *Best American Travel Essays, The Oxford-American Book of Great Music Writing, Best Food Writ-ing,* and *Best American Science Writing.* His one-man show, titled *Making Up the Truth,* toured the country in 2012–13. His book about walking the road to Santiago in Spain, *Off the Road,* was made into the movie *The Way* (2010), and his *Esquire* article on computer amateurs was made into the cult movie classic *Hackers* (1995).

BRANDEN JACOBS-JENKINS is a Brooklyn-based playwright. His plays include *Everybody* (2017, Signature Theatre; Pulitzer Prize finalist), *Gloria* (2015, Vineyard Theatre; Pulitzer Prize finalist), *War* (2014, LCT3/Lincoln Center Theater), *Appro-priate* (2014, Signature Theatre; Obie Award), *An Octoroon* (2014, Soho Rep; Obie Award), and *Neighbors* (2010, The Public Theater). A Residency 5 Playwright at Signature Theatre, his most recent honors include the Charles Wintour Award for Most Promising Playwright from the *London Evening Standard,* a London Critics Circle Award for Most Promising Playwriting, a MacArthur Fellowship, the Windham-Campbell Prize for Drama, the Benjamin H. Danks Award from the American Academy of Arts and Letters, the PEN/Laura Pels International Foundation Theatre Award, the Steinberg Playwriting Award, and the inaugural Tennessee Williams Award. He sits on the board of Soho Rep, and with Annie Baker, he is an associate codirector of the Hunter College MFA program in playwriting.

CHENJERAI KUMANYIKA is a researcher, journalist, and artist who works as an assistant professor at Rutgers University's Department of Journalism and Media Studies. His research and teaching focus on the intersections of social justice and emerging media in the cultural and creative industries. He has written about these issues in journals such as *Popular Music and Society, Popular Communica-tion, The Routledge Companion to Advertising and Promotional Culture and Tech-nology,* and *Pedagogy and Education.* Currently, Kumanyika is the co-executive producer and cohost of *Uncivil,* Gimlet Media's podcast on the Civil War. He has also been a contributor to *Transom, NPR Codeswitch, All Things Considered,*

Invisibilia, and *VICE*, and he is a news analyst for Rising Up Radio with Sonali Kolhatkar.

CAMERON LEADER-PICONE is associate professor of English at Kansas State University. His research focuses on the politics of identity in twenty-first-century African American cultural production. His research has been published in the volume *Post-Soul Satire: Black Identity after Civil Rights* (2014) and in the journals *Contemporary Literature* and *MELUS*. He is currently working on two book manuscripts. The first, *Black and More Than Black: African American Fiction in the Post Era*, theorizes how the connection between the proliferation of "post" concepts in the early twenty-first century and the discourse around Barack Obama's presidency defined a transitional era in African American fiction in which antiessentialism led authors to privilege individual racial performance and reject prescriptive limitations on black art and black identity. The second analyzes the significant body of literature produced by the growing numbers of immigrants from continental Africa to the United States during the post–civil rights era.

DEREK C. MAUS is professor of English and communication at the State University of New York at Potsdam, where he teaches numerous courses on a wide variety of subjects in contemporary literature. He is the author of *Jesting in Earnest: Percival Everett and Menippean Satire* (2019), *Understanding Colson Whitehead* (2014), and *Unvarnishing Reality: Subversive Russian and American Cold War Satire* (2011). He has also edited several scholarly collections, including *Conversations with Colson Whitehead* (2019), *Post-Soul Satire: Black Identity after Civil Rights* (2014, coedited with James J. Donahue), and *Finding a Way Home: A Critical Assessment of Walter Mosley's Fiction* (2008, coedited with Owen E. Brady). He is currently at work on a project comparing African Canadian and African American fiction in the context of the post-soul aesthetic. He divides his time between northern New York and Montréal.

DEREK CONRAD MURRAY is an interdisciplinary theorist specializing in the history, theory, and criticism of contemporary art and visual culture. Murray works in contemporary aesthetic and cultural theory with a particular attention to technocultural engagements with identity and representation. He is currently professor of the history of art and visual culture at the University of California, Santa Cruz. His most recent book is *Queering Post-Black Art: Artists Transforming African-American Identity after Civil Rights* (2015).

CHRIS NEARY is senior development producer at Gimlet. He has produced and reported episodes of *Heavyweight, Reply All, Conviction*, and *Uncivil*, which won a 2017 Peabody Award. Prior to moving to Gimlet, he was a producer at NPR's *On the Media* and WNYC's *Freakonomics Radio*. His work has appeared on those shows and *This American Life*.

MALIN PEREIRA received her PhD in English at the University of Wisconsin–Madison, where she studied with Nellie McKay, Craig Werner, Lynn Keller, and Susan Stanford Friedman. Her scholarship focuses on the generation of contemporary African American poets following the black arts movement and has been published in several journals, collections of essays, and reference works, including *African American Review, Contemporary Literature, Hecate, MELUS, Southern Quarterly,* and the *Dictionary of Literary Biography.* Her books include *Rita Dove's Cosmopolitanism* (2003) and *Into a Light Both Brilliant and Unseen: Conversations with Contemporary Black Poets* (2010). She is professor of English at the University of North Carolina at Charlotte, where she teaches African American literature and leads the Honors College. Her current book project concerns black poetry and visual art.

ILKA SAAL is professor of American literature at the University of Erfurt, Germany. She holds a PhD from Duke University and worked at the University of Richmond before returning to Europe. She is the author of the award-winning book *New Deal Theater: The Vernacular Tradition in American Political Theater* (2007) and coeditor of *Passionate Politics: The Cultural Work of American Melodrama from the Early Republic to the Present* (2008). Her essays on American theater and literature have appeared in various journals and essay collections, including *MFS: Modern Fiction Studies, Canadian Review of American Studies, Journal of American Drama and Theatre, Amerikastudien, South Atlantic Review,* and *Oxford Handbooks Online.* Ilka is the recipient of a Humboldt Research Fellowship for Experienced Researchers. From 2016 to 2019, she worked as editor-in-chief of *Theatre Annual: A Journal of Theatre and Performance of the Americas.* She is presently completing a monograph on Suzan-Lori Parks and Kara Walker.

INDEX

Malcolm X, 83, 87, 102n22
Marshall, Kerry James, 17, 226
Marshall, Paule, 87
Martin, Trayvon, 96, 105n50, 107, 110, 113
Maus, Derek C., 13, 43–64
McDowell, Deborah E., 11–12, 17, 20nn46,47
McQueen, Steve, 91; *12 Years a Slave*, 91, 104n40
melancholia, 4, 208
melodrama, 35, 38, 211, 221, 223
memory, 3, 10, 12, 27–28, 35, 51–53, 108; counter-memory, 10, 17; postmemory, 10; rememory, 17
Mercer, Kobena, 123n47, 142, 156n7
Mercy, A, 4, 5
metanarrative, 13, 46, 50, 107, 160
Metz, Christian, 26, 41n4
Middle Passage, 15, 54, 108, 164
Miller, Arthur, 141, 155–56
minstrelsy, 15, 29, 71–72, 128–29, 140–52, 206–7, 221
Misrahi-Barak, Judith, 3, 4, 5, 17
Mitchell, Angelyn, 88, 162–63, 179n9
Morrison Toni, 8, 11, 53, 102n12; *Beloved*, 3, 4, 5, 46, 50, 162; *A Mercy*, 4, 5; "The Site of Memory," 10, 19n40, 168
Moss, Thylias, 8, 16, 160–81, 174*fig.*, 176*fig.*, 177*fig.* See also *Slave Moth*
Moten, Fred, 146–47, 153, 154
Murray, Derek Conrad, 6–7, 9, 12–14, 21–42, 66, 79n6, 143
myth, 36, 50, 60, 107, 143, 151, 155, 168, 173. *See also* demythologization

NAACP, 69
National Geographic, 122n38
nationalism: black, 14, 85–87, 89, 115; postnationalism, 45; white, 47, 127
Neal, Mark Anthony, 18n18, 49, 50, 53, 84–85, 120n8

Neary, Chris, 15, 124–39
Neighbors, 17, 200–228; and affect, 200; and blackface, 148; and the grotesque, 151; and humor, 151–53; as meta-theater, 149; and minstrelsy, 148–50, 152; and realism, 149; and stereotype, 15, 147–55; and theatricality, 147–55
neo-slave narratives, 3–5, 11, 83–87, 100, 102n12
Nicholas, Teddy, 158n58
Nozick, Robert, 72, 81n31

Obama, Barack, 8, 13, 43, 47, 51, 86, 107, 110, 228
Octavia Butler's Kindred, 14, 92*fig.*, 94*fig.*, 95*fig.*, 97*fig.*, 98*fig.*, 100*fig.*; and black feminism, 14, 96; and collectivity, 14, 98–100; and colorblindness, 84, 89, 99–100; and gender, 93; and intersectionality, 14–15, 84–86, 93–94, 96, 99; and postblackness, 14–15, 84–85, 100; and postracialism 84, 86, 99. *See also* Butler, Octavia; Duffy, Damian; Jennings, John; *Kindred*
Octoroon, An, 9, 17; and affect, 221–23; and black bodies, 205, 207; and humor, 205–6, 208–9, 224; and melodrama, 221, 223; and minstrelsy, 206; and stereotype, 205
O'Hara, Robert, 11
O'Neill, Eugene, 216
oppositional gaze, 106, 119

Parker, Nate, 91
Parks, Suzan-Lori, 142, 143, 155, 199; *The Death of the Last Black Man in the Whole Entire World*, 142; *Venus*, 143, 155
parody, 73, 75, 191
pastoral, 80n19, 175
Patterson, Orlando, 72, 79n4, 81n29